NGUNA
VOICES

For my parents,
who never told me what
I could or should become.

Ellen E. Facey

NGUNA VOICES

VOICES

Text and Culture from Central Vanuatu

THE UNIVERSITY OF CALGARY PRESS

ISBN 0-919813-72-0

The University of Calgary Press
2500 University Drive N.W.
Calgary, Alberta, Canada T2N 1N4

Canadian Cataloguing in Publication Data

Facey, Ellen E., 1954-
Nguna voices

Bibliography: p.
ISBN 0-919813-72-0

1. Folklore - Vanuatu - Nguna. 2. Ethnology -
Vanuatu - Nguna. 3. Nguna (Vanuatu) - Social
life and customs. I. Title.
GR385.V35F33 1988   398'.0993'4   C88-091271-5

Cover design by Rhae Ann Bromley

Printed in Canada

Table of Contents

List of Maps and Figures

List of Plates

Acknowledgements

As this work is based on materials generated during my doctoral research, I would like to express my appreciation to the Australian Commonwealth Department of Education and their Commonwealth Scholarship and Fellowship Plan Committee for the opportunity to undertake doctoral studies at the Department of Anthropology of the University of Sydney. In addition to four years of fellowship stipends (1977-1981) they generously gave a special grant to cover my second field trip to Nguna. For their underwriting of my first trip I am endebted to the Department of Anthropology, University of Sydney, most particularly to the Carlyle Greenwell Bequest Fund administered by that department. I want to thank especially the government of Vanuatu which enabled me to complete my research plans in a most trying political era, one in which they might have been forgiven for being less welcoming to foreign researchers. I hope that this work will go some of the way toward repaying their trust. The preparation of the present document itself has been made possible through a two-year, postdoctoral fellowship granted by the Social Sciences and Humanities Research Council of Canada, administered most efficiently and helpfully by its Fellowship Division, and by the Department of Anthropology at the University of Western Ontario which, in tight financial times, carved out space and technical support.

The nature of anthropological fieldwork is such that we ask a great deal of our subjects of study and, although we try to offer something in return, it often turns out that our "goods", material or otherwise, have little local currency. Consequently, it is difficult to operate other than as a child,

viii

taking much and able only partially to reciprocate. To the Ngunese who had the graciousness and compassion to accept me as a person even when I had little to offer and to treat me as their sister, daughter, or even "little mother", I give my thanks. Sadly, some of these have already left us: Thomas Tavirana, who never tired of discussing customs, canoes and whatever, and who always made me feel welcome; Kaltaᵽau M̃asemata, a master story-teller and spell-weaver in any language or culture; and Chief John Mariwota and John Kos of Tikilasoa village. It is my greatest hope that this collection of oral knowledge will give pleasure and pride to those who remain and will stand as a testimony in honour of the skill and wisdom of those who are now gone but who cared so deeply for both the history and future of Ngunese culture. There are numerous others who either allowed me to record their narratives, which I have been unable to include, or gave me ethnographic assistance of various sorts: Leisei Alick, Emil Jack, Samuel Kalkoa, Jack Manuwia, Stephen Kaloris, John Mariᵽoᵽogi, Roland Woota, Kalosike Tariᵽoamata, and so many others. I would like to thank in particular the chiefs and people of Tikilasoa and Nekaaᵽa villages with whom the great bulk of my time on Nguna was shared; but the people in all Nguna's villages, and likewise those I encountered in Ᵽele, north Efate and Port Vila were all most kind. Theirs is a fine tradition of hospitality.

The following people, however, far surpassed the demands of propriety and tradition. As mother, father and sisters, they gave me comfort for both body and soul when I entered their homes or sat by their sides at meetings, weddings and wakes: Leisei and Minnie in Tiki; Merly and Miurriel in Nekaaᵽa; and, above all, mama Jack and teete Chrissie who found it in their hearts to take me not only into their home, but even into their family.

A number of people with abiding interests in Nguna, Vanuatu or Melanesia in general have rendered inestimable assistance, sharing their knowledge and experience either in person or by correspondence. Among these are Dr. Albert Schütz, whose grammar and collection of oral texts were of considerable assistance, and who has shown remarkable forbearance in our differences over linguistic issues; and Dr. Ross Clark, who generously supplied a copy of his edited compilation of Ngunese vocabulary collected by Schütz, Clark and myself.

In addition, a very personal thank-you goes to two very special people: Mr. Robert McCallum who, for kinship's sake and for the challenge itself, gave freely of his time and computing expertise to a novice sometimes slow to catch on, but inevitably in a rush; and Ms. Jane McAndrew, who rendered valuable technical assistance as well as emotional support through the troughs in my cycle of enthusiasm.

Finally, I wish to express my gratitude to those colleagues who have advised, consulted and cajoled: Drs Susan Hornshaw, Bil Thurston, Rick Goulden and Bill Rodman; Dr. Margy Rodman, who had the courage to be frank and the insight to dare me to do what I wanted; Drs Chet Creider and Larry Gorbet whose MacHelp was sorely needed and greatly appreciated; Dr. Margaret Seguin, who gave helpful comments on numerous drafts as well as solid advice on other related matters; and, finally, Dr. Carole Farber, whose imagination, encouragement, criticism and support have touched so many aspects of this work and my experience of doing it. While this piece shows the mark of the contributions of all of these individuals, I take full responsibility for any failings it may have.

This book has been published with the help of a grant from the Social Science Federation of Canada, using funds provided by the Social Sciences and Humanities Research Council of Canada.

Linguistic Notes

There are three sounds in the Ngunese language which are quite difficult for native English-speakers to pronounce. These are: the bilabial lenis implosive stop, /ɓ/; the bilabial nasal with dorso-velar constriction, /m̃/; and the voiced dorso-velar nasal, /g/ (Schütz 1969b: 15-16). The non-linguist reader might treat the first two as "pw" and "mw" respectively, and the third as "ng"; but, as these are only approximations, I follow the Ngunese' and Schütz' example and transcribe the first two using the tilde [~]— or, as some Ngunese-speakers know it, the "wriggle"— and the third using the symbol [g] alone. Also note that *aa/oo/ii/ee/uu* represent long vowels.

A more complex issue is that of the distinction between /t/ and /d/. These are described by Schütz (1969b: 14-15) as allophones of the apico-dental stop, /t/, which are in free fluctuation, except in certain environments in which they, like several other consonant pairs, display morphophonemic alternation. For these reasons Schütz chose to use only /t/ in his transcriptions, and it is here that our paths diverge. I have chosen instead to employ both forms, compelled by ethnographic or cultural rather than linguistic forces, in the sense that for the Ngunese with whom I discussed this question, there were two quite distinct sounds involved. I feel it only appropriate to bow to their intuitions and prefrences; therefore, in my transcription of these, as well as that of the other comparable pairs of consonants (p/v; p/w; g/k; and t/r), I have attempted to reflect faithfully the contrasts between these sounds as perceived and produced by native speakers.

This, and likewise the occasional inconsistency in the spellings of words, may irk the reader, the linguist in particular. While this is unfortunate, I have chosen this as the lesser evil, preferring to let the orthography reflect variation in pronunciation and, sometimes, in grammar, rather than taking the liberty of levelling the variation in order to produce artificially standardized spellings or grammatical usages. A case in point is the use of both *ni* and *ki* ("of") in the apparently identical environment in the titles of four of the first set of texts (see the Table of Contents). I see no reason why this variation should be eradicated in the interests of the mere appearance of consistency; and numerous reasons why it ought to be reproduced so that interested parties with more linguistic training than I, not the least of whom might be some Ngunese individuals, might have the opportunity of trying to sort out "what is going on" in these cases.

After Schütz (1969a and 1969b) the following modified set of terminological conventions will be used in the inter-linear transcriptions:

Imp = imperative and conditional or incomplete action (*p̃a*)
Int = intention, where the action referred to by the verb has definitely not been completed (ga)
"will" = future (*woo*)
"if, might" = conditional (*pe*)
Inc = "still, yet" (with negative); incomplete (*ko*)
Comp = perfective, completion (*poo* and *sua*)
Prog = progressive, indicating habitual action, or action definitely in progress (*too/doo*)
"of"/Obj Mkr = possessive preposition/object marker (k*i/ni/si*)
Pass = passive prefix, though passivity is not apparent in every occurrence (m*a*)
Caus = causative (*vaka*)
Ord Mkr = ordinal marker prefixed to numerals (*ke*)
N Mkr = noun marker (*na*)
Inr = interrogative (*kite?*)
PL = plural marker (*maaga*)

Chapter One

Dilemmas of Transforming Performance Into Text

The Hearer/Listener

This project began as a way of giving whoever might be interested in Pacific textual materials, most especially the Ngunese people who had given me so much assistance in my doctoral research among them, written documentation of the oral tradition which the latter so highly prize. I wanted to do something with this body of texts, given that it is substantial in size, intrinsically interesting in content for the imagination's pure enjoyment, and important both for the Ngunese themselves, for their own purposes, as well as for Oceanic scholars with linguistic or ethnographic concerns.

As a result I have designed this volume with a view to making it as useful and as accessible as can be to the widest possible audience, from the people of Nguna and other ni-Vanuatu to various types of academic specialists. I hope that it might serve the Ngunese in three main ways: first, to those of you who hoped, and a few who doubted, that you would see anything come of the numerous investigations conducted by colonial government officials and foreign scholars on the island over the years: this is a piece that I believe you will find readable, one that I hope you will appreciate more than a dissertation or scholarly papers written for purposes and in a kind of language that tends to be irrelevant and/or inaccessible to the people whose cultures are their focus. Second, being presented in the language of Nguna as well as in English, the texts in this volume could become a valuable learning tool – perhaps one more enjoyable than others – for students of English in the Ngunese primary schools. Third, what may ultimately prove to be the most significant use of this volume for the people of Nguna is simply whatever they choose to make of it vis-à-vis their own vision of who they are. To all of you let me say: these are your histories. Your elders gave them to me, and I now return them to you with the hope that you will feel that the editing I have done and the form I have chosen does them justice.

With the non-Ngunese reader in mind, I have made a number of other decisions in the production of this volume. I initially (naïvely) planned to present each text in a tri-partite format, with an inter-linear translation linking the fluent Ngunese and English versions. It soon became apparent, however, that this would be impossible given the enormous amount of space inter-linears take. Consequently, bowing to the more important goal of presenting as many texts as possible without having to expand into a second or even third volume, I have tried at the same time to accomodate linguists' requirements by appending complete inter-linear translations of two texts, as well as a glossary cum dictionary of the Ngunese vocabulary for the whole corpus.

Finally, there are the non-Ngunese and non-linguist readers, those more interested in "folklore" and/or "textual studies" or "textual analysis", as well as those, anthropologists or otherwise, who simply want to be informed readers of Ngunese texts and, simultaneously, Ngunese culture. For all of these, and not the least for myself – the most interested and curious of all of these characters – I offer several chapters of introduction to and analysis of Ngunese textual form and content as well as an introduction to the culture of Nguna, Vanuatu, as I have come to know it, at first hand from 1978 to 1980 and, in retrospect, over the years since.

The Nature of the Enterprise

Before going further some prefatory remarks concerning my intentions are in order. It has been my primary concern to produce written versions of the texts recounted by Ngunese individuals in a way that faithfully *re*-presents the particular characteristics and eloquence of the originals. Typically (with only a handful of recent exceptions, discussed below) one finds the "stories" or "folklore" of non-Western cultures as well as their raconteurs portrayed as sub-standard or second-class literature and second-class citizens of the world literary community. Too often, through lack, rather than malice, of forethought, linguists, folklorists and anthropologists produce translations which are literally faithful to the linguistic structure and content of the text, but mockeries of their personal and/or cultural style, import and impact. Anyone who has taught an introductory anthropology class will have seen the reaction of students to texts presented in such a way. If the people's oral literature appears so stilted and simplistic when written down, the people themselves must be "simple" and must have a "primitive" culture.

If the anthropologist as textual scribe/interpreter is to avoid fostering such ethnographically disastrous misconceptions in a public who, sadly, is already predisposed to them, he/she has two related problems to overcome: how to create accurate transcriptions and how to create proper translations. He/she has the task of transforming oral and (in the Ngunese case) relatively informal, singular events into written, thereby formal, documents or texts, and the task of transforming fluent verbal performances in one language into comparable events in another language. The goal of both these processes of transformation is to effect them without losing the individual particularity of each narrative, set as it is in time, space and personal idiosyncrasy as well as in the particularities of culture.

Transcription has for too long been treated as a "simple" matter of putting the oral into written form. Even with the enormously important advent of the ultra-compact, portable tape recorder, the guidelines which would appear to inform many researchers' efforts must be something of this order: "Make the tapes, then write down what you hear. Put a period at the end of each sentence; maybe split it up into paragraphs so it doesn't look so boring, and that's it! Simple!" Rather more care than this has been taken in the process of translation in the recent past, few ethnographers nowadays being content to render purely literal translations. But here, too, there is often still a great deal that escapes, falling through the cracks and holes between different languages and worldviews.

I am very pleased to have discovered a number of works, primarily those of Dell Hymes (especially 1981), Ralph Maud (1982), Peter Seitel (1980), and Dennis Tedlock (especially 1972, 1982 and 1983), which prove that there are others who are not only concerned about this cavalier treatment of oral literature, but have also analyzed the problem and suggested new approaches to deal effectively with it. Tedlock's conclusion is that,

> The apparent flatness of many past translations is not a reflection but a distortion of the originals, caused by the dictation process, the notion that content and form are independent, a pervasive deafness to oral qualities, and a fixed notion of the boundary between poetry and prose. Present

> conditions, which combine new recording techniques with a
> growing sensitivity to verbal art as performed 'event' rather
> than as fixed 'object' on the page, promise the removal of pre-
> vious difficulties.
>
> (Tedlock 1983: 54-55)

The notational system Tedlock devised to *re*-present oral narrative,
along with his conviction that many, possibly all cultures' *oral* narratives
are comparable to Western poetry or poetic forms rather than to Western
prose or prosodic forms have provided my work with powerful tools and
direction. The following is his own summary of the "argument that [as
one specific case] American Indian spoken narratives are better understood (and translated) as dramatic poetry than as an oral equivalent of
written prose fiction...":

> The content tends toward the fantastic rather than the
> prosaic, the emotions of the characters are evoked rather than
> described, there are patterns of repetition or parallelism
> ranging from the level of words to that of whole episodes, the
> narrator's voice shifts constantly in amplitude and tone, and
> the flow of that voice is paced by pauses that segment its
> sounds into what I have chosen to call lines. Of all these re-
> alities of oral narrative performance, the plainest and gross-
> est is the sheer alternation of sound and silence; the resultant
> lines often show an independence from intonation, from
> syntax, and even from boundaries of plot structure.
>
> (Tedlock 1983: 55)

It is clear to me that Tedlock (1983: 54) is correct in saying that
treating oral narrative as dramatic poetry yields both analytical and
aesthetic rewards. Considering the present body of ni-Vanuatu oral
narratives in the light of the preceding set of characteristics has led me
to hear and therefore to find ways of transcribing much more than I
would have otherwise.

The silent act of reading, when what is read began as what was
listened to, calls for a great many more and imaginative visual cues than
we have previously seen employed in texts, in order to convey literary
features absolutely critical to and formative of the narrative moment
and of its experience, understanding and/or interpretation by the hearer/
reader. Among these are: voice tone, quality and volume; physical
gestures; variation in pausing (i.e., the narrator's management of the
semantics of silence); differential stress; syllabic elongation; repetition;
and alliteration. If these fail to be relayed visually to the reader, the

written text can only be said to be a shadow, not even a reflection of its
real self, like the score of a musical from which all the stage directions
and the music itself have been omitted.

In the next chapter the reader will be briefly introduced to Ngunese
society and culture. Then, in Chapter Three, I bring him/her "into the
kitchen" by explicitly sharing my translatory trials, and solutions. The
culinary metaphor is a good one, as anyone who has ever attempted to
re-create a heavenly, exotic dish without the identical ingredients
knows. Months of experimentation are encapsulated here, organized
into seven categories of linguistic/cultural conundrums, gaps (inter-lan-
guage "voids" or "lexical anisomorphisms" in the current terminology),
and various kinds of "tricky bits" (in my terminology). Chapter Four
discusses three sorts of "style" visible in the textual transcriptions and
translations: first, those features common to the texts as a unified body,
cultural productions specific to one culture in a certain time frame (the
texts' "Ngunese-ness"); second, "style" in the sense in which each text is
representative of a particular type of narrative, according to an explicit
set of criteria, some of indigenous and some of extrinsic definition; and,
third, "style" referring to the idiosyncratic features of the individual
narrator's style— the distinctive literary "signature" peculiar to each
major contributor. The final prefatory piece, Chapter Five, supplies
advance information on two central cultural themes which is essential
to the reader/hearer's comprehension. There I also take a single text and
illustrate in detail the kind and degree of interpretive bridging that the
fullest possible reading demands. The texts themselves, presented
using a Tedlockian sort of notational system, as originally recorded, then
in English translation, make up Chapters Six through Eight. Then
follows a brief biographical sketch of each of the narrators, with photographs where possible. Chapter Ten completes the main body of the
volume in exploring the range and cultural significance of inter-textual
variation. Appended are: two inter-linear translations; musical transcriptions of sung passages of certain texts; a Ngunese-English glossary/
dictionary for the corpus; an index of narrators, by name and page
numbers of their texts; a list of scholarly works cited.

Scribe of Kastom

A few final, and especially significant, introductory remarks remain
concerning this volume's genesis and the nature of narration on Nguna.
While in the field my initial interest in "folklore" was a means to an end
other than collecting and investigating oral history or literature. It was
an excellent and enjoyable, though exhaustingly intensive, way of learn-

ing the language in the shortest possible time, made possible by the experience, limitless patience and enthusiasm of my associate, Elder Jack Taviṁasoe of Nekaaᵽa village. For approximately the first three months of my fieldwork, while the community and I got used to each other, this was my major occupation, along with preliminary demographic survey work in the villages in my immediate vicinity and the usual round of participant-observer activities.

Eventually I decided that it was time to move on to a different phase of my research and to pursue the ethnographic interests for which I had at last gained sufficient linguistic competence. But when I attempted to do so, I discovered that people had assigned me to a certain niche; based in part on my early and intensive concentration on oral narrative and local history, I had been classed as a recorder or scribe of their *kastom* ways.

At that time, mid-1979, the Bislama word, *kastom,* was becoming a very powerful, extremely evocative term throughout the New Hebridean archipelago (see the articles by Keesing, Tonkinson, Lindstrom, Larcom and Jolly in Keesing and Tonkinson 1982). Roughly, it designates indigenous cultural forms: social, economic, political and religious institutions, as well as language and technology. From approximately 1971 it grew to be one of the two paramount symbols of the country's new, and only indigenous political party, later named the Vanuaaku Pati, which eventually came to power and led the island group into nationhood. My arrival in January of 1978 coincided with the build-up of political momentum and rhetoric by the Vanuaaku Pati prior to the archipelago's irst national elections. The concept of *kastom,* paired with that of Christianity, proved to be their most effective ideological tool. Together these two notions undoubtedly constitute one of the most symbolically potent, unifying dualities ever created in the history of the Pacific region (see Facey 1983; Tonkinson 1981 and 1982b); and, in the central region of the country, in which Nguna lies, the Vanuaaku Pati enjoyed widespread, staunch support.

Given the nature of my early activities, the general political ambience, plus the fact that I was preceded by a few years by both a historian, Gordon Parsonson, and then a linguist, Albert Schütz, who himself collected and published a set of oral texts (Schütz 1969a), it is no wonder that my presence and purpose on Nguna were perceived in historical and linguistic terms. It was only with considerable effort that I was able to convey to my Ngunese companions, then pursue with them, the wider ethnographic interests that provided the basis of my eventual doctoral dissertation (Facey 1983).

Throughout my stay on Nguna, however, I remained a *kastom*-recorder in the eyes of some, who held the hope that I would produce a written account of their *kastom* so that others, ni-Vanuatu and those of foreign lands, might come to know and appreciate it better. In order to fulfil these hopes, and to repay the generosity of a number of people from several different villages who had recounted texts and explained features of traditional culture to me, I served as scribe, editor, translator and publication agent in writing a bilingual (Ngunese/English) pamphlet covering several major aspects of traditional Ngunese culture, from political structure to culinary customs. With the kind assistance of the national Cultural Centre in Port Vila and its Curator, Kirk Huffman, and the British Department of Education, this document was reproduced and distributed on Nguna and also lodged in the Cultural Centre where it is available to the public. The present volume likewise is in large part written for the people of Nguna in order to give them what they so hoped I would.

Given this consummate interest in and commitment to their own cultural history, two recurrent features of Ngunese narrators' performances stand out. First, none of the texts in this volume was related as a collaborative group effort, nor do I possess tape-recordings of any such accounts. This is *not* because stories are never related in this fashion on Nguna. Indeed, it is a fairly common occurrence that a narrator will confer with his/her fellows who are present to confirm points of fact, for example, person or place names, the chronology of narrative events, or a song's tune. When this happens, however, the narrator or some other person will always request that the tape recorder be shut off until these deliberations have been completed and the narrator has the point under consideration "straight" or "correct". The narrative then resumes as if without break.

Second, while the strength of this concern for narrative correctness or accuracy is not surprising, I was surprised by one of the reasons behind it. As often as not, this concern is explicitly linked to the reaction of the projected, non-Ngunese audience rather than to the internal judgement of members of the Ngunese community itself. Knowing that their texts would ultimately be seen and read by English-speaking Whites, be they in Vanuatu, Australia, Canada or wherever, Ngunese narrators frequently expressed concern over how that absent audience would evaluate their cultural productions and, by extension, their culture and themselves. From time to time they would turn to me asking whether what they were saying was acceptable or even whether I thought it accurate. I witnessed a similar phenomenon when preparations were under way on Nguna for their contribution to the national Arts Festival in December, 1979. In listening to a discussion regarding customary clothing that was to be made for exhibition there, I heard an exchange that went something like this:

> Person 1: "Well, how was it we used to make [a certain item of apparel]?"
> Person 2: "Uh, I think the *kastom* way was like this [...ex planation...]."
> Person 3: "Well, we'd better get it right; because, if we don't, if it isn't the real *kastom* way, those Whites in Vila are going to look at it and just laugh at us."

While I had no ethical difficulty with playing an editorial or translatory role, I was shocked and certainly reluctant to being put in the position of a cultural judge or arbiter, especially if I was to do so as a representative of the White reading community! I believe that I managed to resist that role, encouraging people to "tell it like it is/was" to the best of their knowledge and ability; for it is indeed *their kastom* and *they* who know it best. But the legacy of colonial rule and judgemental reactions from people such as some of the early hard-line missionaries and (to say the least) culturally insensitive plantation owners is an ethnic or cultural insecurity that continues to run deep on Nguna even in the face of the Vanuaaku Pati's attempts to imbue *kastom* with a new respect and to restore its ancient legitimacy. So, while I urged them to be their own guides, I cannot say to what extent narrators may still have engaged in an internal editing process as they spoke. I can only hope that those Ngunese who read this work will offer their "scribe of *kastom*" the benefit of their reactions in the future.

Chapter Two

Introduction To
The Ethnographic Context

Nguna, Vanuatu

Nguna is a relatively small island, measuring some five by ten kilometres and lying about seven kilometres off the north coast of Efate, from which it is separated by the usually calm Undine Bay. It is only one of several islands clustered about Efate. Mooso, Leleppa and little Retoka or "Hat Island" run down to the southwest of Nguna in that order, and P̃ele, Kakula and Emau lie roughly to its east, P̃ele's westernmost point being no more than two hundred metres from *Nagisu Taare* or "White Point", Nguna's southeastern tip (see Map, next page).

To reach Nguna from the nation's capital, Port Vila, one bumps along a coral road originally constructed by American troops in the early 1940s. Leaving Vila, it climbs steeply, then runs along the plateau, passing in and out of scattered hamlets. Barring breakdown or mishap, within an hour and a half one's Vila taxi or local (generally, Toyota) pickup should be descending to Emua wharf on the north shore.

When first glimpsed from the road at a point about halfway between Leleppa and Mooso, Nguna appears dominated by the two volcanic cones that flare high at either end (see Plate One). But as one's vehicle slithers down the clutch-wrenching slope toward the coast, the island's outline is transformed into a soft, nearly symmetrical curve of green, highlighted by a brilliant white beach that traces the length of most of its southern face. "Transport" from the wharf comes in the form of one of several local, communally owned motorized launches. The crossing itself takes only about fifteen or twenty minutes, unless a strong wind

9

Efate, Nguna, and Surrounding Islands

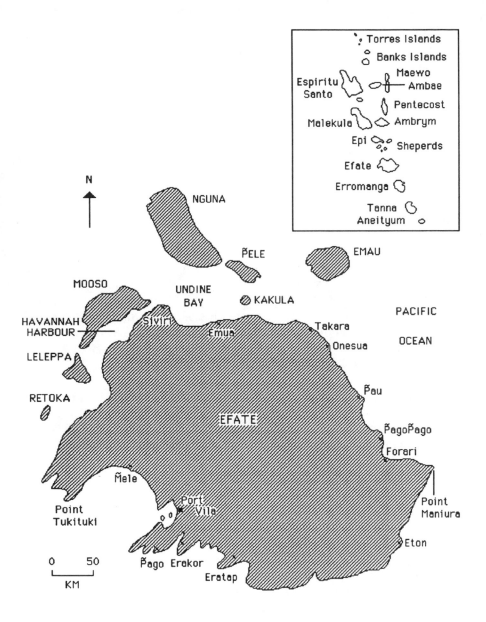

prevails, forcing the launch operator to proceed cautiously, hugging the protective shore of P̃ele rather than heading straight out across the open expanse.

A frequent destination is Tikilasoa, whose population of about 200 makes it the largest of Nguna's twelve villages (see Figure, next page). While atypical in terms of its size, "Tiki" is like the others in general appearance. My first impression was of neatness, compactness and orderliness: grass is kept short and the remarkably straight main paths of beaten earth are swept and weeded with regularity. The homes are arranged in a highly nucleated, roughly rectangular shape. Flowering plants, croton and various types of bushes as well as wooden fences create borders around individual houses and/or compounds made up of more than one dwelling.

Houses in the Western style—cement-block squares or rectangles with corrugated iron roofs—mingle with "*kastom* houses", modified traditional structures done in various combinations of sheet iron, thatch, wood and bamboo. In addition, even the smallest villages have some type of church and *varea* or "meeting-house", the largest and most imposing of which are found in Tikilasoa (see Plate Two). Another significant element found in four villages is the copra co-operative storage shed and retail store. While some of these are referred to as "British" and others "French", all "co-ops" are organized in the same fashion: a committee of local share-holders employs and oversees a "secretary" who keeps the books, runs the store, dispensing all the necessities and desired luxuries, and manages the sale of the members' copra production.

Making copra is certainly the universal, primary source of cash for the Ngunese. A few individuals, most of them teachers in the island's two primary schools and Nguna's Pastor, are able to earn a salary while still living at home (they are liable, however, to be transferred elsewhere in the country). In addition, some people derive a portion of their cash income from part-time "taxi" driving, which means running launches as well as ferrying goods and people by truck on the island or in Vila or operating taxis in Vila and around Efate. Some also raise stock—cattle or pigs—but only on a very small scale. For all of the island's cumulative population of just under a thousand (981 as of 1979 according to official census records), slash-and-burn gardening of taro, manioc, yam and other vegetables is the essential necessity of life.

Nguna's Villages

Deserted Villages

1. M̃alasoro
2. Fanuatapu
3. P̃ogimao
4. M̃alanaruru
5. Komalikasua
6. M̃alamea
7. Em̃oi
8. M̃alarei
9. Raitoa
10. Sierau
11. Tanorop̃o

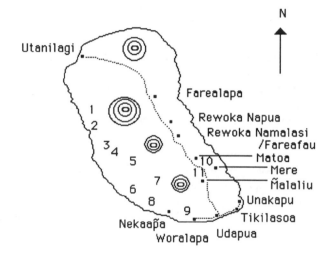

Unity and Continuity

In many, perhaps even most respects, Ngunese culture and society manifest contrary forces and contrary values. The members of Ngunese society live at the intersection of opposing pressures and espouse values which are likewise in direct opposition to one another, but which they choose to and indeed seem able to maintain. Take Ngunese social structure as one example. There are two essential principles of social organization: locality and descent, colloquially glossed as "(same/one) blood" (*nadaa sikai maau*) and "(same/one) line" (*nakainaga sikai maau*) respectively. It is the interplay of these two principles, sometimes conflictual, sometimes complementary, which shapes this society.

The Ngunese are concerned with maintaining various social units, among which are the "family", the village and the matrilineal descent group (*nakainaga* or "matriclan"). The co-resident agnatic cluster is the basic family group in which people live and work; the village, a collection of such clusters, is a highly bounded entity both spatially and politically. In the former the members are united under the authority of the male head while, in the latter, villagers unite as one "people" (*narei*) under their high chief. Thus, co-residence at village and sub-village levels can be seen by the outsider, and is envisioned by the Ngunese themselves, as effecting unity in space.

On the other hand, matrilineal descent joins those who do not share space in their everyday lives. It does so through exogamy, the outward dispersal of women, from the family in the first instance and very often also from the village and even from the island itself, the vast majority of wives leaving their homes for those of their husbands. This loss of women is divisive and disunifying given that social unity depends on closure, that is, on maintaining boundaries either by inclusion or exclusion. Therefore the loss of women is negatively valued vis-à-vis the desire for unity.

At the same time, though, there is an explicit recognition that to "let go of women" (*doropusi nagoroi*) is necessary if they are to fulfil their critical social role of bearing children. Parents who refuse to allow their daughter to marry are criticized for wanting to "hang onto" or "keep her" (*mauti a*) like a selfish child who hoards its toy and refuses to share with another. This attitude derives from the complementary value of social continuity, something which necessitates movement or transaction *across* boundaries. Therefore, vis-à-vis the desire for social continuity, the loss of women is positively valued as, in a sense, personal sacrifice made by individuals and their families for the sake of the reproduction of the social whole.

In their religious life the Ngunese also find themselves caught between opposing alternatives. In this regard Nguna superficially demonstrates a high degree of stability in that, since adopting Christianity at the turn of the century, they have made no major reversions to pagan beliefs; nor have any competing denominations emerged that substantially threaten this Presbyterian stronghold, though this has happened elsewhere in Vanuatu (for the Ambrym case, see Tonkinson 1981). Recent gains made on Nguna by the Seventh Day Adventist Church are small and the local Presbyterian Session has successfully taken steps to retard converts' attempts to strengthen their position locally.

The Presbyterian Ngunese see themselves as rightful heirs to their forefathers' faith. In their thinking, since the island was "brought into the Light" by a Presbyterian missionary, only this church has historical validity. For its adherents, then, any person who abandons it for another church and faith is betraying, even denying, the faith of his or her fathers. There are, nevertheless, those who choose to leave; and there are a few who have tried several different denominations in succession. These tend to be looked on by their peers as insincere, as merely "playing at" being believers of any faith at all. Then, there is the occasional person who tries to use a change of religious affiliation as a threat or point of leverage when criticized for his or her behaviour.

But, more than these, there are all those whose attitude is basically one of disinterest. Especially amongst young, unmarried men there are many who do not actively demonstrate a Christian affiliation by going to church. Some even display open contempt for those who do. In part this is an aspect of youthful rebellion; some of these individuals see fit to act in a more orthodox fashion as they grow into adulthood, especially when they marry and assume adult status and responsibilities. The numbers of people involved, however, and the fact that they are not restricted to those in this rebellious category, suggest a nascent secularism. This is fairly predictable, seemingly an unavoidable consequence of Westernization. In Vanuatu, as in so many other parts of the world, the changing socioeconomic situation has provided competing systems of values along with opportunities for individuals to adopt them and the different lifestyles that go with them without social penalty.

In Ngunese political life similar trends are evident. Traditional politics here were never characterized by ostentatious public competition between individuals, actual or aspiring "Big Men", nor are they today. Nevertheless, there are a few men whose words carry more weight than others', and this fact is not satisfactorily accounted for by comparing their relative positions in the chiefly hierarchy. Personal attributes and skills, such as a good command of local history, oratorical eloquence, and sheer charismatic presence, certainly single out some chiefs over others. There are also interpersonal conflicts between chiefs, but their supporters do not operate publicly as followings in open opposition. Political differences are not thrashed out by rival factions as they often are on Tanna, Ambae and elsewhere in Vanuatu. This, of course, does not mean that there are no differences, no long-standing animosities or scores to settle. But, in order to realize their desire for unity or, at least, to give the impression of striving toward it, such conflicts are suppressed as people attempt to conceptualize and to portray their community as a cohesive, coherent whole.

Ngunese Identity

Two notions together form the basis of the Ngunese conception of their society, embodying its essential distinctiveness as an integral entity distinct from all others. One of these notions, *kastom*, simultaneously invokes the unity and the continuity through time of the social whole. The Ngunese equivalent of *kastom, natoomariana ni navanua*, means literally "the-way-of-doing [things] of the Land" in a progressive or continuous sense. The Ngunese feel that contemporary activities and behaviour should approximate customary standards but, at the same time, there is considerable difference of opinion as to the actual substance of those standards.

The core of *kastom* for the Ngunese is still the traditional chiefly system. Yet, contemporary generations now regard Christianity as traditional as well, even though it originated with Europeans. The essence of Ngunese culture for the Ngunese themselves, then, is a dual identification which Tonkinson's phrase "*kastom* within Christianity" (1982b) describes well, in that it implies that the only elements of *kastom* which may be included are those that are compatible with Christianity's social and moral tenets.

The Ngunese' evaluation of their own culture relative to European culture, however, is sometimes negative. The obvious wealth and technological complexity of European society combined with Europeans' historical condemnation of many aspects of indigenous culture have resulted in the Ngunese' tendency to perceive their own culture as inferior in many ways. Only within the last decade and a half have educated ni-Vanuatu begun to achieve the perspective that Howard observed among educated Rotumans. This growing segment of the population now, as Howard puts it, "...recognize[s] the value of Rotuman custom for its own sake, from a moral-ethical point of view" (1970:150).

Moreover, Howard goes on to say that the educated élite "...can also recognize [custom's] significance as a source of common identity and make efforts to endow custom with dignity." This, along with the statement quoted above, could just as well be used to describe what happened during the late 1970s and early 1980s in Vanuatu. The following thoughts of the country's first Prime Minister, Father Walter Lini, aim at a radical restructuring of the country's self-concept:

> We believe that small is beautiful, peace is powerful, respect
> is honourable, and that our traditional sense of comunity is
> both wise and practical for the people of Vanuatu.

(Lini 1980:290)

I would suggest that the Ngunese of the last two decades have found themselves in a situation rather like that which faced their great-grand-parents at the end of the last century. The major influences of that era (the labour trade, the introduction of wage labour and cash-cropping, combined with a sudden, severe drop in population due to epidemics of novel diseases) produced effects similar to those experienced in the last two decades òn Nguna. Over the last twenty years, a large number of people, particularly the young, have been absent for extended periods and often, upon returning, they have brought with them new values and habits that are socially disruptive or in conflict with local values.

In both periods these processes have resulted in what may be re-garded as a state of ideological crisis in which contradictory notions abound and proponents of different social constructions of reality vie for ideological control. In the historical case the new Christians emerged victorious from this ideological confusion and in the present the support-ers of a particular political party have done likewise. For reasons too many and too complex to go into here (see Chapter Five in this volume and Facey 1983), just as the entire Ngunese population at the turn of the century eventually adopted Christianity, so have virtually all Ngunese now become supporters of the Vanuaaku Pati. What singles Nguna out from other ni-Vanuatu cultures which have gone through similar crises is the fact that, in both instances, not only have the pre-existent leaders managed to maintain their dominance, but the society has also main-tained an appearance of unity no matter what degree of controversy and debate continues to exist below the smooth surface of everyday life.

Plate One: Nguna, as seen from north-west Efate

Plate Two: Tikilasoa's Varea/Meeting-House, front view

Chapter Three

Transformations

A: The Act of Transcription

Finding the Form

As discussed earlier (see Chapter One), this volume takes off from Tedlock and others' well-documented proposition that oral narrative as a genre ought most profitably to be treated as poetry rather than as a form of prose; and that, similarly, any given oral narrative should be understood and treated as a poetic event or performance rather than as a written text.

While Hymes' attitude toward oral literature is much the same as Tedlock's, I do not follow the former's scheme of "discovering" the form in terms of verses, stanzas, scenes and so on (cf. Hymes 1981). While Hymes forcefully argues for their appropriateness in the bodies of oral texts with which he deals, I doubt that such sub-divisions necessarily reflect inherent structural properties of all cultures' oral literature. Therefore, I prefer to make as few alterations and additions to the textual flow as possible. I use only the following few devices, most of which are borrowings from Tedlock's notational system (for other possibilities, see the "Guide to Reading Aloud" in Tedlock 1983).

1. A carriage return to the left-hand margin indicates a pause that marks the clear end of an utterance. In many of the Nguna texts this includes more than one grammatically complete clause or phrase, so the end of each clause/phrase that occurs within a single utterance is marked by a period. Note that this enables the reader to compare relative textual intensity within a text and across different texts and narrators merely by glancing through a text to see how much gets said

between major pause breaks ("textual intensity" meaning the combined effect of the degree of continuousness of verbal flow plus the speed of delivery);

2. Indentation indicates continuation of an utterance that is longer than one line;

3. A pause longer than that which normally follows an utterance is indicated with the symbol (°) placed at the left margin, or two (°°) for a pause of approximately twice that duration;

4. Elongation of a syllable to mark passage of time or movement is indicated by repetition of the vooowel involved or, in translation, of the vowel in the appropriate wooord;

5. A word or phrase pronounced in a louder than normal speaking voice is placed in **bold** typeface;

6. Where physical gestures are performed by the narrator, they are described in italics [*isolated from the text proper*] in square brackets;

7. In addition, musical transcriptions of passages that are to be sung are collected following the Appendix.

Devising Novel Features of Form

While the Nguna texts do not have titles as such, I have taken minimal liberties in assigning titles to them. In some cases the narrator employs a phrase within the first few sentences which introduces the subject of the narrative. Where this is so, the speaker's phrase or some more succinct version of it has been designated as the title; for example, one of Kaltap̃au M̃asemata's texts begins with the statement, "I will recount the origin of **Marimaraki**." Consequently, I entitle the text "The Origin of **Marimaraki**".

In instances in which this is not done by the narrator, I have chosen the name(s) of the most salient charac ter(s), event, place or object(s) and let this constitute the title. In Lui Taatalele's "The Death of Mariameara" the text begins with this general statement: "[There's] one war story that goes like this. It took place long ago." The text's end, however, comes abruptly upon the death of Mariameara: "And it was [only] then that the chief died, for they had shot him with the sacred arrow." It is apparent that Mariameara's death is the point of the account and it therefore is taken for its title.

With any textual corpus one of the most significant factors in its presentation is the decision to divide the corpus into different types of text[1]. Each of chapters Six, Seven and Eight corresponds to one of three major categories of texts which have been delineated with reference to the following two basic criteria:

1. The local terms used to refer to narratives, which are (Ngunese/ Bislama): *naatuusiana/stori*[2]; *nariwota/histri*; and *natukunoa/stori*;

2. The general theme, subject, or apparent raison d'être of each narrative, be it explicit or implicit.

Regarding the first criterion, use of these three terms in discourse follows two unwritten rules: any narrative may be referred to as a *naatuusiana/stori;* and, any text referred to as a *nariwota* may *not* be referred to as a *natukunoa*, and vice versa.

With respect to the second criterion, it is easiest to distinguish the *nariwota* from the *natukunoa*. Each *nariwota* recounts the origin of either a chiefly title, from its first to last incumbents, or a specific matriclan. The latter always begin with a woman of that matriclan who (or whose female matrilineal descendant) was the first member of that clan to come to Nguna. Thereafter, that "line" is traced, uterine descendant by uterine descendant, until it (and the account) reach and name the present day, local representatives of that clan. For this volume, however, I have chosen only *nariwota* that are explicitly chiefly ancestries. Ancestries of the other (more malleable) variety tend moreso to be employed in support of land claims and, as that is always a hot political topic on Nguna (as elsewhere throughout Vanuatu), it is incumbent upon the ethnographer to avoid fanning the flames. While this creates a textual gap from the ethnographic viewpoint, from the fieldworker's viewpoint it is an ethically unavoidable one.

Texts called *natukunoa* bear no resemblance to *nariwota* (with the notable exception of the *nariwota* recounting the origin of the two highest chiefs, Taripoaliu and Taripoamata). The dramatis personae of the *natukunoa* are animals rather than humans, although these non-humans do act very much like people. Not only do they speak; they also also exhibit human emotional, moral and social characteristics and engage in human- like economic, political and military activities.

The texts that make up the rest of the corpus, classed here under the general term of *naatuusiana/stori*, would never be called *natukunoa*[3] or *nariwota*. Like *natukunoa*, each has a discursive structure in which events are recounted; but the actors, even those with unusual powers, are definitely human, many being accepted as historic individuals. Moreover, realistic geographic and other sorts of details are supplied, grounding these accounts in known features of the real world– specific, named places and landmarks such as particular rock formations, hills or trees. The subjects of these texts are also unlike those of *nariwota*: they include historic battles, intra-familial rivalries and the origins and/or attributes of sociocultural institutions.

Having considered these factors, it is clear that the three terms used to describe narratives do correspond to distinctly different types recognized by the Ngunese.   Given the nature of each, they are most appropriately translated for English-readers as follows:

1. *Nariwota ni naveinawotaana maaga* or "chiefly ancestries". (Again, although there are *nariwota* that relate more generally to matriclans rather than to specific chiefly titles, only the latter type are presented here for the reason stated above);
2. *Naatuusiana maaga* or "accounts" of events of various sorts; and,
3. *Natukunoa maaga* or "tales" featuring non-human actors.

One other rather complex feature in support of this tri-partite division (and the English terminology chosen) needs explication. This is the issue of truth value or historic authenticity.   Narrators occasionally make explicit declarations within the texts, distinguishing a "true" story from "just" a story. This is not found in the *nariwota*, because all *nariwota* are universally narrated and accepted as descriptions of actual historic events and individuals.   In addition, at the conclusion of some of the chiefly *nariwota* (texts #3 and 4), plus all of the matriclan *nariwota* which do not appear in this volume, a connection is made between the recited historic characters and one or more known living person who is their descendant.   These first-hand reference points lend such accounts authenticity by grounding them in the present social context.

Texts designated as *natukunoa* are understood to be "just stories", and are often explicitly stated to be "just for children". Yet, in some *natukunoa*, the narrative ends with what, in his discussion of the "poetics of verisimilitude", Tedlock terms "tale-ending paralogic" (1983:164-166; 177).   This is an assertion that the text provides an explanation of a known fact or feature of reality, along the lines of, for example, "And that's why the ___ fish has so many sharp spines." When questioned about such "paralogical" statements in their texts, Ngunese narrators tend to respond to this effect: "Well, maybe it's really the reason; maybe it isn't. Who knows?..." It is clear from this sort of response that whether a *natukunoa* is taken as true or historically accurate is not of great moment to its narrator—truth value is not a primary attribute of the *natukunoa*. It certainly is, however, for the *nariwota*.

As for *naatuusiana*, some contain explicit declara tions of their truth intended to distinguish them from the usual "story". In Kaltap̃au M̃asemata's text #15, "How the Destruction of M̃alasoro was Ended", for example, there is an explicit declaration of the narrative's veracity: "I shall tell the origin of this story. It is not just a story; rather, it is a true story, one which actually happened." Similarly, one of Ronneth Manutukituki's texts (#22) is placed in a specific year: "The War of 1874". Many *naatuusiana*, however, contain neither such declarations nor real-time markers.

Given this variability, it might be possible to argue that declared-as-true versus not-so-declared might be the only categorical, indigenous basis for categorization of the corpus of texts and that, therefore, it and only it should be employed as the basis for that categorization. I find the idea unacceptable, though, because it is an ethnographically sterile one, utterly ignoring the substantial, indigenous evidence discussed above concerning shared themes and/or structure and types of characters involved, all of which have been considered in constructing the proposed system of categorization. Moreover, such a simplistic categorization also ignores both the intra- textual and extra-textual indigenous evaluations of whether a given narrative is true/ not-true/maybe true(?).

B: The Act of Translation

While I have diverged from Hymes' approach concerning form, I could not agree more with the opinion he expresses in introducing his recent book, *"In vain I tried to tell you": Essays in Native American Ethno-poetics:*

> The great linguist Leonard Bloomfield used to tell students that in published work one should not bring the reader into the kitchen. But it is in keeping with the canons of science to let the kitchen sometimes be seen. Always to conceal the turmoil behind the scenes is ultimately to be misleading.

> (Hymes 1981:12)

The following assembles under seven different headings the knotty problems or difficulties that occur and recur in the process of Ngunese

to English translation.   Each is illustrated with one or two prime
examples representative of that type of phenomenon.

1. Non-equivalents

(a) In more than one text (John Mariwota's text #27, "Lawomidimiidi", for example) the term *m̃aau* is problematic. A *m̃aau* is a warrior
of the most fearsome variety. When scenes of combat are depicted, it is
inevitably one or more *m̃aau* who lead the attack, who live to fight the
longest, and who deliver and/or carry out sentences of execution imposed
by the high-ranking chiefs with whom they are associated. The closest
English approximation of *m̃aau*, then, could be something like "champion warrior"; yet the executioner aspect of the *m̃aau's* role suggests
instead such modern, colloquial phrases as "trained assassin" or "hit
man". Given how culturally "loaded" these choices are, the better option
is not to attempt to translate at all, and instead, once having discussed
its meaning, to maintain the original Ngunese term throughout the
translations.

(b) To coin a bizarre phrase, the "modern archaism" is often as
problematic as the true archaism such as *m̃aau*. In Kaltap̃au M̃ase-
mata's text #8, "Chief of the Birds", the term *narup̃a* occurs. It was
translated by my transcription assistant as "concubine", based on his
experience in Biblical translation and, no doubt, an inherited missionary
attitude regarding the indigenous practice of polygamy. In Nguna's past
it was customary or, at least, common for men, particularly powerful,
high-ranking chiefs, to have more than one wife. Historic accounts of
men co-habiting with women without benefit of Christian ceremonies
can only be understood within present Presbyterian terms of reference,
however, as "possessing 'concubines' ". But use of such a term conflicts
with the usual, non-judgemental ethnographic presentation of polyga-
mous relationships in traditional societies. Consequently, I feel compelled to employ a translation which is neither Bible-specific nor culturally judgemental. The solution arrived at is to translate *narup̃a* as either
"lover", "wife", "second wife" or even simply "woman", whichever is most
appropriate given the immediate context of occurrence.

(c) The term *mariki* is also sometimes difficult to translate effectively.
In some contexts it is roughly equivalent in meaning and use to "fellow";
in some it clearly means "husband"; and, in *mariki nawota*, where it is
in apposition to "chief", the phrase can be translated as "the old chief",
although this fails to capture the nuance of respect that is present in
many occurrences of the phrase (see, again, Mariwota's "Lawomidimiidi"). Seitel deals with a comparable problem regarding the Haya

word *Ta*, which is a derivative of *tata* or "my father". As "[it] is used as a title, like 'Mister' in English" (1980:40), Seitel maintains the original word rather than translating it. While *mariki* plays a remarkably similar role in Ngunese, this is only one of its roles. Consequently, I have opted to translate it wherever possible, using whichever of the alternatives listed above most closely approaches the intended contextual meaning.

(d) Occasionally the perennial ethnographic problem of being unable, in the absence of a dictionary, to obtain English (and here, even Bislama) equivalents for particular linguistic items leaves one no option but to use the original terms. This is the case with a number of species of fish and birds (e.g., the *masoni* and *takeo*, both species of fish). All other identifiable animal, fish or bird names appear in translation. I would greatly appreciate the assistance of any Ngunese person, linguist or anyone else who might be able to supply the correct English equivalents for these species or any others that appear in the volume.

2. Variations on a Term

Exclamations are bound to be poorly translated unless one pays a great deal of attention to context and does a lot of experimenting. They comprise a very complex set of meanings some of which demand explication in a footnote, while for others equivalent translations can be devised. For yet others, the only acceptable route is to leave the term as is, untranslated, though perhaps accompanied by an italicized notation or modification in brackets.

Here is one example (from Kaltap̃au M̃asemata's "How the Destruction of M̃alasoro was Ended", text #15): "*Eee*, we think we should go back." This "*Eee*" can best be translated as Well,..." or perhaps "So,...". But "little differences" make a great deal of difference in such expressions. There are instances of the same expression in which, in addition to being elongated, there is extra stress, as "*Eee!*", which is a dramatic expression of shock or dismay. Elsewhere in the texts "*E!*" occurs with an exclamation point to indicate a moderate amount of stress in what functions as a marker to introduce a decision that has been made or an intention to take some action. In other instances it is "*E!*", the bolding indicating more forceful delivery, suggesting moderate surprise (like "Hey!", "Oh, no!" or "What?!"). These four forms—"*E!* / *E!* / *Eee!* / *Eee!*"—are distinctly different communications, establishing qualitatively different emotional tones and expectations in the listener/reader. On top of this, "*Ee*" often simply means "No", and when used in this sense and further lengthened and/or given extra stress, it becomes a negative with more emotional "oomph".

An intriguing expression which, although phonologically different, must surely be placed somewhere along the "*Ee*" spectrum is used almost exclusively by women. "*Iiii*!", with its distinctive parabolic falling and rising of tone, is an expression of ignorance in response to a request for information. It carries a definite overtone (undertone?) of reluctance to consider the request. While this does not occur in any of the texts, it would be best translated as, "How should I know?" or "Why are you asking me?!"

"*Aai*!" is a strong expression of disappointment and annoyance. For example, in Masemata's text #29, "The Crab and the *Strongbak*", a spirit-person steals the two animals' meat under the guise of helping them cut it up. On discovering that they have been cheated out of the entire carcass, left with nothing but the entrails, they say to each other, "*Aai*! That old man took all the good meat." This has been left untranslated, as I hesitate to try to capture it with an English obscenity, even though this might best convey the characters' reaction. A more poignant example from the same narrator occurs in the following situation: the people of a village who have for years been under intermittent attack by another group have just suffered a substantial loss of life in the latest incident. Having discovered how many of their number are missing, they utter this heartfelt, and quite untranslatable, expression of pain: "*Ai*! All the time we have lived here, we have suffered from the people of Utanilagi coming and attacking us. They are devouring us...."

A more positive feeling is conveyed with the expression "*Oo*!". Again in "The Crab and the *Strongbak*", the spirit-person says this to himself when he realizes that the meat he has put into the earth oven to bake must be done, so his ill-gotten feast should be ready to eat. This pleasurable thought occurs to the spirit, with "*Oo*!" translated simply as "Oh!": "Oh! I must take out my meat. I must take out my meat and leisurely eat it."

It hardly seems necessary to add that, as Seitel puts it in speaking of similar expressions used by a female Haya narrator,

> These and other nonlexical utterances are 'phatic' in nature— they speak to the feelings rather than to the intellect. They open affective channels of communication.... Through these phatic utterances, the narrator coaxes greater emotional participation from herself and the audience.
>
> (Seitel 1980:43)

3. Meaningful silence

In text #14, "How the Slit-Drum was Discovered", there is a good example of the translational difficulty frequently presented by the concept of *paapaa*, which roughly translates as "until":

"Goo eu peani **vaatu** seara waina eu doo duki lua naɱelevara maaga wanogoe asa. Paapaa e noopu. Eu mari ɱata ki nia."

The strict translation of this is:

"And they had **stone** some which they PROG knock out coal PL those with-it. Until it finished. They make well of it."

What is problematic when transforming this into fluent English is the dual role of *paapaa*. It simultaneously conveys that (1) the described action took place in the ongoing past imperfect (or theatrical present) and (2) that it has come to an end, i.e., that that action has also been completed. The crux of the problem is to find a way of saying this in English using the verb concerned—"knock out"—in a tense that will convey the sense of continuous action, i.e., "knocking", while combining this with the sense of the end or completion of that action.

In the Ngunese the passage of time is carried partly by the aural space—the unspeaking silence—between *asa* at the end of the first utterance and *paapaa* which initiates the next utterance. While the pause is reflected in the Ngunese transcription with a period, for the translation one might join the two utterances, using the word "until" followed by an ellipsis to suggest the continuousness of action as well as its termination:

"And they had certain stones they would use for knocking out the coals until... it was all done, [then] they would properly finish it."

In like instances throughout the texts, this strategy has been employed. In this particular case, however, another solution was chosen, one which comes closer to capturing another significant feature of the original passage— the way in which the narrator, using pauses, divides the passage into three separate utterances. The final English result is:

"And they had certain stones they would use for knocking out the coals. When this was all done, they would then properly finish it."

This single translational issue points up a critical linguistic and cultural difference between English and Ngunese: for Ngunese speaker/

hearers, it is the pause, the *silence* itself which dramatically expresses the passage of time in the narrative, while the word *paapaa* gives closure to the dramatic moment. For English speaker/hearers, by contrast, it is the *word* itself– "until", especially if dragged out as "untiiil", or modified by the addition of an ellipsis as "until..."–which conveys the equivalent meaning and experience. This is a case in which, for the Ngunese, silence speaks equally, perhaps even more loudly than the word.

4. Grammatical Non-Equivalence

(a) In some ways the Ngunese language can be used to express much using little, such that the English translator must add information or vary the translation from context to context as needed. For example, many extremely common verbs take a number of verbal completions that call for quite different translations. A very common one is *dape* meaning to "take, carry, pick up". With *pano* ("go") as its verbal completion, it generally means "take" in an outgoing or away-going direction; with *umai* ("come") it becomes "bring" or "take" in a direction going toward the narrator's point of reference. Consequently, these frequently require a translation other than simply "take" or even "bring" depending on the context, which includes the narrator's and audience's point of reference as well as those of the characters in the text. Thus, the expanded English version may be an expression such as "bear [it] away" or "carry [her] off".

(b) Another feature of Ngunese grammar that calls for additional information in translation is its neuter (or neutral vis-à-vis gender) pronouns. The third person singular form (*e*), for example, may designate he, she or it. When this occurs in reference to a person, the English translation cannot settle for he/she. One has to choose the appropriate alternative. This becomes unfortunate, though, in instances in which the neutral gender component of the Ngunese pronoun has a dramatic role to play. This is the case, for example, in Lui Taatalele's text #4, "The Origin of Mariamearaliu". Here the neuter *e* is used up until the tenth line of the text in referring to the arrival on Nguna of the first chief Mariameara. Most adult Ngunese listeners will know that the chief in question was female, notwithstanding the masculine prefix (*Mari*) on her title. But both children hearing the account for the first time and English readers will most certainly be ignorant of that fact. Consequently, in having to translate the early pronominal references as "she", the revelation of the new chief's gender, which comes only when she has journeyed to and then been installed as chief in the village of M̃atoa (ten lines into the story), loses some of its revelatory punch.

5. Referents, Muddy or Missing

(a) In many of the texts knowing who from where did what to whom
can be a trial when listening as a non- native speaker/hearer; but trying
to make these things clear in the English translation can be a daunting
task. In a text such as Kaltap̃au M̃asemata's "Marikori goo/ and Leilega"
(#16), there is a veritable morass of ambiguous antecedents.

The following selection begins as two men decide to find out the
identity of the person or thing that has been attacking and killing
hapless passersby at the seaside. One of the men offers to present
himself as bait to lure out the killer while his companion hides to make
the identification (and live to tell of it). The literal translation of the
passage demonstrates the complexity of the Ngunese use of pronouns
and antecedents:

"So the second person of them remained **hidden.**
But, the one who himself agreed to it that he should die, went until
he was right on that path and that person came up.
He came up and **attacked him.**
He attacked him and they-two **fought!**
But that one remained hidden.
They-two remained until
and he beat that person and he **struck him,**
he killed him."

For the sake of comprehension, one is compelled to add the killer's
name as well as some other points of clarification, yielding this:

"So the second man **hid** there.
Meanwhile, the one who was willing to die, went on until he struck the
    path and the man [Marikori] came up [along it toward him].
He came up and **attacked him.**
So the two of them **fought!**
But the other one remained in hiding.
They kept on...
until finally [the m̃aau] defeated the man, and **beat him,**
beat him to death."

(b) Apart from the problem of antecedents unclear to the foreign ear/
eye, the above passage also had to be revised to accomodate understanding of the physical dimension of the action itself. Similar difficulties
arise in many of the texts, among them Lui Taatalele's text #18, "The
Death of Mariameara". These derive from two other referencing prob-

lems: first, English lacks distinctions that are inherent in some Ngunese conjunctions when paired with demonstrative pronouns; and, second, the non-Ngunese reader lacks the everyday knowledge required to make certain kinds of connections immediately.

A specific example of the first of these problems can be found in "The Death of Mariameara". Simplifying, the men of Group A want to fight Group B; so they proceed to B's village and call out to them, tauntingly:

"You should act like **men**, and come here.
We will do battle."

Then the narrator again speaks as himself (literally translated):

"Then those people could **not** go up.
But they had something called a sacred arrow."

Here the subject of the first statement, "those people", refers to those of Group A whose taunt has just been pronounced. Since it is they on whom the narrator has been focussing immediately prior to this statement, the antecedent of "those people" is reasonably clear—it is Group A who cannot "go up". (The problem of what not being able to "go up" signifies will itself be addressed in 5d below.)

Now, the second sentence, "But they had something called a sacred arrow", is bound to completely baffle or at least make the non-Ngunese reader misinterpret the action. The conjunction or connector *maa*, translated here as "but", suggests to the Ngunese reader a shift in focus, while the non-Ngunese reader tends to assume that "they" is the same "they" as encountered in the previous statement, namely Group A. In fact, it is the beleaguered Group B who have the "sacred arrow". Consequently, in the translation necessary extras are supplied to assist the non-Ngunese reader:

"But the [others, the people of M̃atoa], had something they called a sacred arrow."

(c) Throughout this same text, as literally translated, there are many, many instances of this kind of referencing which make the flow of events and actions virtually in- comprehensible to the non-Ngunese audience. The same kind of ambiguity arises over and over in the texts in references to "the chief", and to chiefly titles that stand for particular villages and vice versa. For Ngunese reader/hearers all of this is perfectly clear. The pairing of chiefly titles with village/dominion names is "second nature" to them, such that they immediately recognize as such any name which is a chiefly title, understand any reference to a chief as a reference to whatever bearer of a chiefly title has been previously referred to, and take any citing of a chiefly title to imply a certain village and vice versa.

(d) Ngunese "ethnogeography" includes a set of relative primary reference points. Up/down and above/below are the most commonly used of these, referring to the lay of the land—up the slope as opposed to down the slope or, equally, inland versus seaward. The use of these reference points requires exegesis only in telling to a non-Ngunese. One example is the line quoted above, in 5(b): "Then those people could not go up". This utterance is problematic only if one lacks the geographic referents that make it meaningful. Ṁatoa is situated on one of a number of closeby hills; knowing this, one would already be aware that, in approaching, attackers would be coming from downhill, from below. So the statement "...those men could not go up" implies that the aggressors' position is too vulnerable for them to attempt a direct attack. This explains why they taunt the men of Ṁatoa—they are hoping to lure them out of their protected position to come *down*, level with their attackers.

6. Repetition

(a) Repetition of events is one feature of the Ngunese narratives that is likely to be misread or unappreciated by a foreign audience. Oftentimes a narrator will present a sequence of familiar markers, a string of commonplace, homey events such as the following from Kaltaᵽau Ṁasemata's "The Chief of the Birds" (#8):

"They baked the fish, until it was done.
They ate in the evening.
And when they had finished eating, they slept.
Then in the morning they returned as before to the gardens."

At various points throughout this narrative he repeats slight variations of the same sequence. This serves two purposes: it enables the narrator to register the passage of time via these landmarks of everyday existence; and it provides an emotional "down-time" between more active phases of the narrative. The result is that the listeners get an emotional breather; then, when the more active segments come, not only will the audience perceive them as more dramatic by contrast, they will also be able to respond more strongly to them.

(b) Since repetition does not *always* add to the import or meaning of the text, it will be represented/ reflected in the translation only where it is evident that it *does*. One example in which repetition of a single word is dramatically important occurs toward the end of Ñasemata's "Matokoaale, Leilolo, goo/and Tariliu" (text #10). A certain stone is named twice, as follows:

"Then the chief led the people of the two villages to
    Ƥaukaroa, a stone that lay on the shore.
It is still there today.
Its name is Ƥaukaroa.
And he pointed,
and said, "From here to Worakoto, is the small holding
    that we are giving to you."

The repetition plus the narrator's voice quality make it evident that he wants to emphasize the stone's name. A literal English translation of what he says, however, reads somewhat heavily. To avoid this, one might choose to conflate two or even three of his statements, reducing the repetition by providing that name only where it would have the most force or effect. But, since the narrator clearly intends to stress the name of the stone– as he often does elsewhere with proper names– such editing would constitute an inappropriate anglicization. Consequently, the translation of this passage cleaves close to the original in order to retain this aspect of the narrator's style as well as to fulfil his dramatic intent.

(c) A very common feature in the texts, and one which has both mnemonic and dramatic functions is that of line or clause-linkage in which the repetition of a whole clause or phrase joins or pairs successive utterances in this fashion:

A
AB
BC

Tedlock (1983:52) points out that, while this feature is rare in Western prose and poetry alike, it commonly occurs in epic poetry. It is found to greater or lesser degree in the works of all of Nguna's narrators.

(d) In one important sense repetition *is* always significant. It is a critical component of any body of oral literature which, after all, must be retained if it is to survive the passing of human generations. Repetition carries a substantial portion of the burden of making oral narrative memorable, i.e., rememberable. Therefore, for the scribe or translator, the reduction of textual repetition must be regarded as a rare necessity to be under- taken only cautiously and conservatively.

Footnotes

1. For an interesting comparative case, see Dorothy Counts' (1982) volume of New Britain texts, *The Tales of Laupu/Ol Stori Bilong Laupu.*

2. This spelling, true to its Ngunese pronunciation, differs from that given by Camden in *A Descriptive Dictionary: Bislama to English, as store.*

3. But never say never! Text #14 is one exception: in the first line of "How the Slit-Drum was Discovered", the narrator refers to it as a *natukunoa*. I have chosen, however, to class this text with the *naatuusiana* because of the differences between it and the other *natukunoa*, most particularly that the central character in text #14 is a human rather than an animal. The narrator's classification of the text as a *natukunoa* may derive from the obverse of this, i.e., that the birds in the text act like people.

Chapter Four

Style And Rhetoric

In examining this corpus several essential questions have been asked of each text: (1) What stylistic and/or rhetorical devices are present? (2) What role do these play with respect to emotional tone, dramatic flow, bounding segments of the story, etc., and, (3) Which of these are common to all narrators and which peculiar to individual speakers? In this chapter I discuss the results of this exploration, in so doing delineating the three different sorts of "style" mentioned in Chapter One:

1. "Cultural" Style, which is composed of features common to the texts as a unified body, as cultural productions specific to a certain culture in a certain time frame— in other words, the texts' "Ngunese-ness";
2. "Text-Specific" Style, in the sense of each text being to some degree representative of a particular type of narrative, according to an explicit set of criteria, some of indigenous, some of extrinsic definition;
3. "Idiosyncratic" Style, referring to features of the individual narrator's typical style, that is, the distinctive literary "signature" peculiar to each.

1. Cultural Style

(a) The greatest single, shared feature of the texts is that of repetition. As discussed in Chapter Three, this can involve utterances of any length, from single words to whole clauses that are repeated and paired so as to link succeeding lines. Also, set sequences of familiar, commonplace activities or events often recur within a single text. In different contexts

35

repetition may serve any of the following purposes: to suggest continuous action; to emphasize a single piece of information such as a name; to mark or register passage of narrative time; to provide a hiatus between one passage and another which has more action or unexpected events; and simply to reinforce specific details—to make them memorable.

(b) Another common feature of the texts is the means of altering the pace of the narrative flow. Variations in speed can be generated in several different ways. By making grammatical "mistakes", e.g., dropping final vowels or even syllables (as when *ragi* becomes *rag, natasi* becomes *natas, paki* becomes *pak,* or *pano* becomes *pa*), the narrator speeds up his/her delivery. Slowing the flow is achieved by elongating words as well as by some of the types of repetition discussed above. Another means lies in what is not said, or omitted. In Ñasemata's text #12, "The New Diviner", for example, the absence of a connecting phrase, such as "he said", to introduce the son's response to his diviner/father simultaneously speeds up the interchange and indicates the character's emotional tone at the moment; that is, it implies the son's impatience and his difficulty maintaining sufficient self-control to act with the proper degree of deference.

2. Text-Specific Style

To a considerable extent, this issue has been covered in Chapter Three, where the three types of narrative in terms of which this volume is organized are differentiated from one another as: the *nariwota* or "ancestry"; the *naatuusiana* or "account"; and the *natukunoa* or "tale".

(a) The Nariwota

What most typifies the *nariwota* is concern with historicity or authenticity. On occasion in such texts the narrator injects his own identity, as in the following example from text #15:

"When he got there he went to the dancing-ground of
Ñasemata's meeting-house.
(Today it is I, [Ñasemata], who have this meeting-house.)"

If told by a direct descendant of one of the individuals featured in it, a narrative is considered to be more reliable than that which might be told by any other person, because it is the person closest to the source and *only* such a person who has the right to narrate it. Therefore this interjection serves at least two implicit purposes: the narrator simultaneously asserts both the veracity of his recounting of these particular events and the legitimacy of his right to do so.

Demonstrating textual authenticity can also be achieved by presenting certain kinds of information. The first paragraph of text #3, for example, being the ancestry of a specific chiefly title, provides these bits of information: the chiefly title itself; its village and/or dominion of origin; the pre-existing high chiefly title in the village to which the new chief goes; and the name of the original meeting-house associated with the title. All of this is delivered within the first seven utterances of the story; indeed, I would suggest that these identifying details are the entire point of the early lines of the recitation. A little further on, additional details are given, marking each stage in the narrative: the personal name(s) and clan name of the chief with which the story is concerned; the names of the harbours at which she began and ended her journey; the name of the individual who ferried her across; that of the clan stone which went with her, and so on. All of this lends the air of veracity and of historicity to the narrative.

Where a narrator lacks such information, he/she may make an explicit assertion regarding the text's veracity. Such a meta-comment occurs in text #17:

"She lived theeere... and eventually she bore two children, two boys.
(I don't know their names, but she did have two sons.)"

Unable to provide the names that would substantiate it, the speaker felt compelled to make this aside in which he re-emphasizes the narrative fact of the existence of the two sons.

The narrator may also attempt to draw in the audience and the present time. This is done by referring to a point of either contrast or commonality between the Ngunese present and past. In the text just quoted, for example, Taatalele uses contrast: "You know, in those days children could defecate anywhere." Likewise, M̃asemata refers to the difference between pre- and post- Contact technology in text #14: "But in the olden days they had nothing at all. No axe and nothing else." On the other hand, in text #5 the narrator, Manutukituki, melds past and present, recalling the location of a contemporary feature to the listeners in order to give them a vivid picture of the scene of the narrative's historic action:

"The path was there, by Vaatup̃auna, and that's where he put her ashore, and she followed the path upward, came up and up untiiil
she reached the road, and went on up to...
Today we [can] see the cemetery by the road—the village

where she settled was on the lower side of the cemetery.
So Leiameara settled in that spot, and built a house there."

Occasionally narrators choose pronouns which, by virtue of certain of their semantic features, constitute explicit, grammatical recognition of the presence of the listeners and of their participatory role. This is the case in Manutukituki's text #19, where in his second statement one of the main characters, Tariwiawia, uses the first-person plural exclusive pronoun (*kinami*–"we-more than 2-exclusive") in referring to himself along with a group of women, his fellow characters. With no awareness of the audience, the inclusive variant of the pronoun (*nigida*) would be appropriate as there is no-one else present at this point in the narrative, nor is any absent person implied; consequently, what the narrator conveys by choosing this pronoun is the sense that the textual character himself recognizes and takes into account the existence of the audience as silent actors in the drama.

A last point regarding this type of text has to do with one characteristic which, while not exclusive to either of the other two general text types, is totally absent from the *nariwota*. Singing occurs in 6 of the texts presented here, 5 of these from the *naatuusiana* group, the other a *natukunoa*–although if we take the narrator's classification of #14 as a *natukunoa* (see footnote to Chapter Three), then one might say that singing occurs in 2 *natukunoa* and 4 *naatuusiana*.

(b) The Naatuusiana

Naatuusiana are either descriptive or discursive, consisting in large part of either descriptions or explanations of features of traditional culture (e.g., texts #7 and 9) or of the landscape (e.g., #8 and 11), or recitals of historic or seemingly historic events such as wars, feuds between villages and conflicts between individuals (e.g., #10 and 15). In the latter the emphasis is on the events themselves rather than on some general moral, a single interaction, or the tracing of the history of a group or title. In other words, the "point" of the narrative is the whole narrative itself and, as stories with plots, many of them are charged with emotion, quick of pace and full of action–violent attacks, ambush, murder and mayhem, people plotting, victims fleeing, chiefs dying.

(c) The Natukunoa

Four related characteristics tend to typify the *natukunoa*: a formulaic conclusion, what Tedlock (1983: 177) terms "tale-ending paralogic" ("The War of the Fishes" (#30) and "The Dove, The Turtle and the Rat"

(#32) being two examples); a rather transparent moral lesson; a narrower dramatic scope than that of most *naatuusiana* or *nariwota*; and they tend to be shorter and more simply phrased than narratives of the other two types. What no doubt relates these general characteristics is the fact that *natukunoa* are intended moreso for a juvenile than an adult audience.

3. Idiosyncratic Style

There is a multitude of features of personal style which might be mentioned: introductory and conclusory formulae, patterned shifts in voice quality, frequency and kind of accompanying gestures, and so on. Texts transcribed via Tedlock's notational system allow the reader to see visually stylistic differences between one narrator and another. In his book, *See So That We May See*, Seitel characterizes each Haya narrator's style with a single descriptive adjective, for example, "lyrical", "plodding and cautious", "cerebral", "epic" (Seitel 1980: 44-47). As one reads the texts of the different narrators back-to-back, these differences are discernible on the page.

One might do likewise for Nguna's raconteurs; but, given that the content or subject matter of a narrative itself affects the style in which it is told, and the fact that not all narrators produced narratives of each kind to be recorded, I prefer not to gloss each individual's style with a single adjective. Rather, broad descriptions are given below for each of the following narrators: Ronneth Manutukituki; Kaltap̄au M̃asemata; Lui Taatalele; and Jack Tavim̃asoe. The others' contributions constitute too small a sample for stylistic generalization.

Ronneth Manutukituki

In comparison with other narrators, Manutukituki tends toward long, rapid-fire utterances, between which the pauses are very short. This feature makes his texts unusually difficult to transcribe accurately from the oral recordings; but, for the listener, it lends his narratives considerable force and momentum. Moreover, though his oratory so often achieves breakneck speed, Ronneth also varies both the speed and precision of his speech to create markedly contrasting passages. The following is a clear example from "The War of 1874" (text #22). The first six utterances are separated from one another by the briefest possible pauses. They are delivered furiously fast, the words running together, their enunciation blurred. Then, there is a clause of moderate length and speed that reprises the outcome of the wild scene; and it is all capped by a remarkably anti-climactic, brief phrase:

" They kept firing on and on and on and once it was fully light they
   entered the village, they burned down the houses, killed the pigs,
   killed the chickens,destroyed all of their belongings, until there was
   absolutely nothing left.
The meeting-house was the one and only thing remaining.
They left."

Ronneth is also capable of employing sound to artistic perfection, as
in this selection from "The Family of Matoa (Part One)" (#19). Drawn out
and repeated, the long a, e, o and u grow heavy and sonorous, conveying
beautifully the heaviness of heart of the bereaved heroine, Konamsese,
and the ponderousness of the funeral procession for her late husband-to-
be:

"Ragi waina eu dape a,
te doo peea,
e peea, te doo dagi peea, maa taina maaga, tanari maaga,
eu dape a, teu doo dausi a."

["When they picked it up,
she went first,
she went ahead, wailing in front, while her sisters, [and] his friends,
carried him along, following after her."]

Kaltaṗau Ṁasemata

The late Kaltaṗau Ṁasemata's oratory gifts were many and varied.
From the moment he began to speak, the audience was gripped. He
would visibly gather his forces before starting, then mark the commence-
ment of any narrative with a loud "Io!" ("Yes!" or "Alright!"). His
narratives are generally finished off equally emphatically with a conclusory statement of this sort: "That's it!", "There it is!" or "That's all!".
Throughout many of his texts, Kaltaṗau acted all the parts in extremely
realistic conversations which were often interspersed with evocative
colloquial exclamations. In addition, minute description characterizes
many passages in his texts. His "How the Slit-Drum was Discovered"
(#14), for example, is a veritable how-to on the traditional means of
felling trees and carving them into gongs through the use of fire and
stone implements alone. Another stylistic feature that sets his narratives apart is neatly illustrated in the following passage from "The
Origin of Marimaraki" (#3):

"When he ferried her across,
the wind was blowing from the direction of **Emau** [island]. The easterly.
   Blowing so **hard**
that it [kept] submerging the **outrigger.**
So they put **the stone** they had brought along on the sideopposite the
   outrigger."

The details regarding the direction, force and effects of the prevailing
winds during the crossing give vitality and immediacy to this account
which, up until that point, is largely a string of identifying features: the
woman who came from P̃au village, whose meeting-house was named
Vareatapu, whose dancing-ground was named M̃alatapu, who left P̃au
via the passage called Naworalapa, etc.

Kaltap̃au invariably made the utmost of his voice. It might fall very
low, yet forcefully resound to lay stress on one passage, then become a
foreboding whisper at a point in the narrative where danger lurks. Some
of his texts are particularly finely crafted. In one example mentioned
already, from "The New Diviner" (#12), Kaltap̃au sets up a particular
semantic framework before describing the diviner P̃akae's son's reaction
to his father's seemingly irresponsible behaviour. The narrator comments that the people of Farealapa village and, perhaps of Nguna in
general, had yet to realize the extent of the new diviner's recently
acquired powers. Then follows the interaction between father (cum
diviner) and son in which Kaltap̃au uses the phrase "the son 'speaks to'
his father". Given the aura of doubt established immediately prior to this
phrase, it implies that the son is being verbally aggressive, possibly even
harassing or reprimanding. He behaves disrespectfully toward P̃akae
both as his father and as the new diviner, not only in expressing doubts
that the food, which is his father's responsibility to supply, will be
forthcoming, but also in asking questions more than once, effectively
challenging his father as to whether he is going to deal with the situation
at all. The repetition of this element of their verbal exchange further
builds suspense over whether P̃akae will indeed be able to rise to the
occasion; for salvaging the situation–along with his reputation, as well
as that of his village– will require an even greater feat than any
accomplished to that point.

Lui Taatalele

Compared with Kaltap̃au's, Lui Taatalele's style tends to longer utterances. But, like Kaltap̃au, his action scenes are characterized and set
apart by short, snappy statements. The conclusion of his "Roimata,
Roimuru and Leimaarona" (#17) is a striking demonstration of Lui's use

of variation in utterance length to build to a punchy finale. The two
young men's terse reply to their mother Leilolo's admonition that they
ought not to kill their uncles is followed by three lengthy statements
describing their preparations for the ambush, followed by a single line
depicting the attack itself:

"So five days later
they went to the shore, and stood there waiting for them.
Their uncles came; and as they came along, the [boys] cut and cast spells
   on [a few] blocks of wood from the white canoe tree.
They cast the spell then stood ready, as the canoe ran up and reached the
   reef's edge, like here [*gesture* indicating the reef behind the
   narrator].
Then they heaved the pieces of wood smashing open the [hull of the]
   canoe."

The dénouement is delivered in three crisp verbal blows plus a curt
variation of the common text-ending marker:

"The canoe **sank**.
Their **uncles** were killed.
They were **dead**.
That's it."

While Lui's voice does not have the compelling force of Kaltaᵱau's, he
nevertheless obtains fine dramatic effect in his texts through stylistic
means. There is a nice point of irony near the end of one text (not included
in this collection) wherein the people of Utanilagi village, unknowingly
imprisoned in their own meeting-house, are soon to be attacked. They
playfully tease each other with what they think is a fanciful possibility
of a surprise attack on them by their enemy village, M̃alamea. The
narrative's audience, however, knows that the terrible vision is not fancy
at all, but about to come only too true. The audience is witness to the
M̃alamea warriors lying in wait all around the meeting-house in the
darkness and driving rain. The irony doubles as the narrator tells of the
waiting warriors overhearing their intended victims' banter as they
themselves are on the very point of attack. Here Lui simultaneously
employs irony at two levels to intensify and sharpen the tension.

Jack Taviṁasoe

While Kaltaᵱau M̃asemata is the most talented and prolific narrator
of all of those whose texts appear in this volume, Jack Taviṁasoe has far
and away the most para- professional linguistic experience, having acted

for many years as a Biblical translator, amongst other things (for more information on Jack's background, see Chapter 9). As a result he has an extraordinary degree of concern with correctness of grammar and accuracy of vocabulary, plus an acute awareness of the comprehension difficulties foreigners encounter in listening to oral speech. These factors account for the characteristically slow, overly careful beginning in "The Ten Brothers and Rovemao". As the narrative grips its narrator, however, he both speeds up and begins to speak more freely and naturally, so that the account achieves its own (considerable) dramatic momentum. In addition, Jack has a particularly fine singing voice, and adores singing, so those of his texts which include such passages benefit greatly from this.

Chapter Five

Between The Lines

What follows is not intended as a thorough-going content analysis; nor does it pretend to be an analysis of Ngunese culture via the texts as cultural artifacts. It is neither of these for two reasons: first, the volume's primary intended audience is the Ngunese people themselves, whose interests are not anthropological theory or an anthropological analysis of their culture. Second, given the goals of the present volume as stated in its initial chapter, such an analysis lies beyond its boundaries. The intended aim of this chapter, then, is twofold: (1) to bring to the reader's attention two central themes that appear in the corpus: the conceptualization of different cultural periods and of chiefs and the chiefly system; and (2) to give the reader general information and explain terms essential to any reading of the texts. (More specific, particular details appear as footnotes within the individual texts.)

The second section of this chapter is an extended discussion of numerous significant elements in a single text. Lui Taatalele's "The Death of Mariameara" is a prime example of what an enormous amount of cultural knowledge may be required for proper understanding of any one text.

A: Hearing the Texts

Central Themes

Seitel refers to the "social landscape" depicted in any body of texts. For the Hayas of Tanzania this is:

...a particular view of the world that indicates places which
are important to the life of an individual and to the continued
existence of society, an aspect of an ideology by which Hayas
comprehend and interpret their lives.

(Seitel 1980:7)

Seitel's discussion of the Haya "social landscape" focusses on contras-
tive pairs such as inside/outside and civilization/wilderness. At the
heart of the Ngunese "social landscape" is an image of their own culture
as a trio (or trinity?) of contrasting eras that constitute a Ngunese meta-
cultural commentary. These three are:

1. *Namaligo* or "The Darkness", i.e., the pre-Christian, "pagan" period;
2. *Namarama* or "The Light", i.e., the early Christian period;
3. The present.

1. Namaligo

"The Dark" and its Ngunese equivalent, *Namaligo*, are unambiguous
terms for the pre-Christian period on Nguna. They were introduced by
the first missionary, in contrast to "The Light" of Christianity; and this
is how the Ngunese still refer to it.

The negative connotations implicit in the dichotomy represent one
aspect of the Ngunese view of the pagan period. It was a "hard" time,
people say; a time when war was rife, and men always kept their
weapons at hand. This is quite apparent in many of the texts, as they
recount how warring groups attacked each other's villages by night; how
warriors were shot with poison arrows, women raped, whole groups
forced from their lands, and so on. All in all, these were evil times during
which things contrary to Christian moral teachings were done. Moreover, these times are widely held to have a certain contemporary reality,
in the sense of their having retained a potential for evil. Young people
are warned that it is unwise to talk or think too much about things such
as sorcery lest they reappear from times gone by and reassert their hold
over both individuals and society.

Apart from what is clearly perceived as negative, though, this "dark"
chapter in Nguna's history has a positive side. The word "hard" can also
mean "strong", the people of the "pagan" era being portrayed as taller
and stronger than recent generations because they ate no "weak"
European foods and drank only coconut water or rainwater. This
positive side is reflected in many texts which stress physical and political
might in accounts of these same wars and in communal achievements

such as great feasts, dances and the erection of slit-drums and meeting-houses. People believe that before Christianity came, not only the people but the yams and other crops were bigger and better, and men were rich with pigs to the extent that gardens had to be fenced to protect them from the free-ranging pigs. By contrast, today it is the pigs that are fenced in, and they are few and small.

There are several other elements of this period of which people speak with a nostalgic sort of admiration, even awe. This is particularly so with *munuai* (the diviners cum miracle-workers) and chiefs. Their extra-ordinary powers, in so far as they represent the exercise of legitimate authority, make them, and therefore the period as a whole, admirable.

Munuai are said to have performed super-human feats such as trans-forming stones into snakes or lizards, transporting themselves under-water to distant islands or, as in one text in this collection, calling fire down to earth from the sky to rekindle cold hearth-fires. The greatest feat of all, of course, and the one that establishes the reputation of the "new diviner" in the same text, is to produce magically the most highly valued kind of food (coconut puddings filled with pork and chicken) to save the day when the diviner's village is host to a visiting work-party.

In a similar way chiefs of this era are portrayed as having cared for their people, as having husbanded them as a man does his pigs. A family would not go homeless as long as the chief was there to see that all the villagers helped to build them a house; and a whole village would not go hungry as long as the chief wisely managed its resources. Furthermore, in "pagan" Nguna, chiefs upheld the law of the land in no uncertain terms. While today's church elders usually stress love and Christian charity, when they are discussing how things used to be, they laud the enforcement of society's traditional laws by chiefs who would have had a man killed for committing adultery. They uphold the Commandment, "Thou shalt not kill", but, when it is a matter of the exercise of chiefly sanctions, they suffer no pangs in saying that those harsh times were good times because chiefs defended the law of the land.

2. Namarama

Namarama covers roughly the period from 1900 to the death of the paramount chief, Suasavi Tarip̄oaliu, in the early 1930s. The island's first resident missionary, Rev. Peter Milne, arrived in 1870 and lived there almost without break until his death in 1924. He and Tarip̄oaliu are both described as men of strength, one as religious leader and the other as both political leader and strong Christian.

The few remaining people who were young during Milne's later years give witness to his forcefulness of personality and strict approach, in classroom and pulpit alike. A story is told of how he insisted that Nguna's last known *munuai* (the "new diviner" of text #12 in this volume) shake hands with him, and thereby overcame the power of the *munuai* who died shortly thereafter (for this account, see Schütz's *Nguna Texts* and Chapter Ten in this volume). This was a demonstration of Milne's, and God's, greater power. (In yet other versions of the story, as well, the *munuai* further shows his own power or superhuman aspect by rising from the dead three times before disappearing forever.)

Milne also organized some long-term native proselytization in which there is still pride taken by devout Ngunese. They say that, once converted themselves, they took "The Light" to virtually every island in the Group. They were dispatched by Milne as lay missionaries, called "Teachers", like the Polynesian Christians who performed the same function in the early years of the ni-Vanuatu church.

Somewhat ironically, Milne is also seen as the first recorder of *kastom* for posterity. On one occasion, when a few older men and I were working on the manuscript documenting their knowledge of traditional customs, one of them brought along a copy of Don's short biography of Peter Milne. It was treated as a reference text on funerary sacrifices for chiefs. The individuals with whom I was working clearly felt that the examples quoted in that book represented authentic norms of behaviour in this regard. I suspect, however, that this was a case of artificial standardization, i.e., reinventing tradition in the process of trying to recapture and encode it. (For details on reconstructed pre-Christian political structures, see Facey 1983.)

The strength of Suasavi Tariɓoaliu, the paramount chief during the early Christian period, is usually expressed in terms of social control. One is told that he kept the law strong and that, in order to do so, he had a number of "policemen". When some infringement of the rules was committed, the high chief of the guilty party's village could send him or her to the paramount chief to be judged. He would assign the appropriate fine or punishment—in the form of money, goods, labour on community works, or incarceration in his "calaboose", a small building near his house—which would then be enforced by his "police". In extreme instances punishment was the destruction of the guilty party's gardens. Consequently, there was a strong incentive to heed the chiefs' word and to express deference toward them. These days are remembered as a time in which crimes were inevitably met with punishment and young people behaved circumspectly, especially young, single men vis-à-vis young women. In fact, one of the "policemen's" duties was to keep apart single people of the opposite sex, especially in the inviting darkness of evening. A blast on the shell- trumpet in mid-evening served as curfew and young men found abroad after then would be chased home with blows from sticks or even a whip to speed them towards a decorous destination.

One point about these portraits of the past should be made in passing. From my historical reconstruction work, it is clear that in the pre-Contact period secular and sacred authority or, more precisely, political and mystical or religious power were closely linked. These two phenomena were bound together in the traditional world-view, chiefs and their ritual experts constituting necessary complements of one other. Likewise, much stress is laid on this combination in the ideal views of the early Christian past just outlined. As chiefs and ritual experts of "The Dark" are described, so are Suasavi Taripoaliu and Rev. Milne of "The Light".

3. The Present

The third era covers the time from Suasavi's death in the early 1930s to today. These modern times are seen as fraught with problems—rising numbers of unwed mothers, more instances of drunkenness and its social consequences, and so on— whose origins are frequently attributed to moral slippage, in comparison with the pristine early phase of "The Light". In the eyes of many of the older and more devout, that "Light" has grown dim. To these as well as to other sectors of the community, many of the disconcerting issues in the present derive from "weakness" at the leadership level, caused less by personal failure of key individuals than by a hypothesized severing of the tie between the two complementary types of power, the secular or political and the mystical or religious. Let me expand on this.

Elsewhere (Facey 1983) I have delineated four behavioural ideals that are espoused by the Ngunese: humility, respect, truthfulness and generosity. Underlying these are three general propositions about human behaviour:

1. that people are essentially unpredictable, having motivations, desires and feelings that cannot be known with certainty from outward signs, i.e., primarily, what they say;
2. people are dependent upon one another, particularly upon those with whom they live and cooperate; consequently, great stress is laid on the individual's actions as it is through them that he/she is judged;
3. in conflict with the second tenet, people are seen as being ideally independent and autonomous. Everyone is conceived of as having

jurisdiction over something, be it material possessions, the organization of a household or merely their own opinions. Even an infant's refusal to eat is interpreted as the expression of an idiosyncratic preference, a conscious choice that it asserts.

Rooted in these three fundamental conceptions about human behaviour are two universal preoccupations: one's reputation and the inviolability of authority in all its forms and contexts. Likewise, in each of the above- mentioned four behavioural ideals respect for and obedience to figures of authority are central; and, not surprisingly, those who most appear to subscribe to these ideals and who are most vocal in propagating them are those who hold positions in the local authority structures.

When such people talk about these ideals, they are in fact putting forward an argument to account for the discrepancy between the idealized past and the imperfect present. They are asserting that today's troubles are a result of everyone failing to live up to traditional norms of behaviour, and that, therefore, the solution to today's problems is for everyone to act more closely in accordance with the ideals.

In addition, they assert the necessity of directly reinvigorating the chiefly and church systems themselves, saying that in order to strengthen Ngunese society as a whole both chiefs and church must be strengthened. This led, in 1980, to discussion of inviting a well-known evangelical group from one of the islands to the north– Tongoa– to come and hold revivalist meetings on Nguna. Similarly, the local Presbyterian Session's stand against a few individuals' desire to be married by *kastom* alone (i.e., married by virtue of traditional gift-exchange, with no Christian wedding ceremony) and against the spread of new denominations such as the Seventh Day Adventist church constitutes an attempt to re-assert the church's authority.

Also in 1980, in Tikilasoa, token monthly prestations of food to the church's Pastor and to the village's high chief were instituted as lapsed, traditional gestures of respect and deference, affirmations that chiefs and church leaders are working for their people. There was also some talk of reviving the more expensive yearly tribute (*nasautoga*) in traditional goods—pigs, mats and kava—but even those who proposed it admitted that it would be impossibly onerous given how few pigs people have nowadays.

Even with all this emphasis on past glories and strengths and the desire to recapture valued old ways, there are still many facets of the present period which are appreciated in comparison with the distant, "pagan" past. While dimmed it may be in some people's eyes, "The Light" still prevails today on Nguna. Likewise, certain of the highly valued aspects of traditional society, such as the clan system, continue to have a lively existence and social role. The Ngunese are happy to have local, trained paramedics and access to modern hospital services in Port Vila, and to participate in the Western education system. No-one would choose to relinquish these or various others of the positive aspects of modern life. This is demonstrated in "How the Slit-Drum was Discovered", in an explicit statement of how dull and technologically impoverished life was in the long, long ago, when the slit-drum had yet to be invented, let alone the steel axe.

Chiefs

The word for chief, *nawota*, is clearly a cognate of terms in use elsewhere in Vanuatu (see, especially, Layard 1942:704-5 and Patterson 1976:99). The northern variations, like the Ngunese term, are linked with special stones at which pig-killing rituals took place. In the Ngunese case, however, this was not part of an open, competitive, ritual grade-taking system; nor were the pigs actually slain on these stones. Nevertheless, the metaphor of standing up on a stone to legitimate claims to authority (and to land rights) ritually is occasionally still employed on Nguna.

In my observation, *nawota* is used metaphorically in two other contexts: as a term for "husband" and for "boss", for example, as a leader of a group of workers or a student's teacher or supervisor. *Naveinawotaana*, however, while in one sense a synonym of *nawota*, is used in many contexts. Literally it means the "being-a-chief". But one might also gloss it as "possession, dominion (over), control (of), right of/to control (of)" in its various occurrences. For example, one may have *naveinawotaana* over a decision whether to lend a "possession" such as an axe or a piece of land. What this word denotes more generally, then, is the power of disposal of some object or the power of decision on some issue.

Schütz observed that in Ngunese there are two forms of the possessive preposition "of": *ni* and *ki*. The latter is used in phrases such as "the x of y" ("y" being a person/animate being) only when a relationship of "active control" (Schütz 1969b:41-2, following Buse 1960:131) obtains between "x" and "y". The significance of this for the present discussion is that the relationship between a chief and his people is conceived of in these terms. Just as one says "the book of Jack" using *ki* as the possessive preposition (because the actor has control over his inanimate possession, a book), so does one say "the assistant of the chief" or "the people of the chief" using *ki*, even though the objects of the preposition are animate beings. Furthermore, a chief "has/possesses" (*peani*) his people, his *varea* or "meeting-house", and his *namarakiana* or "dominion" just as other people "have/possess" (*peani*) their belongings, tools, etc.

The controlling and judicial role of a chief with respect to his people is nowhere so evident as in the symbolism of certain aspects of the *varea* itself. A chief is said to be above and to hold his people, as the walls of a *varea* do, curving upwards to form the roof. A chief is often likened to a banyan tree for similar reasons: its domineering size, strength and ability to shelter many birds. A metaphor of nurturance is evident in several of these texts wherein feeding and being fed stand for the chiefs' duty to provide for their people and the reciprocal duty of allegiance to them by their people. This duty on the part of chiefs is tied to their titular ownership of the land on behalf of the members of their group. In apportioning rights to land within his dominion a chief supplies the means of earning the food of life. A central feature inside the *varea* is a large pile of fire-rocks for baking communal meals. While this is part of the symbolism of chiefly nurturance, it also suggests the authority of the chief in the sense that the rocks are sometimes likened to the chief's people and the oversize bamboo tongs that lie next to them to the chief, who may reach into his dominion to pluck out and mete justice to any person who commits a crime.

Traditional chiefly investitures involved to some degree a process of depersonalization in that a successor's personal name was discarded as he was invested with the chiefly title born by each of his predecessors (as explained by the narrator in text #7). The bestowal of a title was also once thought to entail a transference of mystical power, a sacred spirit, to the new title-holder. Ideally, then, the chief was one who was set apart from the common people through this ritual. Therefore he had a special nature by virtue of which he both controlled and maintained his people as "his subjects" (*narei aneana*).

Traditionally inheritance of chiefly titles passed through the matriline from mother's brother to sister's son, be he a consanguineal or classificatory nephew (*p̃elemata*). (While all present chiefs are male and past ones have been likewise, it was not entirely the case long ago. For further discussion of this point, see the preface to Chapter Six). With the advent of Christianity, however, a shift to succession from father to son occurred, this new convention being termed *nanatu* (meaning "[going to] the offspring"). At the time of large-scale Ngunese adoption of Christianity about the turn of the twentieth century, this widely replaced the previous convention as is mentioned by Lui Taatalele in his "The Origin of Mariamearaliu".

In the final paragraph of the same text the narrator refers to a second significant shift which also took place then: "And, likewise, the son of his who became Mariameara did not kill the one hundred." "Killing the one hundred" refers to the number of pigs that had to be slaughtered ceremonially by a successor to any of the approximately half dozen titles designated as *nawota ni p̃onotia* or "chief of a hundred". The chiefly system is a hierarchical, three-tiered one in which the highest title, known in English as the "paramount chief", is the one and only *nawota ni tivilia* or "chief of a thousand" for which a successor had to slaughter 1,000 pigs. Below it, in intermediate rank, were the chief of a hundred titles; and on the bottom rung were all other chiefly titles, for which traditionally there may have been up to as many as 50 pigs required. Abandonment of the custom of pig sacrifice by successors to chiefly positions occurred more or less concurrently with the universal adoption of Christianity and the shift to successsion by sons rather than by sisters' sons.

B: Mysterious Motivations

Note: This section concerns a single text narrated by Lui Taatalele. I have placed the discussion of this piece here rather than immediately before the text itself because it is a particularly intriguing one. Since, when faced with a bulky corpus of texts, readers' tendency is to pick and choose among them, reading only those whose titles "grab" them, I hope to expose this discussion to more readers than might otherwise be the case. I would recommend, then, that one first read "The Death of Mariameara" (text #18) closely, then return to the analysis below.

(a) In the opening lines of "The Death of Mariameara", the Ngunese logic depends on common cultural knowledge of what is a "sacred arrow" (*natip̃a tapu*), most particularly, how it acts differently from any other kind of arrow. The sacred arrow has a type of poison on the tip which, while slow-acting, is inevitably fatal. The person struck by even a single sacred arrow is and *knows that* he is doomed, destined to survive for eight days thereafter, but no more. This comes into play here in the opening scene where the attacking war party from Taava village tries to get the men of M̃atoa to come out to fight. The beleaguered villagers are able to stay put in the safety of their village because they hold the most lethal of all weapons— they have a sacred arrow. With this single shaft, and without endangering any of their number, they are able to rout their enemies by shooting it into the air. When it plummets into the valley below, it magically seeks out the attacking force's chief and leader, striking and fatally wounding him.

(b) At the text's end, another well-known feature of the sacred arrow is manifested. In this story, as likewise in others recorded (for example, Kaltaɓau M̃asemata's text #19), it is clear that being shot with a sacred arrow evokes a particular state of mind in the victim. In this case, having been struck with a sacred arrow, Mariameara, accompanied by his trusty champion (m̃aau), keeps going, searching for his enemy. The first potential victim Mariameara finds turns out to be a clansman of his champion, so he goes unscathed (for further explanation of this, see c below). The next old man he finds, though, is evidently not in danger (for an explanation as to why this is so, see d). The latter realizes that Mariameara has been fatally wounded and offers him both his own warclub and information that the old man automatically knows (again, see d) Mariameara is seeking, i.e., that some of the Taava people who fled the attack on their village are hiding in a nearby cave. Mariameara and his champion then go and find them and proceed to slaughter the lot of them in spite of their being women and children rather than warriors: "Then Mariameara took that club and ran with this man and killed women and children until it was finished". It is only when his killing spree is complete that Mariameara returns to his village to await his death.

It is reasonable to conjecture, and there is a certain amount of ethnographic evidence to support the idea, that before the Ngunese adopted Christianity, they held beliefs regarding the positive impact on a warrior's condition in the after-life of his accumulating as many killings as possible during his earthly existence. Consequently, knowing that one has "only eight days to live" would be a sufficient, even necessary, impetus for the warrior to kill and keep on killing his enemies as long as he is able.

(c) The term "line" derives from the common Ngunese use of the Bislama word "line" to translate nakainaga, which translates into English as clan or, more precisely, matriclan. In the following passage, common matriclan membership serves to unite two men whose relationship is hostile given their current relative situation:

"[Mariameara] and [one of] his [own] m̃aau ran;
and he—Mariameara—seized [the old man], calling to his m̃aau to come and kill [the old man].
But when the m̃aau saw him, he recognized him as a member of the fish clan.
So then

he couldn't kill him because he was of his own blood, [a fellow clansman];
and so [the old man] was released."

The champion warrior has been commanded by his chief, Mariameara, and is about to, summarily murder the old man whom the chief
has seized. But then the champion recognizes the old man as one of his
clansmen. We are not told whether he knows him by sight or recognizes
his clan identity through visible signs—a clan-specific design on an
adornment such as an arm-band, for example—or whether perhaps the
old man makes his clan identity known in some other way to avoid being
killed. The strength of the clan bond is so great that it overrides the
champion's loyalty to his chief. Although it goes unsaid in the narrative,
the champion evidently conveys to his chief his moral dilemma at the
prospect of having to kill someone to whom he owes friendship and
protection; for it is then that Mariameara releases his intended victim
and he and his champion go off in search of another.

(d) Shortly thereafter, having further descended to the village of
Mere, the two men come across what the reader/hearer might presume
is another prime, potential victim—a lone old man. But what happens?
We read:

"They went to Meere,
and there they found an[other] old man.
It was [chief] Marimasoe's assistant,
Taivakalo.
And
he realized that, even though the chief was still going, still he bore a
    sacred arrow [in his body].
So then he took out his club, and threw it to [Mariameara].
And he said,
'Some people,
[went by] running for their lives; they're [hiding] in the cave over there,
    [in] the cave in the rock.'"

This passage raises a whole host of questions in the minds of the non-
Ngunese audience: Why isn't this man a potential victim—or is he? and,
if so, why is he not seized and killed? Of what relevance is his chiefly title
and function? Why does he offer Mariameara his club and reveal the
location of the refugees whom he has seen fleeing the attack on their
village?

There are numerous possible, in the sense of culturally sensical or
meaningful, answers to these questions:

1. Perhaps the old man, like the first one they encounter, is also a clansman of either Mariameara or his champion and is therefore an ally rather than a potential victim.
2. Perhaps the old man is an ally of Mariameara's by virtue of an alliance between either his village and that of Mariameara, or by virtue of an alliance between the old man's chief, Mariñasoe, and chief Mariameara. Certainly there were such inter-village alliances traditionally.
3. Perhaps none of these is the case, but rather, knowing that Mariameara has been struck with a sacred arrow, and therefore also with an insatiable desire to kill, the old man is merely trying to save himself by giving Mariameara what he wants—readily available victims and the means of dispatching them.

I cannot say with authority which, if any of these, is the "correct" explanation; moreover, it may be that any (or even more than one of them) is "correct", that is, meaningful and/or sensical to the Ngunese audience. Conversations with the narrator and with my linguistic assistant about this story's content did not yield definitive metacommentary on these points. Moreover, presented with such questions, the typical Ngunese response is: well, it may have been that way, or it might have been the other way—who can say?

It is more useful anyway to consider the possibility that there are *no* "correct" answers; rather, that the narrative event's dramatic role is to recall to the listeners' minds all of these "answers", as fundamental, semantic connections, cultural themes. The dramatic impact of this may be the provision of a kind of vicarious role-playing exercise in which particular scenes and events (be they of accepted historical status or fictional status, as in texts designated as "tales") are evoked, giving the listeners an opportunity to mull over or grapple with typical, recurrent interactions, moral dilemmas and symbolic themes of their culture. It seems evident that this is a significant and central role of oral textual performance as it is of ritual action or performance, as Victor Turner, Clifford Geertz, and numerous others have demonstrated so clearly.

Chapter Six

Nariwota Ni Naveinawotaana Maaga/ Chiefly Ancestries

The first group of (6) texts represents the genre *nariwota ni nave-inawotaana*, or the chiefly ancestry. The first three, narrated by Kaltap̃au M̃asemata, tell of the origins of the following chiefs of high title: Tarip̃oamata and Tarip̃oaliu (M̃alaliu village); Marip̃op̃ogi (M̃alamea) and Mariwota (Tikilasoa); and Marimaraki (Unakapu). The other three texts, by Lui Taatalele, Ronneth Manutukituki and Jack Tavim̃asoe respectively, recount the arrival of the first Mariamearaliu (M̃atoa), Mariameara (M̃atoa), Manaruru (M̃alanaruru) and Uusam̃ooli (Rewoka/Fareafau).

Among the many issues raised by these texts one is of particular interest: the historical existence and crucial role of female chiefs. In texts #3, 4 and 5 the original bearer of the title in question is a woman. Likewise, in one of the *naatuusiana*, "Roimata, Roimuru and Lei-maarona" (#17), there is another example of a female chief which, while understated, is clearly one of quite high status. These instances would tend to surprise the non-Ngunese audience, knowing already that Ngunese women do not bear such titles today, and that neither do they function fully as chiefs even in historical cases in which a chief's widow temporarily performed as an interim chief until such time as a proper successor could be installed. Nevertheless, these are apparently authentic instances in which the original bearer of the title was indeed a woman; moreover, in the case of Leimaraki (text #3), even though she was surrounded by male aides who took on certain of her chiefly duties, she maintained her position until her death. (It is important, too, to remember that every chief of high rank also has/had numerous aides who perform a similar range of duties to those taken on by Leimaraki's retinue.)

What significance might one place on these facts? Looking at the sequence of events in text #5, it is clearly stated there that there were chiefs in (and of) M̃atoa before the arrrival of Leiameara from Efate. Though his link to Tariwiawia is left ambiguous, the chiefship is said to have started with Manaatamate, who was then succeeded by Manatai and he by Marikoroi, each following the customary practice of slaughtering one hundred pigs. Generally stated, "...it was still men who ruled up until Marikoroi died and [then] it was Leiameara." Leiameara's origin is then recounted and, once again, the narrator reviews the sequence of events: "And Marikoroi died. When he died Leiameara began as the first female chief. She was a female chief Mariameara. ... So Mariameara began at that time."

I draw your particular attention to the final statement. This text inarguably records the process whereby a series of male, indigenous chiefs is supplanted by a woman, and most importantly, a woman who bears a titled chiefship of foreign origin. Leiameara, brought from Efate by a holder of another chiefly title (Maatap̃au, himself the first chief of Unakapu), becomes the founder and first incumbent of the chiefly line of Mariameara. The men who preceded her, though considered chiefs of M̃atoa, were *not* holders of the title, Mariameara. It is only with Leiameara that this title comes into existence; consequently, each of her successors down to the present day drops his personal name and is identified instead by that title: "The names they had had first they did not keep. So Mariameara began at that time."

I suggest that what happened here was the invasion of Nguna, in this instance and in others recounted in other texts (e.g., M̃asemata's text #3 and Taatalele's #4), by foreign chiefs who were possessed of Efate-based titles. For reasons about which one could only speculate—such as a need to expand due to land/population pressure on the mainland of Efate—these individuals immigrated to Nguna. For reasons that are also opaque, they were allowed to displace the extant indigenous leaders, founding new lines of succession to their imported chiefly titles.

Text No.1:

"Nam̃eluana ni Tarip̃oamata goo Tarip̃oaliu"
pae
Kaltap̃au M̃asemata

A ga woo atulake nalo ni nawota duua,
doko Efate, Siviri.
Tarip̃oamata, goo
Tarip̃oaliu.
Naara nam̃eluana adeada ero pae **sagalegaale**.
Goo naka ni Siviri maaga eu doo p̃osiwosi, eu mari roara doko
Lap̃oa
Goo eu lawo naadi,
goo eu lawo nawii,
goo eu lawo noopa maaga.
Goo eu punusi naga noopa maaga e dakiusi waina eu doo p̃akuti a, e
    dakiusi naatam̃ooli.
Goo eu punusi naadi maaga eu doo gani a, dakiusi naatam̃ooli.
Maa e pei sagalegaale, waina e piragi natuna.
Goo ragi sikai
naatam̃ooli maaga ni Siviri eu masau naga eu ga sai ki navatuuna
    wanogoe waina e doo gani naadi adeada.
Goo eu mari sua nasum̃a sikai, nalakena eu atae naga e pei sagalegaale.
Goo p̃oogi eu pa raki naadi wanogoe.
Goo ragi waina eu pano,
sagalegaale p̃ilana e pagi doko elagi ni naadi wanogoe.
Goo e doo ganikani.
Goo ragi waina e doo elagi goo e doo dua natuna paki natano.
Goo ragi waina natuna e gani sua aneana, goo e noa ki natuna, e noa
    naga, "Ku namnam sua?"

Goo e naga, "Io!"
Goo te nadi ki [na]waa pota dua e asa.
Goo naatamooli maaga naara eu doo sai ki nia.
Goo ragi waina eu pano eu dae naio maaga,
ni nakopesi.
Goo ragi waina eu pano pilana e pagi doko elagi.
Goo, eu lawo namalo ni naadi ki naio maaga wanogoe naga pilana ragi
    waina e ga siwo e ga woo doo gona naio maaga wanogoe.
Naga e ga mari daliali goo **naara** eu ga vuati natuna poo sava.
Goo ragi waina eu pano seara eu dape naio goo eu lawo namalo naadi asa.
Goo seara eu dape natuna doko **sava**, paki esuma.
Goo eu duti natoara maaga pae napua, pae nadigi napua duua, naga e
    ga sava umai poo moro dapilagona naga e ga towo, naga e ga mari
    daliali paki esuma.
Goo naara eu dape natuna poo pa sili ekopu wanogoe.
Goo sagalegaale wanogoe e marisara paapaa e paki natano, goo e moro
    sava dausi ra.
Goo e dapilagona natoara maaga wanogoe waina eu duti a goo e dowo.
Goo ragi waina e pano, kite
sagalegaale natuna te doko sua ekopu. E pei nagoroi.
Goo e doo daliepu nasuma!
E doo kai poo doo daliepu nasuma!
Maa naara, eu suui nakapu goo eu daragi napati naau
poo doo pokati sagalegaale wanogoe asa naga e ga lua ki sara naleo saa
    maaga waina e gani a doko namaritana.
Goo nae e doo kai goo e doo lua!
Maa nae e doo daliepu,
e daliepu nasuma.
Paapaa, nasuma e **kasua**, goo e pagi paki natalie sikai waina e doko
    maladigi ki nasuma wanogoe.
Goo e doo pasa pakii da,
e noa naga,
"Koroi kiiki wanae e pei namata ni naveinawotaana.
E pei namata ni nawota duua
Taripoamata goo Taripoaliu.
Ku ga leo paraati ki nia.
Ragi waina e pe toko paapaa e pe matua,
e pe tape natuna,
sikai e ga woo pei Taripoamata, goo sikai e ga woo pei Taripoaliu."
Goo ragi wanogoe, pilana te liliu paki namalasi.
Maa koroi kiiki wanogoe te doko.
Paapaa, eu mari mata ki nia a paa[paa] te dakiusi gida naatamooli,
maa nadaligana e daa panopota e pei sagalegaale doko.
Maa paapaa e noopu, goo naatamooli sikai ni Siviri e poo piragi

natu ni sagalegaale wanogoe waina e pei nagoroi.
Goo ragi waina e piragi a, goo e maneana dape natuna duua.
Sikai e pei naanoai goo sikai e pei nagoroi.
Goo tea waina e pei naanoai
e pei Tarip̃oamata.
Goo **kerua** e pei **nagoroi**.
Goo e pei tea tip̃akiana umai paki Nguna.
Goo ragi waina e umai paki Nguna, goo naatam̃ooli sikai, e moro piragi
tea waina e umai paki Nguna.
Goo ragi waina e moro piragi a,
goo nae e moro dape natuna naanoai sikai.
Goo tokora wanogoe e pei waina Tarip̃oaliu navavakawoOraana aneana
    eu atulake m̃elu asa.
Goo sagalegaale wanogoe e doko paapaa e mate.
Goo e pei tea ovakiana doko M̃alaliu.
Goo matigona
e doko taikesa ni M̃alaliu e doko nap̃aunako kakana, goo tokora wanogoe
    eu soso e ki Matigo ni Sagalegaale. E pei matigo varau, nalakena koroi
    wanogoe, e pei koroi varau.
Goo matigo wanogoe tokora wanogoe waina eu ova ki nia asa eu soso e
    ki Matigo ni Sagalegaale.
E doko paapaa paki masoso waia.
Te noopu.

"The Origin of Tarip̃oamata and Tarip̃oaliu"
by
Kaltap̃au M̃asemata

Let me tell you of the two chiefs
of Siviri, Efate.
Tarip̃oamata, and
Tarip̃oaliu.
Their origin derives from the **sagalegaale**[1].
And the people of Siviri were working, making gardens at
Lap̃oa[2].
They were planting bananas,
and yams,
and island cabbages.
And they saw that something, perhaps a person, had been picking the
cabbages.
And the bananas looked as if someone had been eating them.
But it was a *sagalegaale*, she and her child.
This particular time
the Siviri people decided that they would catch the thing that had been
eating their bananas.
They had already constructed a building [to hold it in], because they had
realized that it was a *sagalegaale*.
So that night they went to the banana tree.
When they got there,
the [little] *sagalegaale*'s mother was up in the banana tree.
She was eating.
While she was up in it she was giving [food] to her child beneath.

62

When her child had finished its food, she said to it, "Have you finished
  eating?"
And it replied, "Yes."
So she threw down another fruit for it.
Then the men devised a plan to catch it.
They went and cut spikes,
of *nakopesi* wood.
When they returned, the mother climbed way up high.
So they stuck the spikes in the trunk of the tree such that when the
  [child's] mother came down she would get caught on them.
This would slow her down so that then they could grab her child and flee.
So some of them went and speared the trunk of the banana.
Meanwhile the others grabbed up the child and ran.
And they bound together the grass, from both sides of the path, so that
  again when she came running along she would stumble and fall, and
  this would slow her down in coming to the building.
So they carried off the child and went and hid inside [it].
Meanwhile the *sagalegaale* struggled and struggled until finally she
  managed to reach the ground and started running after them.
But she stumbled on the grass that they had bound together and fell.
Finally she [got loose and] went [after them], but
her child- a female- was already hidden inside.
Then she began circling the building!
She began to cry and circle the building!
But [inside], they built a fire, and heated reeds [over it]
and [using them] started to whip the [little] *sagalegaale* to make her
  throw up all the evil things that she had eaten, that were still inside
  her.
She cried and vomited!
And the other one kept on circling
going around and around the building.
But in the end, the house stood **fast**, so then she climbed a *natalie* tree
  that stood near the house.
And she spoke to them,
she said,
"That little girl is the source of the chieftainship.
She is the source of two chiefs
Taripoamata and Taripoaliu.
Look after her.
If she should live to adulthood,
and bear a child,
one shall be Taripoamata, and the other Taripoaliu."
At that point the mother went back into the bush.
But the little **girl** remained.

In time, they transformed her until she became human, like us,
except for her ears which never changed and remained like those of a
    sagalegaale.
And eventually, [after she had been transformed], a Siviri man took the
    sagalegaale's daughter for his wife.
After they were married, she bore him two children.
One was male and the other female.
The boy
was Tarip̄oamata.
The **second** was the **girl**.
She was sent over to Nguna.
Likewise, when she went to Nguna, a man married her,
the one who came to Nguna.
And, likewise, after he married her,
she bore him a son.
It was there that the descendants of Tarip̄oaliu originated.
The *sagalegaale* [woman] remained there until her death.
She was buried in M̃alaliu.
And her grave
lies in the M̃alaliu graveyard, on the far side, the place they call the
    "*Sagalegaale*'s Grave". It is a long one, because she was a tall woman.
The grave where they buried her is called "*Sagalegaale*'s Grave".
It is still there to this very day.
That's it.

Footnotes

1. *Sagalegaale* is a kind of humanoid being with long, dangling ears and
   long, sharp nails.
2. Lap̄oa is known today as where the Harris coconut plantation is
   located on Undine Bay, North Efate.

(Reference: Kalo-7. April 11, 1978, Unakapu. Tape 3A, 0-19.)

Text No.2:

"Nam̃eluana ni Marip̃op̃ogi goo Mariwota"
pae
Kaltap̃au M̃asemata

Io, a ga woo noa naatuusiana ni nam̃eluana ni naveinawotaana duua,
Marip̃op̃ogi, goo Mariwota.
Naara ero m̃elu pae **Tukutuku.**
Goo nam̃eluana adeada,
ragi waina ero atulake m̃elu, ero m̃elu pae nakainaga ni **kukusue.**
Goo ero m̃elu pae Tukutuku.
Goo ragi waina ero umai, paapaaa
ero rumai doko **Esema.**
Goo ragi wanogoe ero maromaaro doko tokora wanogoe.
Goo naatam̃ooli maaga eu doo pakilina tokora wanogoe
ragi waina eu doko Esema.
Goo eu doko parau **kiiki.**
Ragi waina eu doko parau kiiki, goo naatam̃ooli maaga waina eu doko
 sua,
eu naga, "Ee! Tea maaga waia eu ga toko paa[paa] teu ga maripueli ki
 gida!
Goo e p̃ia eu ga m̃elu."
Goo nam̃eluana adeada waina eu m̃elu pae Esema,
e pei nalakena natu ni kukusue maaga, eu poo soso ra ki Esema.
Goo ragi waina eu m̃elu
poo umai paki Mooso,
eu doko Mooso tokora sikai eu soso e ki **M̃alavakalo.**
Goo eu doko tokora wanogoe, eu doko parau kiiki.
Goo ragi waina eu doko paa[paa] goo tea ni Mooso maaga
eu naga, "Ee!

65

Tea maaga wenaga!
Teu duu paapaa teu ga maripueli ki gida!
Goo e p̃ia eu ga m̃elu.
Eu ga laaga tokora waina eu ga vaki asa."
Goo eu m̃elu tokora wanogoe, poo umai paki navanua kiiki sikai.
Eu soso e ki Eradagana.
Goo eu moro doko parau tokora wanogoe.
Goo ragi waina eu doko asa, poo m̃elu umai poo paki euta Nivaau,
doko Nguna.
Goo ragi waina eu paki euta Nivaau goo eu sake.
Eu sake, maa Mataapaga e doko sua namarakiana ni M̃alamea.
Goo eu dua ra tokora seara waina eu mari nasum̃a asa.
Tokora maaga waina eu doko asa eu soso e ki Sum̃anitaupilelu.
Maa ragi wanogoe eu ko diika nawota.
Maa eu noa naga, Mariwota goo Marip̃op̃ogi
e pei nam̃eluana adeada.
Goo ragi waina eu rumai, eu doko parau M̃alamea.
Goo eu doo laaga naga seei e ga woo dape naveinawotaana ni M̃alamea,
    seve nagisa.
Goo eu doko varea adeada,
varea wanogoe eu soso e ki Vareanimatawola.
Maa uusa e p̃owo.
Goo tuai wanogoe naveele e p̃arua pae napaga maaga.
Goo ragi waina eu doko, goo eu dogo,
manu sikai waina eu soso e ki mapula.
E doo p̃oruru.
E p̃oruru maa nadaleona e daa p̃arua, e kiiki.
Goo eu naga, "O! Nagisa veea ni namarakiana waia wanogoe,
Mapula."
Goo ragi waina eu doko kiiki,
goo eu dogo manu wanogoe sikai waina nadaleona e moro p̃arua,
waina e moro p̃oruru maa nadaleona e p̃arua.
Goo e naga, "P̃og! P̃og! P̃og!"
Goo ragi wanogoe eu naga, "O! Ragi waia tu poo pap̃ai nagisa warua.
Te pei Marip̃op̃ogi."
Goo ragi wanogoe
teu sike naveinawotaana wanogoe.
Maa naveinawotaana maaga eu peani nagisa dolutoolu.
Nagisa veea ki Marip̃op̃ogi e pei Mapula.
Goo nagisa warua e pei Marip̃op̃ogi.
Goo nagisa ketoolu
e pei Manaveele,
nalakena manu maaga wanogoe eu pagi doko naveele, poo doo p̃oruru.
Goo ragi wanogoe Marip̃op̃ogi te maraki lua narei aneana maaga seara

  teu duu darogo.
Maa,
taleeva ki Mariwota eu ga woo moro m̃elu.
Eu ga woo m̃elu paraki Tikilasoa.
Goo eu m̃elu, poo pae elagi umai.
Eu rumai paapaa paki Sum̃anitanomiala.
Goo eu moro mari natokoana tokora wanogoe.
E pei Sum̃anitanomiala, waina eu doko asa.
Maa natokoana sikai e doko sua doko tokora wanogoe.
Waina e pei M̃alalolo, e doko elagi kakana.
Goo ragi waina eu doko paapaa
goo tea ni M̃alalolo maaga eu noa naga, "Ee! Tea maaga waia,
eu mariatae duu paa[paa] naga eu ga kopasi gida namarakiana anigida
    waia!
Goo e p̃ia eu ga m̃elu."
Goo naara
eu peani m̃alala sikai waina e doko tokora wanogoe.
M̃alala adeada e pei M̃alavunuta.
Eu naga teu m̃elu mau goo teu mataku.
Goo eu naga, "Tu ga toko paapaa p̃oogi. Tu ga woo m̃elu."
Goo eu doko paapaa p̃oogi goo eu m̃elu.
Goo tokora sikai eu soso e ki Sum̃animalasi, e pei natusum̃a adeada
    maaga.
Goo eu peani dumu sikai waina e doko elagi kakana.
Eu soso e ki Lip̃alip̃a. E pei noai wanogoe, e pei luku wanogoe waina eu
    doo pue navinaga adeada asa.
Goo eu m̃elu p̃oogi.
Eu poo m̃elu paraki Tikilasoa.
Goo ragi waina eu rumai, pae elagi,
eu rumai poo doko tokora sikai waina eu soso e ki Sum̃anitapuragona.
Eu rumai paki tokora wanogoe, goo eu gonasokisoki asa
poo doko tokora wanogoe doko, paapaa, goo eu mari varea,
goo eu peani m̃alala.
Goo m̃alala waina e pei m̃alala veea ki Mariwota, e pei M̃alanumea.
Goo varea adeada e pei Vareanumea.
Goo ragi wanogoe naara maa eu poo moro sike naveinawotaana adeada.
E pei Mariwota. Maa Marogoe e doko sua.
Goo ragi wanogoe Marogoe te dua Mariwota namarakiana aneana.
Goo Mariwota wanogoe
nae e maramara doko [paapaa] paki masoso.
Naatuusiana waia e noopu.

"The Origin of Maripopogi and Mariwota"
by
Kaltapau Masemata

Alright, I will tell the story of the origin of the two chiefs,
Maripopogi, and Mariwota.
They came from **Tukutuku.**
And their origin
where they came from originally, was the *kukusue* matriclan.
They came out of Tukutuku,
coming aloooong, untiiil
they reached **Esema.**
And there they stopped.
And they bore some [children]
while they were living in Esema.
They stayed for **quite** a while.
And when they had been there a little while, the people who were there
    first said, "Hey! These people will stay until they've gotten rid of all
    of us!
They will **have to leave."**
So the reason the children of *kukusue* are called Esema [as part of their
    second personal name, their *namavesi* name]
is that they came from Esema.
When they left,
they came to Mooso,
and stayed in a place on Mooso called **Malavakalo.**
They lived there, for quite a while.
They stayed for some time until the people of Mooso
said, "Hey!

Those people!
They will stay until they have gotten rid of all of us!
They will **have to leave.**
They should look for somewhere else to go."
And they left that place, and went to a little island.
They call it Eradagana.
And they then stayed there for a long time.
From there they left and came to the landing-place, Nivaau,
on Nguna.
When they reached the landing-place they went up inland.
They went up inland, but Mataapaga was already there, in the dominion
    of M̃alamea.
And they granted them some land on which to build houses.
The place where they lived was called Sum̃anitaupilelu.
And at that time they still had no chief.
But they say that, for Mariwota and Marip̃op̃ogi
this was their origin.
So when they came, they stayed in M̃alamea a long time.
And they tried to find out **who**— which title— would take the chiefship
    of M̃alamea.
And they stayed in their meeting-house
which they called **Vareanimatawola.**
And it rained.
In those days the *naveele* vine was long and hung down from the
    banyans.
One time they heard
a bird called *mapula.*
It was cooing.
It cooed but its voice wasn't loud, it was quiet.
And they said, "Well, we've found the dominion [chief's] first name-
Mapula."
And a little while later,
they heard one of those birds whose voice was **louder,**
when it cooed it was **louder.**
It said, "*P̃og! P̃og! P̃og!*"
So they they said, "Well, we've found the great name.
It shall be Marip̃op̃ogi."
So then
they raised up the chief.
Chiefs all have three names.
Marip̃op̃ogi's first name was Mapula.
And his great name was Marip̃op̃ogi.
His third name
was Manaveele,

after the birds that sat on the *naveele* vines, and cooed.
And then Maripoᵽogi led his people out, (though) some did stay behind.
And,
Mariwota's group also left.
They headed for Tikilasoa.
They left and went up
until they came to Sumanitanomiala.
And there they made a village once again.
It was Sumanitanomiala where they settled.
But there was already a village there.
Malalolo lay up above it.
And they lived there until
eventually the people of Malalolo said, "Hey! These people,
they will remain until they have chased us from our own dominion!
They will **have to leave.**"
And [the new-comers]
had a dancing-ground there.
[It] was called Malavunuta.
When [the others] told them to leave they were **afraid.**
So they said, "We'll stay until nightfall. [Then] we'll leave."
So they stayed until dark then left.
And there is a place called Sumanimalasi, their old dwelling-place.
And there was a pool up above it
called Liᵽaliᵽa. It was the water of that pool that they put in their food.
So they left by night.
They headed for Tikilasoa.
They left, passing along above,
until they came up to a place called **Sumanitapuragona.**
Whey they reached there, they stuck to it
living there until, eventually, they built a **meeting-house,**
and had a **dancing-ground.**
That first dancing-ground of Mariwota's, was Malanumea.
And their meeting-house was Vareanumea.
It was only then that they raised up their chief.
He was **Mariwota.** But **Marogoe** was already there.
At that time Marogoe gave his dominion to **Mariwota.**
And Mariwota
ruled from then right up until today.
That is the end of this account.

(Reference: Kalo-13. April 19, 1978, Unakapu. Tape 4A, 50-60.)

Text No.3:

"Nam̃eluana ki Marimaraki"
pae
Kaltap̃au M̃asemata

A ga woo atuusi nam̃eluana ki **Marimaraki**,
waina e m̃elu pae taleeva ni P̃au, poo umai paki Unakap[u].
Goo ragi waina Marimaraki e ko **daa** umai, Matap̃au e doko sua doko
   navanua, ni Unakap[u].
Goo ragi waina Marimaraki **e** m̃elu, e m̃elu umai e pei **nagoroi**.
E pei nagoroi waina e m̃elu P̃au.
Goo varea waina e m̃elu asa e pei **Vareatapu**.
Goo m̃alala kakana e pei M̃alatapu.
Goo ragi waina e m̃elu umai, e m̃elu pilake vaatu sikai waina eu soso e
   ki Newoatau.
Goo, e m̃elu nawora sikai waina eu soso e ki **Naworalapa**, nawora
   wanogoe e doko P̃au.
Goo e peani naatam̃ooli **sikai** waina e musagi a umai.
E musagi **Leimaraki**, eu peea soso e ki **Leimaraki** nalakena e pei nagoroi.
Goo ragi waina e musagi a umai,
nalagi, e sau pae taleeva ni **Emau**. E pei ruatu. Goo **e kasua**.
Goo e doo p̃okapupugi **nasama**.
Goo ragi wanogoe e musagi a pilake **vaatu sikai**, waina eu doropusi a
   doko katea.
Goo naatam̃ooli waina e musagi a umai, nagisana e pei
Marakip̃owolau. Marakiwowolau.
Goo e musagi a umai paaa paki euta nawora ni Unakap[u], waina e pei
   Naworalapa.
Goo rarua wanogoe te moro liliu.

Maa ragi waina nagoroi wanogoe e umai, nagoroi eu daa peani nakasuaana.

Goo seei e ga silae nawosiana aneana? nalakena e umai ragi ni navakalo.

Goo e peani naataɱooli seara waina nagoroi wanogoe e pilasaisai ki tea
ni natokoana,

poo naga, "Seei maaga eu ga silae au pae taleeva ni navakalo seara e pe
vakiliina?"

Goo e puati naataɱooli seara

waina eu pei tea tapenelikau aneana, paki tokora sikai waina eu pe
midoaki naga eu ga mari navakalo [asa] diɓa tea ni Unakap[u].

Goo sikai e pei
o

Marakiwola.

Goo sikai e pei
o

Marakiteere.

Goo sikai e pei **Marakivanua.**

Maa e pei Marakiɱaau e pei waina nae e doo piragi ra paki navakalo, nae
e pei naɓauda.

Maa Marakivanua, nae e pei waina e doko sikoti vitariki wanogoe
nalakena e dape naraperape ni naleoparaatikiana ni namarakiana.

Goo vitariki wanogoe te doko.

E maramara doko.

E maramara doko paapaaa

goo naataɱooli sikai e piragi a.

Naataɱooli sikai e piragi a, maa e pei nakainaga ni naniu, vitariki
wanogoe.

Goo naataɱooli sikai e piragi a, goo e dape piakiiki naanoai sikai goo
nagoroi sikai.

Goo vitariki wanogoe e doko paapaa te mate

goo natuna wanogoe, natuna naanoai wanogoe, te ɓarua.

Goo e moro dape nalia ni ɓilana.

E pei Marimaraki.

Te pei nawota **kerua.**

Goo e doko paapaa

mariki wanogoe te **matua,** tea waina e dape nalia ni ɓilana, te matua.

Goo e doo midodoa naga, "E ga tapala [e]sava?"

Goo gorena wanogoe e laki.

E laki, e moro peani natuna naanoai sikai maau.

Goo ragi waina e doko pano paa[paa] te matua,

goo

tea **wanogoe** e pei ɓelematana, waina nae te moro dape nagisa wanogoe,
Marimaraki.

Te pei nawota ketolu.

E pei nakainaga ni naniu.

Goo **teu** doko.

Teu doko paapaa, naataṁooli wanogoe waina e moro dape nagisa ni aloana, **te** doko.

Goo p̃ilana e mate.

Goo ragi wanogoe e masikina doko, goo aloana maa **te** mate.

Goo e doko paapaa, eu masau naga nakainaga ni naniu sikai e ga moro pei **nawota**, doko Unakapu.

Goo eu pano, poo moro daulua naataṁooli sikai ni Farealapa

waina e ga moro umai dape **naveinawotaana** ni Unakap[u], e ga vei Marimaraki.

Goo eu daulua e umai,

poo dovi nap̃auna.

Goo tea **wanogoe** te **matua**.

Goo ragi waina e doko paa[paa] e mate,

naataṁooli wanogoe ni Farealapa nae e moro dape nagisa wanogoe.

°

Te doko.

Ragi wanogoe te pei nakainaga ni **naniu** waina te dape nagisa wanogoe.

Te doko.

E doko paapaa, e **mate**.

Goo e moro pei namalopaa varau kiiki.

Goo te pei nawota kevaati wanogoe.

Goo eu doko paapaa mariki **sikai**, nae e daa pei nakainaga ni naniu, maa e doko paapaa e pei namalopaa varau goo nae te moro dape naveinawotaana **waia**, Marimaraki.

E pei nakainaga ni **noopa**.

Nagisana e pei Marivaleaniwaago

waina nae te moro pei Marimaraki.

Maa e daa pei *laen* kakana, e daa pei namatarau kakana, maa

ragi waina eu doo lagalaga naataṁooli goo, nae e midoaki ṁata ki nia naga e ga tape a.

Goo ragi waina eu noa ki nia naga, "Ee, p̃a toko; maa tea p̃ota e ga tape a."

Goo naririmatana e pevera.

Goo teu dovi nap̃auna, te pei Marimaraki,

Goo teu doko, eu doko paapaa, e mate.

E moro pei ragi varau kiiki.

Goo vitariki sikai e moro peani natuna naanoai sikai.

Nae e moro pei **Marimaraki**.

E moro pei nakainaga ni **naniu**.

Eu soso e ki Marikiteriki.

°

E moro dape a.

E doko paapaa e mate.
E peani namalopaa varau kiiki e doko.
Goo **natuna** e moro dape a.
E pei **Yonah**
waina eu moro dovi nap̃auna e pei Marimaraki.
Goo **wanogoe** e pei nawota kelatesa.
Marikiteriki e pei nawota kelatesa.
  ०

Goo Marimaraki waina e poo pueli, doko 1948, nae e pei nawota kelarua.
Goo pae **ragi wanogoe** umai paki **ragi waia**, namalopaa e doko.
Goo au doo maridogo pusuñaki naga, **naworana** e ga woo moro duu oli
    namadau wanogoe.
Maa au ko daa marimatua.
Naatuusiana waia e noopu.

"The Origin of Marimaraki"
by
Kaltaṗau Ṁasemata

I will recount the origin of **Marimaraki**,
who came from the coast near Ṗau [Efate], to Unakap[u].
When Marimaraki had **yet** to arrive, Mataṗau was already **here**, in
  Unakap[u].
When Marimaraki **left**, it was as **a woman**.
It was a woman who came from Ṗau.
Her original meeting-house was **Vareatapu**.
And her dancing-ground was Ṁalatapu.
When she came out, she was accompanied by a stone called Newoatau.
And, she left through the passage called **Naworalapa**, the passage for
  Ṗau.
And there was **someone** who ferried her across.
He paddled **Leimaraki** across. Originally [the title] was **Leimaraki**
  because she was a woman.
When he ferried her across,
the wind was blowing from the direction of **Emau** [island]. The easterly.
  Blowing so **hard**
that it [kept] submerging the **outrigger**.
So they put **the stone** they had brought along on the side opposite the
  outrigger.
The name of the person who ferried her across, was
Marakiṗowolau. Marakiwowolau.
Eventually he brought her ashore at Unakap[u], through the passage
  named Naworalapa.
Then the canoe went back again.

But [though] the [chiefly] woman had arrived, women are not strong,
and, as she had arrived during the time of war [1], who was there who could
   help her in her work?
So she gathered together some of the people of the village,
and said, "Who all will help me if a war should break out?"
So then she took several men
as her warriors to go to the place where, if war was to be made against
   the people of Unakap[u], it would take place.
One was
○

Marakiwola.
And one was
○

Marakiteere.
And another was Marakivanua.
And Marakiṁaau was the one who would lead them into war, who was
   their leader.
But Marakivanua, he was the one who accompanied that lady
and took responsibility for administering the dominion.
So the woman remained.
She ruled there.
She ruled... until eventually
someone married her.
Someone married her, she who was of the coconut clan, that old lady.
And after marrying, she bore a son and a daughter.
The woman lived on... and when she died
her child, her son, was full grown.
So he in turn took his mother's place.
He became Marimaraki.
He became the second chief.
And this man, who had replaced his mother, lived on... until he grew old.
And he started to worry: "What will happen [after I die]?"
And his sister got married.
She married and also had just one son.
And eventually he grew up;
and
it was he, [the chief's] nephew, who would next take the title,
   Marimaraki.
He was to become the third chief.
He was of the coconut clan.
And they lived on—
they lived on together... until that person in turn took his uncle's title and
   then he was there [as chief].
Then his mother died.

So at that point he was the only one left, his uncle, having died, too.
He remained until... eventually they needed another person of the
coconut clan to become chief, in Unakapu.
So they went, and once more redeemed[2] a person from Farealapa
to take up the chiefship in Unakap[u], to become [the next] Marimaraki.
They redeemed him,
and annointed his head [as the chief-designate].
The other one [,his predecessor,] was growing old.
When finally he died,
the person from Farealapa took his title.
    o

And he remained.
At that point it was the coconut clan who took that title.
And he remained
for a long time... until eventually he died.
Then there was a rather long gap
before the fourth Marimaraki.
They remained [without a chief]... until at last once again another, a man
who was not of the coconut clan, took this title, Marimaraki.
He was of the native cabbage clan.
His name was Marivaleaniwaago;
it was he who became the next Marimaraki.
He was not of the appropriate *laen*, or clan, but
they had been searching for someone and, he wanted very much to take
[the position].
They told him, "No, wait; someone else ought to take it."
And tears poured down [his face].
So they annointed him Marimaraki [3].
And they remained. They lived on until he died.
And once again it was a rather long time [before a successor was found].
Then once again a woman bore a son.
It was he who became the next Marimaraki.
He was once again of the coconut clan.
They called him Marikiteriki.
    o

He in turn took [the chiefship].
He remained [chief] until he died.
Once again there was a rather long gap.
Then his son in turn took it.
It was Jonah
who was annointed to be the next Marimaraki.
The previous chief was the sixth.
Marikiteriki was the sixth chief.
    o

And [Jonah] Marimaraki who has been "gone" since 1948, was the
  seventh chief.
From that time up until now there has been a gap.
We have been trying to choose one of his descendants, who might fill the
  position.
But we have not yet succeeded.
That is the end of this account.

Footnotes

1. This does not refer to a specific conflict in progress, but rather, as in
   several other stories, it is a general reference to the pre-Christian era
   as a time when people spent a great deal of time engaging in
   hostilities, so war was an ever-present possibility.
2. "Redeemed" translates *daulua* which could be literally glossed as "to
   buy out". It describes compensatory prestations made to the person's
   dominion chief, and probably to his extended family as well, in order
   to remove him permanently from his dominion and incorporate him
   into a different one. In this case this was done in order to obtain a
   person of the proper clan as a successor to the Marimaraki chiefship
   since there were no candidates available in Unakapu itself at the time,
   as stated: "So at that point he was the only one left", meaning the only
   remaining member of the coconut clan in the dominion of Unakapu.
3. One might gather from this statement that it is easy to become chief
   by shedding a few well-timed tears, but what this in fact implies, is
   that lineage is not the only prerequisite for taking chiefly titles. It is
   said that the best candidate for such a position is not necessarily
   always the one who is in the precisely correct genealogical and birth-
   order position; rather, it is sometimes the man who shows evidence of
   his genuine desire to care for "his" people. It is all this that the narrator states so very simply and elegantly in Ngunese, in just three
   words: "tears poured down".

(Reference: Kalo-23. June 26, 1978, Unakapu. Tape 7B, 20-39.)

Text No.4:

"Nam̃eluana ki Mariamearaliu"
pae
Lui Taatalele

Nawota sikai [e pei tea] ni Efate.
Nawota wanogoe e pei tea ni **Tapumara**.
Nawora aneana e pei nawora Takara.
E duagoto paki Nguna.
E pei **tuai mau**.
Ragi waina e m̃elu, e m̃elu paa[paa] paki Nguna, e paki euta elau ni
 M̃atoa.
Elau ni M̃atoa wanogoe eu soso e ki Vatup̃aunu.
Goo e sake poo pei paki euta
goo e doko natokoana ni M̃atoa.
Ragi wanogoe e pei nawota ni M̃atoa, e pei nawota **nagoroi**.
Eu soso e ki **Leiameara**.
Nae e doko natokoana ni M̃atoa.
Pae ragi wanogoe e doko paapaa ragi waina e mate.
Goo
naatam̃ooli sikai eu soso e ki **Mantai**.
Nae e atu p̃onotia kakana, nalakena koroi **wanogoe** e pei nawota ni
 p̃onotia.
Nagoroi wanogoe e pei nawota ni p̃onotia.
Goo Mantai wanogoe e atu p̃onotia kakana goo te poo pei nawota, te poo
 pei Mariameara.
E doko paapaaa naga ragi waina Mantai wanogoe e **mate**.
Goo naatam̃ooli sikai waina e doko M̃atoa doko
eu soso e ki Manaatamate,
te moro atu p̃onotia,

79

p̃onotia kakana,
goo te moro pei Mariameara.
Naga e doko paapaaa naga ragi waina Manaatamate wanogoe eu dipe a
  navakalo.
Goo nae te mate.
Te daa moro peani naatam̃ooli seara waina e pei nakainaga ni nawii e ga
  tape nagisa wanogoe.
Ragi wanogoe eu laaga naatam̃ooli paki natokoana p̃ota seara goo eu
  paki Rewoka, natokoana ni Rewoka.
Goo eu pap̃ai nakainaga ni nawii sikai naatam̃ooli sikai e doko asa doko
  e doko varea sikai eu soso e ki Sapuraki, Varea ni Sapuraki.
Goo,
eu pap̃ai naatam̃ooli wanogoe e doko asa e pei nakainaga ni nawii eu soso
  e ki Marikoroi.
Goo Marikoroi wanogoe eu puati a paki M̃atoa.
Nae wanogoe e moro atu p̃onotia ni
Mariameara, goo te poo moro pei Mariameara.
E atu p̃onotia ni Manaatamate.
Goo te poo pei Mariameara.
Ragi waina
Marikoroi wanogoe e doko paapaa naga e mate,
e daa moro peani naatam̃ooli seara.
Maa Marikoroi wanogoe e peani gorena sikai.
Gorena wanogoe e laki paki
natokoana sikai m̃aladigi ki Rewoka,
e pei Rewokanapua [Fareafau].
Goo eu pap̃ai naatam̃ooli sikai e doko asa doko.
E pei nakainaga ni nawii, nalakena e pei Marikoroi gorena
natuna naanoai.
Eu pap̃ai naatam̃ooli wanogoe, eu moro puati a, naka ni M̃atoa eu puati
  a pano, e pa pei nawota.
Eu soso e ki
Taatalele.
Eu moro puati a pano, e pa pei nawota.
E doko paapaaa ragi waina e mate.
Goo *kastom* wanogoe te diika.
Teu doa *kastom* wanogoe, te paki nanatu.
Goo Taatalele wanogoe e pei nakainaga ni nawii, maa natuna, te daa pei
  nakainaga ni nawii nalakena teu doa naveinawotaana paki nanatu.
Natuna nae e pei nakainaga ni noasi,
maa te moro dape naveinawotaana ni Mariameara.
Pae ragi wanogoe e atulake paki nanatu.
Natuna wanogoe e pei Mariameara, nae e daa moro p̃okati p̃onotia.
Goo te atulake paki nanatu pae ragi wanogoe, natuna e pei

Kenneth.
Te dape naveinawotaana, e pei Mariameara.
E noopu.
Kenneth te mate.
Te moro pei
natuna te moro dape naveinawotaana, e pei Abel.
Te moro pei Mariameara.
Kenneth wanogoe te pei kelarua.
E noopu wora wanogoe.

"The Origin of Mariamearaliu"
by
Lui Taatalele

There was a chief from Efate.
The chief was from **Tapumara**.
Her[1] landing-place was Takara.
She crossed over to Nguna.
It was so very **long** ago.
When she left, she came out to Nguna, [and] went ashore at the beach
    below M̃atoa.
They call the beach below M̃atoa Vatup̃aunu.
Then she went up inland
and settled in the village of M̃atoa.
At that time she became the chief of M̃atoa, a **female** chief.
They called her **Leiameara.**
She lived there in M̃atoa.
From then on until the time she died she remained there [as chief].
And
there was a man whom they called **Mantai.**
Now, **he** killed one hundred [pigs] for [the title], because that **young
    woman** was a "chief of a hundred"[2].
That woman was a "chief of a hundred".
So Mantai killed the one hundred for it and he then became chief, he
    became [the next chief] Mariameara.
Mantai remained [chief for some time] then he died.
And there was a man living in M̃atoa
called Manaatamate,

who likewise killed the one hundred,
the one hundred [pigs required] for [the title],
and in turn became Mariameara.
He then remained [chief] until he was shot in a battle.
Then he died.
[At that point] there was no-one else of the yam clan who might take the
    title.
So they began searching for someone in other villages and they went to
    Rewoka, the village of Rewoka.
And they found one person of the yam clan living there, in a certain
    settlement called Sapuraki, the Meeting-house of Sapuraki.
So,
they found a person living there who was of the yam clan and who was
    called Marikoroi.
Then they brought Marikoroi back to Mãtoa.
The latter then also killed the one hundred for
"Mariameara", and he in turn became Mariameara.
He killed the one hundred for Manaatamate['s chiefly title].
And so he became [the next] Mariameara.
Then
Marikoroi remained [chief] until he died,
and there was no-one else [to replace him].
But Marikoroi did have one sister.
His sister had married into
a village near Rewoka,
Rewokanapua [Fareafau].
And they found a man who was living there.
He was of the yam clan, because he was Marikoroi's sister's
son.
Having found this man, the people of Mãtoa brought him back, and he
    in turn became chief.
They called him
Taatalele.
They brought him back, too, and he became chief.
He remained [chief] for some time then he died.
Then that custom was no more.
They altered the custom, to going to one's son[3].
So Taatalele was of the yam clan, but his son was not, for they altered the
    [inheritance of chiefly titles] such that they went to one's son.
So, although his son was of the native cabbage clan,
he was the next to take the chiefship of "Mariameara".
It was then that [succession to titles] started going to one's son.
And, likewise, the son became Mariameara, but he did not kill the one
    hundred.

So it went to the sons from then on, and his son was
Kenneth.
He took the chiefship, becoming Mariameara.
That's it.
Kenneth died.
And once more it was
his son who next took the chiefship, Abel.
He in turn became Mariameara.
[And] Kenneth was the seventh [Mariameara].
That is the end.

Footnotes

1. Some of the punch of the revelation of the new chief's gender is lost
   in the English translation since the genderless pronoun e̲ is used up
   until the tenth line of the text; it is only then, when the chief is already
   installed in M̃atoa, that we learn that it is a she, a woman. (See also
   Kaltap̃au M̃asemata's "Nãm̃eluana ki Marimaraki" (#3) which tells
   that the original bearer of Unakapu's chief Marimaraki was a woman,
   Leimaraki.)
2. *Nawota ni p̃onotia* or "chief of a hundred" refers, first, to the requisite
   number of pigs to be ceremonially slaughtered by any successor to that
   title and, second, to the intermediate rank of that title within Nguna's
   three-tier chiefly system. "Chief of a hundred" titles, of which there
   were approximately half a dozen, fell below the single title of "paramount chief", and above all the rest.
3. *Nanatu* means something like "[going to] the children". It is the
   custom of inheriting chiefly titles from father to son. At the time of
   large-scale Ngunese adoption of Christianity about the turn of the
   twentieth century, this widely replaced the previous custom of passing chiefly titles through the matriclan, the ideal being to pass from
   mother's brother to sister's son. Notice also, in the final paragraph,
   that there was a second significant shift at this time: "And, likewise,
   the son became Mariameara, but he did not kill the one hundred." The
   abandonment of the custom of pig sacrifice/slaughter by a successor
   to a chiefly title occurred more or less concurrently with the shift to
   successsion by sons rather than by sisters' sons (or, at least, by
   clansmen).

(Reference: Lui-2. May 7, 1978, Fareafau. Tape 3B, 31-42.)

Text No.5:

"Naworearu ni Ñatoa"
(Namagovai Kerua)
pae
Ronneth Manutukituki

Naatuusiana waina a noa e naga e noopu ragi wanogoe, maa a ga woo
    moro sokari a ragi waina te umai pei nawota waina e doko masoso,
waina e pae tuai wanogoe umai paapaa paki masoso. Tea waina e pei
    naatuusiana kakana.
Tariwiawia wanogoe ragi waina teu atulake pei nawota teu daa moro pei
    Tariwiawia maa, teu atulake pei Manaatamate. E pei nawota veea
    mau, nawota veea mau ni Ñatoa.
Ragi waina Manaatamate e doko paapaaa, e **mate**.
Goo
tea p̃ota te moro dape naliana.
Tea waina e dape naliana eu soso e ki Manatai.
Te p̃okati p̃onotia kakana pae *kastom* ni naveinawotaana.
E p̃okati waago p̃onotia sikai.
Te moro maraki nalakena Manaatamate te mate sua, maa nae te moro
    dape naliana.
E doko paapaa naga nae e moro mate.
Ragi waina Manatai e mate, goo **Marikoroi** te moro p̃okati p̃onotia
    kakana, te moro pei nawota.
Maa Mariameara e ko daa pakiliina.
Nagoroi maaga wanogoe teu vaivai ki sua waina e dakiusi naworearu
    rualimasikai wanogoe.
Maa teu moro pei naanoai maaga waina eu doo maramara.
Paapaa ragi waina Marikoroi e mate,
goo, te pei **Leiameara**.
Leiameara te atulake.

85

Leiameara wanogoe
e pae **Takara**.
E pae Takara ni Efate, taleeva ni North Efate— East Efate, io!
Mariki waina e musagi Leiameara pae Efate umai nagisana e pei
Maatap̃au.
Maatap̃au wanogoe e pei nawota ni Unakap[u], nae e pei nawota veea,
ni Unakap[u].
Ragi waina e musagi Leiameara, e musagi ra pilake Marimaraki.
E umai paa[paa] e lip̃a ki Marimaraki Unakapu
maa te musagi Marileiameara, doko umai paapaa pae elau pa lip̃a ki nia
vaatu warua sikai e doko elau, wora wanogoe e pei nawora aneana eu
soso e ki Vaatup̃auna.
E doko napua e doko Vaatup̃auna, goo te lip̃a ki nia wora wanogoe e doko
sake lulusi napua sake, sake umai paapaaaa
pakiliina napua, doko sake paki…
Ragi waia au punusi taikesa e doko napua goo natokoana waina e dasake
asa e doko taleeva ni etano ni taikesa.
Goo Leiameara te dasake wora wanogoe, e mari nasum̃a wora wanogoe.
Goo, Marikoroi te mate.
Marikoroi e mate,
ragi wanogoe Leiameara te atulake, te pei nawota nagoroi.
E pei nawota nagoroi doko pei Mariameara.
Nagisa veea maaga waina teu madoko, teu daa moro pei nagisa veea
maaga waina eu peea doko.
Maa Mariameara te atulake ragi wanogoe.
Leiameara e doko paapaa e peani natuna nagoroi sikai.
Natuna nagoroi wanogoe, e pei nagoroi sikai maau saa.
Mariki sikai ni Fareafau te piragi a.
Mariki ni Fareafau wanogoe e piragi a.
Goo
te moro maneana dape natuna naanoai sikai nagisana te pei Marikiliida.
E pei nagisa sikai waina e pei nagisa **kasua**, Marikiliida.
Maa nagisa kiiki aneana eu soso e ki **Taatalele**.
Goo Taatalele wanogoe te moro umai pei Mariameara dape nalia ni taata
aneana.
Ragi wanogoe Leiameara te mate.
Ragi waina te mate sua, nae e umai te moro p̃okati p̃onotia kakana, pae
taleeva ni *kastom*.
Goo e p̃okati p̃onotia kakana, goo e moro pei Mariameara e doko
paapaaa.
Mariameara wanogoe, Marikiliida e mate, Taatalele e mate,
goo **natuna**,
Nap̃ileitia,
te moro dape a, te moro dape naliana.

Ragi waina e dape naliana, nae te daa p̄okati p̄onotia. Te umai paki ragi ni nalootuana.

Ragi waina e pei ragi ni nalootuana p̄onotia, nawokawokaana ni p̄onotia ni naveinawotaana, te noopu.

Pae *nineteen hundred, nineteen hundred* waina eu pusake mariki wanogoe, ragi wanogoe te daa moro dakiusi *kastom* tuai.

Wanogoe stori e noopu tokora wanogoe.

"The Family of M̃atoa"
(Part Two)
by
Ronneth Manutukituki

I've said that that is the end of the story, but I should also continue in
    order to connect it to the presentday chief,
telling how the chiefship passed from long ago up until the present.
    What follows is the account of that.
There were no more Tariwiawia's; instead, the chiefship began with
    Manaatamate. The latter was the first chief, the very first chief of
    M̃atoa.
Manaatamate remained [chief] untiiil, he **died**.
Then
someone else in turn took his place.
The one who took his place was called Manatai.
He "killed a hundred" for [the title] according to chiefly **custom**.
He killed one **hundred** pigs.
He ruled in turn because he replaced Manaatamate, once he was dead.
He remained [chief] until he too died.
When Manatai died, **Marikoroi** likewise killed a hundred for it, and he
    became the next chief.
But [chief] Mariameara had yet to arrive.
The women had been an omen of it, the ten sisters.
But it was still men who ruled.
[This was so] up until Marikoroi died,
and, [then came] **Leiameara**.
Leiameara began.
Leiameara
came from **Takara**.

She came from Takara, on Efate, on the coast of North Efate–East Efate,
  rather!

The fellow who ferried her over from Efate was named **Maatap̃au**.

Maatap̃au was the chief of Unakap[u], the first chief, of Unakap[u].

When he brought Leiameara, he brought [chief] Marimaraki as well.

He travelled along until he had put Marimaraki ashore at Unakapu

and then he continued along the shore with Marileiameara, putting her
  ashore by a big rock that lay on the shore, that place, her landing-
  place, being called Vaatup̃auna.

The path was there, by Vaatup̃auna, and that's where he put her ashore,
  and she followed the path upward, came up and up untiiil

she reached the road, and went on up to...

Today we [can] see the cemetery by the road–the village where she
  settled was on the lower side of the cemetery.

So Leiameara settled in that spot, and built a house there.

Then, Marikoroi died.

After Marikoroi died,

Leiameara took over, became the first female chief.

She became the woman chief, Mariameara.

The names [chiefs] initially had, they didn't keep.

So from that time on she was [entitled] "Mariameara".

After a time Leiameara gave birth to a daughter.

That girl, was her one and only daughter.

A fellow from Fareafau married her.

This fellow from Fareafau married her.

And

she bore him another child, a boy named Marikiliida.

This name, Marikiliida, is a **strong** name.

But his first name[1] was **Taatalele**.

And it was Taatalele who took his maternal grandmother's place as the
  next Mariameara.

Then Leiameara died.

Once she was dead, he in turn killed a **hundred** for it, according to
  custom.

He killed the one hundred, and became Mariameara and remaaaained.

Mariameara, Marikiliida, Taatalele[2] died,

and his son,

Nap̃ileitia,

in turn took [the chiefship], in turn took [Taatalele's] place.

When he took his place, however, he did **not** kill the one hundred. The
  Christian era had arrived.

When Christianity came, the one hundred, the slaughter of one hundred
  for the chiefship, ceased.

Since **1900**, 1900 when they ordained that chief, it has **no longer** gone

according to the original custom.
That is the end of this story.

Footnotes

1. Literally, his "small name" (*nagisa kiiki*), is an individual's first or personal name, one which, as the narrator explains, is no longer used for either reference or address once he/she assumes a chiefly title.
2. The reader should bear in mind that these three names all refer to the same individual: Taatalele Marikiliida Mariameara, who was Nap̃ileitia's predecessor.

(Reference: Ronneth-1. May 5, 1978, Mere. Tape 4B, 4-30.)

Text No.6:

"Manaruru goo Uusaṁooli"
pae
Jack Taviṁasoe

A masau atuusi naatuusiana ni naveinawotaana duua waina ero ṁelu
  pae Mooso,
Uusaṁooli goo Manaruru.
Natokoana adeada nagisana Ṁalanaruru.
Uusaṁooli e pei nawota sikai waina namariana aneana e daa p̃ia, sara
  ragi.
Goo Manaruru e pei nawota waina nadoomariana aneana e p̃ia.
Goo tea ni natokoana wanogoe, Ṁalanaruru, pakalaapa eu dogo kite saa
  nalo ni nawosiana ki Uusaṁooli.
Goo Uusaṁooli, nawota wanogoe, nae e **mate**.
Goo waina eu ova ki nia,
e daa dakiusi naataṁooli **laapa** waina eu kili ṁooru poo lesi ra eu one
  etano ni ṁooru.
Maa **nae eu** ova ki nia, nap̃auna e doko **liina**, goo eu dae **namariu** waina
  e peani **nasaga**.
Eu sara ki **naasina** e doko namariu wanogoe.
Goo e doko paapaa nap̃okasina maaga eu meso **puti**, maa naasina e doko
  nasaga ni namariu wanogoe doko.
Goo nawota **Manaruru** e masau naga e ga tuagoto paki Nguna.
Nae, goo narup̃a aneana maaga, goo nagoroi ki Uusaṁooli waina e pei
  namaleepu, e masau sikoti Manaruru pilake narup̃a aneana maaga.
Goo eu **duagoto** pae Mooso paki Nguna.
Goo tokora waina eu paki euta asa, nagisana e pei **Vaaturiki**.
Goo eu paki euta Vaaturiki, Manaruru e piragi narup̃a aneana [maaga]
  pilake nagoroi maleepu ki Uusaṁooli eu sake

paapaa paki euta paki natokoana ki **Matokainaleo.**
Natokoana ki Matokainaleo nagisana e pei **Komali, Komalikasua.**
Manaruru e noa ki Matokainaleo, e naga,
"Ku mariatae dua au namagovai ni namarakiana aniigo?"
E naga, "Io! A mariatae."
Goo e dap̃ otae namarakiana **aneana** dua Manaruru asa goo Manaruru
     e salagisa ni tokora wanogoe waina Matokai e **dua e** asa e pei M̃ala-
     naruru dakiusi natokoana aneana waina e doko **Mooso.**
Goo Uusam̃ ooli **naasina** eu dape a sikoti ra umai paki Nguna.
Goo nae e pei nawota sikai, goo natuna e sikoti a, waina e ga woo moro
     duu oli tamana.
Maa nawota **duua** ero marisaa doko natokoana sikai **maau,** Uusam̃ ooli
     goo Manaruru.
Goo e pei nalakena Manaruru e dip̃ a ki nagoroi maleepu ki Uusam̃ ooli
     goo natuna goo naasi ni Uusam̃ ooli.
Goo e piragi ra sake paapaa paki taleeva kerua ni namarakiana sake pae
     taava paapaa eu siwo paki namarakiana ki Marim̃ asoe[tap̃ are], **Re-**
     woka.
Goo Marim̃ asoe e moro dap̃ otae namarakiana **aneana** dua [nagoroi ki
     Uusam̃ ooli asa nalakena nae e pei tukurau ni naveinawotaana] naga
     e ga toko asa.
Goo naara eu doko asa paapaa natuna e **paataka** ni naveinawotaana goo
     eu pusake a e pei **Uusam̃ ooli.**
Goo e pei nawota ni Rewoka [Fareafau] doko paapaa paki masoso.
Goo e peani kokoi sikai pae tokora wanogoe, M̃alanaruru, paki Rewoka.
Goo
pae ragi wanogoe ero dum̃ ada **puati** ra, Uusam̃ ooli goo Manaruru, maa
     namarakiana ni M̃alanaruru e pei agi **Manaruru.**
Goo Uusam̃ ooli, **nanoap̃ otaeana** kakana e naga e dakiusi e pei **uusa**
     m̃ ooli.
E **daa** pei navatuuna.
E pei **naasi** m̃ ooli, e pei navatu m̃ ooli.
E daa pei nap̃ atoko.
E dakiusi waina e pei uusa m̃ ooli, ragi waina uusa e nadi [paki natano],
     tu daa moro punusi a, [e pueli].
Goo [tea] waina e pae Mooso umai e pei **Manaruru,** e pei **nawota** wanogoe,
     goo narup̃ a aneana maaga, maa Uusam̃ ooli e pei navatu m̃ ooli.
Goo pae ragi **wanogoe** paapaa paki **ragi waia,** Uusam̃ ooli e doko Rewoka
     goo Manaruru e doko M̃alanaruru.
E pei pae tagona laapa laapa paapaa paki Manaruru natuna maaga
     [waina eu doko] masoso.
Naatuusiana wanogoe e noopu.

"Manaruru and Uusaṁooli"
by
Jack Taviṁasoe

I want to tell the story of two chiefs who came from Mooso,
Uusaṁooli and Manaruru.
The name of their village was Ṁalanaruru.
Uusaṁooli was a chief whose behaviour was **never** good.
And Manaruru was a chief whose behaviour **was** good.
The people of that village, Ṁalanaruru, were often troubled by Uusaṁooli's
   behaviour.
And then that chief, Uusaṁooli, **died.**
When they buried him,
it was not done as is the case for **most** people in that they dig a **hole** and
   then lie [the body] **down** in [it].
Rather, they buried him, with his head **protruding**, and cut a forked stick
   from a *namariu* tree.
Then they hung his [**head**] up on the stick by the **jaw.**
And eventually the flesh rotted away **completely,** and the jaw alone
   remained on the forked stick.
Then chief **Manaruru** decided to go across to Nguna.
He went, along with Uusaṁooli's widow, who wanted to go with him, and
   Manaruru's women as well.
So they **crossed** from Mooso to Nguna.
The place where they went ashore, was named **Vaaturiki.**
So Manaruru took that woman, Uusaṁooli's widow, and his women
   ashore there, going up inland
until they reached the village of [chief] **Matokainaleo.**
The name of Matokainaleo's village was **Komali, Komalikasua.**

Manaruru said to Matokainaleo,
"Can you give me part of your dominion?"
He replied, "Yes! I will."
So he divided his dominion for Manaruru and Manaruru named the area
   Matokai gave him M̃ alanaruru, the same as his village on Mooso.
And they had taken Uusam̃ ooli's jawbone with them to Nguna.
Also there was [Uusam̃ ooli's] son, who was to take his father's place.
But both chiefs couldn't stay in the same village, both Uusam̃ ooli and
   M̃ anaruru.
Because of that Manaruru sent away Uusam̃ ooli's widow, his son and
   jawbone.
He led them up inland until they reached the other side of the dominion
   and descended to Marim̃ asoe[tap̃ are]'s dominion, Rewoka.
Then, likewise, because she was the widow of a chief, Marim̃ asoe split his
   dominion to give [land] to Uusam̃ ooli's wife.
And the two of them lived there until the son was old enough to become
   chief and then he was ordained Uusam̃ ooli.
And he remained chief of Rewoka [Fareafau] from then until this very
   day.
And there is a boundary from there, from M̃ alanaruru, to Rewoka.
Since then
the two [chiefs], Uusam̃ ooli and Manaruru, have supported each other,
   but the dominion of M̃ alanaruru belongs to Manaruru.
Now, the meaning of [the name] Uusam̃ ooli, is that he was "*uusa m̃ ooli*",
   "just rain".
He was nothing.
He was only a jaw, just bones.
He had no body.
It's like when rain falls to the ground, you can't see it, [it disappears].
Likewise, the chief who came from Mooso with his women was Mana-
   ruru, but Uusam̃ ooli [came] as nothing but bones.
And from then until now, [the title of] Uusam̃ ooli has been in Rewoka and
   [that of] Manaruru has been in M̃ alanaruru.
Many, maaany generations have passed since then up until [one comes
   to] the descendants of Manaruru who are alive today.
That is the end of the story.

(Reference: Jack T.-2. July 5, 1978, Nekaap̃ a. Tape 9B,1-20.)

Chapter Seven

Naatuusiana Maaga/Accounts

There are 21 texts included in this section. In terms of general content and particular focus, they can be roughly divided into those which give the origins and/or explanations of particular social institutions, customs or physical/geographic landmarks; those which recount individual battles or long-term, inter-village hostilities; and those which, if they serve any specific purpose as do the others in describing and/or explaining, it is a moral or pedagogical one. "The Ten Brothers and Rovemao", in which a whole family of brothers desire the same beautiful woman, is a good example. The tragic, ironic ending undoubtedly "says something" to the listener about the potential divisiveness of sexual desire if it leads to frustration and envy, transforming brotherly love and commitment into hatred and destructiveness. So, while some of these accounts are clearly intended to be taken as historically accurate, others are of dubious historicity, and yet others would generally be treated as fictional anecdotes.

This, then, is a very "mixed" narrative "bag". My reasons for presenting such a varied assortment of texts under a single broad rubric are detailed elsewhere (see Chapter Three). I would add, however, that I am compelled to take this approach for another reason as well. Oral literature, like "culture" itself, is a strange and varied mixture of the "what We think", "what We believe", "what We think is true", "what We believe is true", "what We would like to believe/think/think is true", and "what We should believe/think/think is true". To the insider, the "native", these are not always entirely distinct from one another;

therefore, if one is to be ethnographically realistic, one must *re—present* such contradictions or ambiguities as they present themselves in a body of oral literature (or, likewise, in a culture), without imposing artificial clarity or fine definition merely in response to outsiders' clamouring for these.

Text No.7:

"Namariana ni Naveinawotaana Maaga"
pae
Kaltaṗau M̃asemata

A poo masau noa nalo ni, stori nalo ni naveinawotaana.
Goo naveinawotaana maaga doko **Nguna**,
goo **Ṗele**,
goo **Efate**,
eu peani nagisa eu **dolutoolu**.
Ragi waina naveinawotaana sikai, e pei naga e ga woo duu oli tamana,
  e ga woo ova nagisa veea.
Goo ragi waina e ga ova nagisa veea wanogoe, goo e ga umai dape nagisa
  ni m̃aleoputo, nagisa veea e ga woo nadi ki nia madoko.
Maa ragi waina e pe toko paapaa e pe ma**tua**,
goo natuna e pe vaataka wia.
E ga woo moro dape nagisa ni m̃a**leoputo**,
maa, tamana e ga tape nagisa **ketolu**
e pei "retired" nagisa, waina te noopu.
Goo ragi waina eu doko paa[paa] eu masau dovi naveinawotaana
  wanogoe.
Eu pıragi a paki weede.
Maa peea
naveinawota lakesikaiana.
Dakiusi, e ga umai poo pua sike a.
Dapala waina e peani navatuuna sikai waina nawota veea e mate e pei
  nal[e]o mauri sikai waina e doko matigo, waina eu pa doni a pilake
  naṗatoko.
Goo navuasikeana e pei naveinawotaana lakesikaiana waina e ga tape
  te navatuuna seara umai,

poo puasike a, dapala waina e puasike nal[e]o mauri wanogoe e pei sup̃e
   ni naveinawotaana.
E ga umai poo sili naatam̃ooli waina eu poo moro dovi nap̃auna, goo
   nawosiana aneana e ga woo moro kasua p̃ia.
Goo ragi waina e ga vuasike a peea,
goo
tea aneana maaga,
e pe vei tukurau waina e doko, kite taina maaga, kite gorena maaga
maa edaku eu ga woo pusi a.
Eu ga woo pusi nagisa wanogoe, poo dua naatam̃ooli waina
e ga woo ova nagisa wanogoe.
Goo ragi waina eu pusi a pano, edaku, eu ga woo piragi a paki weede,
waina e pei vaatu sikai,
goo, e ga woo pei tea toviana asa.
Goo ragi waina nawota wanogoe, e pe toko paapaa e pe **mate**,
doko ragi ni tuai
e pe naga e pe mate.
Goo
eu ga woo pitua ki navasaana paki sara naatam̃ooli,
Nguna daliviri, kite naure, kite Efate.
Goo eu ga woo umai dagisi nawota wanogoe.
Maa
ragi waina eu ga umai, nawota wanogoe e daa pei tea lesiana, e daa
   dakiusi ragi waia.
Maa eu ga woo mari a e ga **ovi**, e ga ovi doko naara ni nasum̃a aneana,
e ga woo dapala tea mauri sikai.
Goo eu ga woo puati waago warua sikai waina napatina e puri
pakaruua.
Poo liko sokasokari viria maaga wanogoe poo umai likoti naru ni
   naveinawotaana wanogoe asa. Eu ga likoti a paki naruna ni matua.
Goo ragi waina, eu pe tagi paapaa e pe maligo.
Goo, eu ga woo pa ova ki nia.
Eu ga woo pa ova ki nia,
maa, tea aneana maaga,
eu ga woo doko, eu ga woo pali, naaleatia rualimaliima.
Goo nap̃oogiana wanogoe eu ga woo dape navinaga seara poo doropusi a
   matigo.
E pei waina eu ga vagani a asa.
Goo ragi waina malip̃oogi eu pano eu daa punusi te navinaga seara e
   doko matigo.
Maa e lagoro pei koriia kite puusi kite nasava e gani a.
Goo naara eu midoaki nia naga naatamate e gani a.
Eu ga toko paapaa kup̃a **lima**
kite nakup̃a rualimaliima.

Goo naara teu ga woo paki natasi poo loloso.

Ragi waina eu midoa ki nia naga eu ga vaki matigo

dapala nigida ragi waia tu doo p̃osiwosi ki nia doko kup̃a lima

maa naara e pei nakup̃a rualimaliima kite nakup̃a p̃onotia sikai.

Goo ragi waina eu ga vano, eu ga woo paki matigo.

Goo ragi waina eu ga vaki matigo,

tea mamauputi eu ga vano.

Goo ragi waina eu paki matigo eu midoa ki nia naga eu ga vavano natasi.

Goo ragi wanogoe

eu ga naga,

"Itoo! Itoo! Taaroa, itoo!" [*tea legaana*]

Ragi wanogoe eu sava naga eu ga kisip̃ai natasi; seei e ga veea kisip̃ai
natasi?

Maa eu midoa ki nia naga ragi waina tea waina e edaku,

saatana ki naveinawotaana wanogoe e ga woo kisip̃ai a goo nae e ga woo
mate.

Goo ragi waina eu ga woo mamauputi sava kisi natasi.

E pe vei euta maaga maa eu masau naga eu ga sava poo kisi natasi.

Eu sava poo gaegae, maa tea waina e kasua

e kisip̃ai natasi peea.

Goo ragi waina eu paki sum̃a,

eu mari navinaga warua, goo eu moro dovi nap̃au ni naveinawotaana
sikai, waina e ga tuu oli tamana

waina te mate sua waina teu ova ki nia.

Goo stori kiiki waia te noopu tokora waia.

"Making Chiefs"
by
Kaltap̃au M̃asemata

I wanted to talk about, to tell a story regarding the chiefship.
The chiefs of **Nguna,**
and **P̃ele,**
and **Efate,**
have **three** titles.
When a man decides to becomes chief, in place of his father, he uses the first name.
After he has taken the first name, then he will take the middle name, and discard the first one.
But if he lives to a **ripe age,**
his [own] son will then be old enough.
Then [the latter] will take the **middle** name,
and, his father takes the **third** name
as his "retired" name, having ceased [being chief].
And then they wait until they are ready to ordain this chief.
They take him to the ordination seat.
But first
[there must be] a chief of shared origin.
That is, he will come to raise him up.
It is as if there were something which the deceased chief [possessed], a living thing that remains in the grave, that was buried with the body.
The raising up means that the chief of shared origin would bring something,
and pull it up, that is, he raises up that living thing, the chiefly spirit.
It then enters the person who is ordained, so that his works will also be good and strong.

So he is raised up [as chief] first,
then
[the dead chief's] family,
his widow, if she is still alive, his brothers or his sisters
afterwards they pass it over to him.
They pass on the name, giving it to that person,
so that he may then bear the name.
And once they have passed it on to him, then, they take him to the
    ordination seat,
which is a stone
and, he will be ordained on it.
And then if in time, this chief should die,
in the olden days,
if he thought he was going to die.
Then
they would send word to everyone,
all around Nguna, or "the small island" [Ƥele], or Efate.
And they would come to mourn the chief.
But
when they arrived, the chief would not be laid down, not as is the case
    nowadays.
Rather they would sit him up, leaning against the wall in his house,
as if he were alive.
And they would take a large pig whose tusks had pierced its jaw
twice.
And take the ropes [with which it is tied] and attach them to the [dead]
    chief's hand. They attach them to his right hand.
Then, they would wail until sundown.
Then, they would go and bury him,
but, his family,
would remain behind, and fast, [for] fifty days.
And during the night they would take food and put it on the grave.
It would be to feed him.
Then when they went in the morning they would not see any food
    remaining at the grave.
But perhaps a dog or cat or something else ate it [*musingly said*].
But they would think that a ghost [the dead chief's spirit] had eaten it.
They would remain there until the fifth day
or the fiftieth day.
And then those [people] would go to the sea to wash.
When they decided to go to the grave
as we do on the fifth day
but for them it would be on the fiftieth day or the one hundredth day.
So then they would go, go to the grave.

When they went to the grave,
everyone would go.
Once they had gone to the grave, they would then want to wash in the sea.
And then
they would say,
"Good-bye! Good-bye! Everyone, good-bye!" [*sung*]
Then they run to the sea [*quickly said*]; [to see] **who** will be the first to
   touch the sea?
And they think that the one who is last,
the **evil spirit** of the [dead] chief would touch him and he would die.
So they all run to touch the sea [*quickly*].
Even if far inland, still they want to run and touch the sea.
They run until they are quite out of breath, but the one who is strong
touches the water first.
And then they go home,
make a great feast, and **ordain** the chief, who is to replace his father
who has died and been buried.
And that is the end of this little story.

(Reference: Kalo-2. March 23, 1978, Unakapu. Tape 1A, 53-63.)

Text No.8:

"Wotanimanu"
pae
Kaltap̃au Ñasemata

Vaatu sikai nagisana e pei
o
Wotanimanu.
Goo tuai! tuai! tuai!
Ragi waina e doko Eromaga, e pei naatam̃ooli.
Goo e pei naatam̃ooli waina
e pei naatam̃ooli araika, e doo daliviri navanua ni Eromaga.
E doo lawo naika daliviri navanua ni Eromaga.
Goo ragi waina e umai paki taleeva ni Efate,
e punusi nagisu varau sikai, waina nagisana e pei Maniura.
Goo e naga, "O! A leom̃ata ki nagisu wanae.
A masau pa lawo naika asa maa a ga vae esa[v]a pano?
E pei uvea saa."
Goo e pano poo sara ki naio varau sikai, waina naturana e parau.
Goo ragi waina e doko Eromaga, e nadi ki navinaga ni naio wanogoe e
    madoko naworaone ni Eromaga.
Maa natura ni naio aneana e umai p̃oka nagisu ni Maniura.
Goo ragi wanogoe e sai lua naio aneana.
Goo e atulake poo lawo naika pae Maniura, poo umai paki taleeva ni P̃au.
Goo ragi waina e umai paki P̃au, e punusi tamadawota sikai ero doko.
E pei naveinawotaana ni P̃au.
E pei mari[ki] Valeawia.
Goo nagoroi aneana e pei Leiwia.
Goo ragi wanogoe e doo lawo naika goo e dape a paki sum̃a ni kiada.
Nagoroi ki naveinawotaana wanogoe e doo mari naika maaga wanogoe e

maaso goo ero doo gani a.

Goo ragi sikai e doo disu umai pae taleeva ni Onesua, paki Epule.

Goo e doo liliu pano

pa punusi tamadawota.

Paapaa, goo ragi sikai, e umai doko doliu

paki taleeva ni Emua.

Goo ragi waina e umai paki Emua,

e punusi nagoroi sikai, natu ni Manalaesinu, nagisana Leinasei,

e naga e ga vautu.

Goo e noa ki nia, "Aleatiwia!"

Goo nagoroi wanogoe e noa naga "Aleatiwia!"

Goo e puati naika seara goo e dua nagoroi wanogoe asa.

Maa tamana ma p̃ilana ero surata puoli.

Goo ragi waina ero rumai paki sum̃a, ero dogo nap̃o ni naika.

Goo ero naga, "Seei e dua ko naika?"

Goo e naga, "naatam̃ooli sikai.

E lawo naika umai paa[paa] e dua au asa maa te moro liliu."

Goo matamai ki nia

e moro pano, nalakena e punusi koroi wanogoe goo te masau na

naga e ga vei nagoroi aneana

natu ni Manalaesinu.

Matamai ki nia e moro pano.

Goo p̃ilana goo tamana ero moro surata.

Goo ragi wanogoe, e moro dua e naika,

e naga, "P̃a umai toro ga rua paki ekopu."

Goo ragi waina p̃ilana ma tamana ero liliu,

ero naga, "Nap̃o ni naika wanogoe."

E naga, "Naatam̃ooli waina e moro umai." Maa ero naga, "Te paki esa[v]a
     pano?" E naga, "E doko ekopu."

Goo naara ero pano poo talova ki nia.

Goo eu mamau doko.

Maa naatam̃ooli wanogoe e pei naatam̃ooli ni naika, naatam̃ooli araika.

Goo sara ragi, e marisaa paki namalasi,

maa e doo araika daliviri Efate.

Goo e doo dape naika umai.

Paapaa goo tamadawota wanogoe,

eu doko eu datuuta ki nia naga natau vaau eu ga woo sike naveinawotaana
     vaau,

Manalaesinu

ni Emua.

Goo tea laapa eu doo marisokisoki, eu doo um̃a.

Goo vitariki e umai goo e noa ki natuda asa e naga, "Te koro pa mamale saa!

Maa kinami au doo p̃osiwosi kasua saa pae namalasi nalakena tu ga mari

naveinawotaana sikai, natau vaau."

Goo koroi kiiki wanogoe e noa ki mariki aneana asa.

E noa ki Wotanimanu asa.

Goo e noa ki nia asa, e naga, "P̃a noa kii da asa naga matamai ero ga tua gida masimasi sikai, toro ga va um̃a."

Goo ragi waina tamadawota ero dua ra masimasi ero dua ra masimasi kaum̃elu sikai, nakauna e m̃elu.

Goo ero puati a poo paki **taava**, naga ero ga um̃a.

Goo koroi wanogoe e peea ki nia goo ero pano, goo e naga, "Niigo p̃a woo punusi tokora waina toro ga um̃a e waina e matemate paki uvea."

Goo ero pano

poo daelua nakau sikai maau poo moro putilua nam̃enau sikai maau poo nadi ki nia, goo ero moro liliu umai paki esum̃a.

Goo ragi waina ero umai paki esum̃a goo tamadawota ero moro liliu, p̃ilana ma tamana,

"O! Maa nimu koro surata dapale sava?

Tekoro pa mamale saa!

Tekoro surata maraverave saa doko umai paki esum̃a!"

Maa koroi kiiki e daa pasa.

E moro lawo naika paapaa, tero pauria paa[paa] tero dao sua.

Eu ganikani sua ragimelu,

malip̃oogi ero moro pano.

Ero moro paki tokora wanogoe waina ero um̃a e.

Ragi waina ero pano, naenum̃a warua waina eu madeada um̃a sua e poo dae nakau asa.

Ragi wanogoe te pei tea marim̃atakiana raki waina eu ga tokoni a.

Nalakena e peani narei eu laapa.

Wotanimanu e peani narei laapa.

Goo matamai ki nia, ero **moro** pano.

Ero moro pano poo punusi waina te kokolo p̃ia, goo ero dape nalisere sikai, poo nadi ki nia asa.

Goo ero dokoni dogoe te madoko maa tero liliu paki esum̃a.

Goo ragi waina ero liliu umai paki esum̃a,

navasaana sikai maau wanogoe tamadawota ero moro noa ki nia asa.

"Nimu tekoro pa mamale **saa**!"

Maa koroi kiiki e daa pasa,

nalakena e maaga nawoslan̄a waina e doo pei tea mariana roara adeada, doko taava.

Goo matamai ki nia ero pano

maa te pei tea tokonisuaana.

Te pei tea marim̃atakiana raki waina teu ga lalawo.

Wotanimanu e noa ki Leinasei e noa naga, "P̃a noa ki tamam̃a goo p̃ilam̃a asa, naga ero ga tua gida nawii e ga sikai maau,

goo sara naleo mamauputi waina eu pei tea lawoana doko lolua maaga, eu ga tua gida e ga sikasikai."

Goo eu dua ra asa.

Goo ero pano poo lawo taki nawii sikai maau e madoko goo sara naleo
maaga wanogoe ero nadi ki nia madoko.

Goo ero moro pano matamai ki nia, ero punusi naga nawii maaga, eu lawo
e paa[paa] e pura tokora wanogoe,

pilake sara naleo—

maniok goo naadi,

noopa, nap̃arae, namaloku, sara naleo mamauputi e[u] pura.

Goo e doko.

Paapaa ragi waina nawii te matua, goo teu datuuta, naga, "E pei atelagi
vaau, tu ga mari naveinawotaana."

Goo eu doo magi sara naatam̃ooli maaga ni Emua, tea laapa.

Woli e doo kai, eu doo madeada dape navinaga maaga, paki esum̃a, eu mari
vaala pae nasum̃a maaga.

Paapaa te noopu.

Maa te naata sikai ni Emua e daa punusi roara adeada wanogoe.

Paapaa adeada maaga e[u] noopu.

Goo koroi kiiki e noa ki tamana ma p̃ilana asa, e naga,

"Waasa!

Tu ga woo maginami surata pae roara aginami paki esum̃a."

Goo naara ero noa ki nia asa ero naga, "E! Aro mataku!

nalakena nimu koro pei tea mamale.

Tu ga vano poo dape nasava?

nalakena nimu koro pei tea mamale."

Goo koroi kiiki e noa ki tamana ma p̃ilana asa e naga, "E pei tea m̃ooli. Tu
ga vano.

Waasa! Woli e ga woo kai, goo tea laapa tu ga woo pano.

E pei namasauana aginami."

Goo ero noa naga, "Io."

Maa naara ero peea pano, masoso, goo matamai ero moro pano.

Ero marisokisoki.

Ero marisokisoki uupu maaga

naga ragi waina eu ga vano eu ga veea gani navinaga maaso peea poo edaku
dape tea mata, dape a umai paki esum̃a.

Goo ragi waina ero pano, ero madoko marisokisoki loriki maaga wanogoe.

Paa[paa] waasa

goo woli poo kai, goo tea laapa eu poo pano.

Ragi waina eu pano,

taoa maaga eu doo sui, nalakena narei aneana eu maneana mari sua
nawosiana maaga wanogoe,

narei ki Wotanimanu.

Goo e naga, "Tu ga too ganikani."

Eu puke.

Eu tuturi pae nasum̃a maaga.

Paapaa e noopu.

Navinaga maaga waina eu ga woo dape a, eu kili sua e, narei aneana maaga
eu maneana kili sua e.

Goo ragi waina eu ganikani sua,

nagoroi maaga eu pai navinaga maaso.

Naala adeada maaga e[u] pura.

Goo ragi waina e noa kii da asa naga, "Tea mata wanae e duu."

Eu dape sikasikai m̃ooli maa sara naleo mamauputi eu maduu

nalakena teu pai tea maaso, te toliu.

Goo ragi wanogoe e noa, "Tea m̃ooli. Tu ga vaki sum̃a. Maa tea mata maaga
waia e[u] ga tuu."

Maa ragi waina p̃oogi narei aneana eu poo maneana dape a umai paki
esum̃a.

Goo eu sawa ki nia paki vaala paa[paa] e pura.

Pilake waago rualimasikai maau, waina eu dape a umai pilake navinaga
maaga wanogoe, paki esum̃a.

Goo teu datuuta, noa naga naaleatia waia e ga vei naaleatia ni naleoana
warua.

Goo teu dovi naveinawotaana wanogoe.

Goo ragi waina naveinawotaana e noopu.

Eu doko kiiki

goo tea ni Emua, eu maeto ki nia nalakena navinaga aneana e doliu
naatatoko maaga,

kite waago maaga, e doliu naatatoko maaga.

Goo eu atulake poo pasa ki nia,

eu naga, "O! Niigo ku pei namusasake, ku pei nam̃enaki,

goo ku umai poo mari doliu gami.

Ragi waia au karae kita ko!

P̃a vano!"

Goo nagoroi p̃ota sikai e moro liko Wotanimanu, e pei nagoroi kerua ni
Leinasei.

E piragi narup̃a.

Goo ragi wanogoe malip̃oogi e noa kii da asa e naga, "Ta ga m̃elu!

Ta ga m̃elu tokora waia!"

Goo naara eu dodomi p̃arua ki nia.

Goo ero m̃elu poo umai paki taleeva ni matigo ni Emua,

paki taleeva ni Saam̃a.

Goo e naga, "Tokora waia ta ga loloso asa."

Goo nagoroi dua wanogoe ero madoo kai tokora wanogoe, poo dagisi a, maa
nae te m̃elu.

E loloso duagoto umai paki Nguna.

Maa tea rua ero madoko namaati ni tokora wanogoe.

Eu soso e ki Nawewelekinarup̃a.

Nagoroi dua wanogoe ero doko paapaa paki masoso, e pei vaatu dua waina

ero doko tokora wanogoe doko.
Eu soso e ki Nawewelekinaruᵽa.
Maa nae e umai poo sake Tikilasoa
poo paki taava, [ni] lake nakim̃au.
E poo doko tokora wanogoe.
Goo ragi wanogoe e naga, "O! Ragi waia a doko ᵽia."
Ragi wanogoe te pei vaatu.
Te daa pei naatam̃ ooli maa te pei vaatu.
Goo ragi waina e doko, e dogo e kite naka ni Tikilasoa maaga eu ᵽokati
    nakᵽea ᵽoogi; e marisaa maturu.
Goo naka ni M̃alalolo maaga, goo naka ni M̃alaliu.
E naga, "O! A doko tokora waia a daa maturu ᵽia ᵽoogi.
Eu ᵽokawoka aleati goo ᵽoogi!
A dogo saa ki nia naᵽaugu e pitinu asa goo naᵽelegu e pitinu!
A marisaa maturu ᵽia.
A ga woo lagoro m̃elu."
Goo e doko kiik[i] e m̃elu,
e m̃elu poo paki taleeva ni Unakapu,
doko natokoana e doko etano maa nae e doko elag[i] kakana.
Goo tokora waina e m̃elu asa doko Tikilasoa, eu soso e ki M̃oruniwota, e
    doko paapaa paki masoso.
Goo e moro m̃elu poo paki taleeva ni Unakapu.
Goo ragi waina e paki Unakapu, maa tea ni Unakapu maa eu ᵽoka nakᵽea,
goo e marisaa maturu,
"Eeee! A dogo kite saa!
Naᵽaugu pitinu.
A daa doo maturu ᵽoogi.
Elagoro a ga woo m̃elu."
Goo e moro m̃elu tokora wanogoe.
E m̃elu tokora wanogoe poo paki taava,
paki taleeva ni Meere.
"O! A doko tokora waia a leo ᵽia, paki natasi,
paki natalovanamalaadi.
Goo elo e sake a punusi m̃ata ki nia ragi waina e sake maliᵽoogi.
A poo doko ᵽia."
Goo tokora wanogoe e m̃elu asa doko Unakapu.
Nae maa nagisana e pei M̃oruniwota e doko masoso.
Goo e dasake tokora wanogoe.
Ragi waina e doko kiiki,
naka ni Meere, naka ni M̃alaliu, naka ni M̃atoa, naka ni Rewoka,
naka ni Sauwia maaga eu ᵽokati nakᵽea ᵽoogi, goo e daa maturu.
E naga, "O, A doko tokora waia maa e paataka sikai,
elagoro a ga woo m̃elu,
a ga woo m̃elu paki natasi."

Goo ragi waina e m̃elu
e paki nataku ni Mataaso
poo doko tokora wanogoe.
Goo e peani narei **laapa** waina eu doko asa doko masoso.
Narei maaga wanogoe waina eu doo maneana p̃osiwosi ki roara aneana
   doko Emua.
Goo **masoso**
tu punusi naga manu maaga wanogoe eu doo diri pano, maa **sala veea**, eu
   pei naatam̃ooli.
Goo manu maaga waina eu doko masoso waina naka ni Mataaso eu doo
   gani ra.
Goo stori waia e noopu tokora waia.

"Chief of the Birds"
by
Kaltap̃au M̃asemata

[There is] a **stone** whose name is
°

Wotanimanu[1], [chief of the birds].
Long! long! long ago!
When it was on Eromaga, it was a person.
And he was a
fisherman, who used to travel around the island of Eromaga.
And one time he came to the coast [facing] Efate,
and saw a long point, whose name is Maniura.
And he said, "Oh! What a lovely point.
I'd like to go and do some spear fishing there, but how can I?
It's so far."
So he went and fashioned a large spear, with a long shaft.
And from Eromaga, he threw the spear so that its end was stuck in the sand
    on Eromaga.
But the shaft of his spear struck the point on [Efate], **Maniura**.
Then he pulled out his spear.
And he began to fish [around the coast of Efate] from Maniura, all the way
    around to P̃au.[2]
And when he arrived at P̃au, he saw a man and his wife there.
It was the chief of P̃au.
It was old Valeawia.
And his wife, Leiwia.
And when [Wotanimanu] had speared some fish, he took them to the
    [couple's] house.

110

The chief's wife cooked the fish, and when it was done the two of them ate it.
And one time he was travelling along from the coast at **Onesua**, toward
    Epule.
He used to go back
to see the couple.
Until, on this particular occasion, he passed on **by**
toward the coast at **Emua.**
And as he was approaching Emua,
he saw a woman, Manalaesinu's daughter, whose name was Leinasei,
who was going to draw water.
He said, "**Hello!**"
And the woman replied, "Hello!"
Then he caught some fish and gave them to the woman.
But her father and mother were away working in the gardens.
And when they got home, they smelled the fish.
And they said, "Who gave you the fish?"
And she said, "A man.
He speared the fish and gave them to me, but then he went away again."
And the next day
he went back again, because when he saw the girl he **wanted** her
for his wife
Manalaesinu's daughter.
So the next day he went back again.
And once again her mother and father had gone to the gardens.
And when, he again gave her [some] fish,
she said, "Let's go inside."
And when her father and mother returned,
they said, "There's that smell of fish again."
She said, "That man has come back." And they asked, "Where has he gone?"
    She replied, "He's inside."
So they went in and shook hands with him.
And [from then on] they all lived **together.**
But this man was one for fishing, a fisherman.
Never, would he ever go to the bush,
instead he continued fishing all around Efate.
And he would bring the fish back.
In time the [older] couple,
promised him that in the **new year** they would raise up the new chief,
[the next] Manalaesinu
of Emua.
And everyone was getting ready for it, clearing the bush for gardens.
And the old woman came and told her daughter [*irritably*], "You two are
    very lazy!
Yet here the rest of us are working very hard in the bush in order to raise up

a new chief, next year."

So the young woman went and related this to her husband.

She told Wotanimanu.

So he said, "Go and tell them to give us a knife tomorrow, and we will go and clear bush."

So the couple gave them a knife, one whose handle had come off, it had no handle.

And they took it and went into the hills, to clear the bush.

Off they went with the young woman in front and having gone a distance, he said, "Go and have a look for a spot to clear, one that is a long, level stretch."

So the two of them went

and cut down a single tree and pulled out and threw aside a single blade of grass, then returned to the house.

After they had returned, the [older] couple, her mother and father, returned [*speaking quickly and angrily*],

"OH! What kind of work do you call this?

You two are so lazy!

You work such a short time and then come home again!"

But the young woman said nothing [*said in a low, flat tone*].

[Wotanimanu] went back to spearing fish again, then the two of them built a fire and baked the fish.

They ate that evening,

and in the morning went back.

They went back to the place they had been clearing.

When they got there, a huge clearing party had finished clearing it and taking out the trees for them.

It had been completely prepared for burning off.

For he had a great number of people.

Wotanimanu's people were many.

The following day, the two of them went back.

They went back and saw that [the field] was good and dry, so they took a single coconut frond, [set it alight] and threw it down on it.

Having set [that single frond] alight they left it and went home again.

And when they returned to the house,

the [older couple] said exactly the same thing as before [*again, angrily*].

"You two are so lazy!"

But the young woman said nothing,

because she was amazed at the work that had been done in their garden, up on the hill.

The following day they went

but the garden plot had already been completely burned off.

It had been all cleaned up ready for them to plant.

Wotanimanu said to Leinasei, "Tell your father and mother, to give us just one yam,

and likewise with everything else that is to be planted in the gardens, they are to give us just one of each."

So they gave them to them.

They went and planted a single yam stalk and likewise with everything else left them lying there.

When they went back the next day, they saw that the place was full of planted yams,

along with everything else—

manioc and bananas,

native cabbage, sugarcane, kava, it was full with every kind of thing.

So they waited.

Until finally the yams were ripe, and then they set the date, "Next month, we will raise the chief."

So they [made a feast] for all the people of Emua, many people.

When the conch shell trumpet sounded, they collected food for them, [and took it] to their houses, making yam storage racks by every house.

Until at last it was complete.

But not one of the Emua people had seen their garden.

Until finally theirs were empty.

Then the young woman said to her father and mother,

"The day after tomorrow!

We will all go to our gardens [to bring food] to the house."

But they said to her, "What! We're afraid!

You two are so lazy.

What could we possibly get there

since you've been so lazy?"

And the young woman said to her father, "Never mind. We're going.

The day after tomorrow! The conch will sound and many of us will go.

That's how we want it to be."

So they replied [*resignedly*], "Alright."

But the [other] two [Leinasei and Wotanimanu] went beforehand, that day, and then again the day after.

They made ready.

They prepared earth ovens

so that when [the villagers] went they would be able to eat pre-cooked food and then take the raw food home.

So they went, they stayed there getting everything ready.

At last the following day

the conch sounded, and many people went.

When they went,

the ovens were [already] steaming, because his people had already done the job for him,

Wotanimanu's people.

So he said, "Let's eat."

They opened the ovens.

They distributed the food household by household.

Until eventually it was all done.

The food that they were to take, had already been dug up, his people had
    already dug it up for him.

So when they had finished eating,

the women loaded up the cooked food.

Their baskets were full.

Then he told them, "There's still raw food left over there."

[Even though] they each took one almost **everything** was still left

because they had already loaded up with the cooked food, there was so
    much.

At that point he said, "Never mind; let's go home. The rest of the raw food
    will have to be left."

But during the night his people carried it all home for him.

They loaded the yam racks until they were completely full.

Along with that were the ten pigs, that they brought with the food, to the
    house.

Then they announced that, that day would be the day of the great feast.

So they ordained the chief.

After the ordination was over,

they stayed for a short time,

but the people of Emua, were angry with him because he had produced
    more food than had the local people,

and more pigs, than any of the locals.

So they started talking to him,

saying [*disparagingly*], "You! You're like driftwood, a stranger,

yet you come along and outdo us.

We don't want you around!

Get out!"

And there was another woman who was attached to Wotanimanu, a second
    wife to Leinasei.

He had taken a lover.

So when morning came he said to them, "I'm leaving!

I'm leaving here!"

But they both loved him very much.

So they left and came to the coast by Emua's graveyard,

toward the coast at Saama.

Then he said, "I am going to swim from here."

And the two women stayed behind, crying, grieving for him, but he was
    gone.

He swam across until he reached Nguna.

But they remained there on the reef.

They call [that spot] "The Lover's Bed."

The two women are still there today, the two stones that are still there today.

They call it "The Lover's Bed."

But he went ashore at Tikilasoa

and climbed [what is known as] the hill of the nakimãu tree stump.

He stopped there.

And he thought, "Oh, this is a good place to live!"

At that point he turned into a stone.

He was no longer a human, but a stone.

And as he continued to live there, he began hearing the people of Tikilasoa beating the slit-drums at night; he couldn't sleep.

And the people of Mãlalolo, and of Mãlaliu [beat their drums all night].

He said, "Living here, I can't sleep at night.

They drum **day and night**!

I can't stand listening to it, my head aches from it and my stomache **aches**!

I can't sleep properly.

So I think I'll move out."

He stayed a little longer and then **left**,

moved along the coast toward **Unakapu**,

the village was down below, but he lived up on the high ground behind it.

And the place that he abandoned in Tikilasoa, is called the Pit of the Chief,

it is still there today.

So he left for the Unakapu coast.

But when he went to Unakapu, the people of Unakapu were beating drums as well,

and he couldn't sleep, [and groaned],

"Oh, nooo! I feel **terrible**!

My head is aching.

I can't sleep at night.

I think I'll move out."

So he left that place as well.

He left there and went up further inland,

toward Meere.

"Oh! From here I have a beautiful view, of the sea,

and the horizon.

And I love watching the sun come up in the morning.

This is a great place to live [said contentedly]."

And the place he abandoned at Unakapu.

It too is called the Pit of the Chief still today.

So he settled down to live there [above Meere].

He had been there only a short time,

[when] the people of Meere, the people of Mãlaliu, the people of Mãtoa, the people of Rewoka

[and] the people of Sauwia all started beating their drums at night, so that
   he couldn't sleep.
He said, "It's just the same here,
I think I should leave,
I'll move out to sea."
So he moved out
[and] went around to the far side of Mataaso to live.
And there were **many** people there then as there are even today.
All these were his people, the ones who had worked his gardens for him at
   Emua.
And **today**
we see those birds flying about [over Mataaso], but originally, they were
   humans.
And these birds are eaten by the people of Mataaso.
And that is the end of this story.

Footnotes

1. Generally known in English as Monument Rock.
2. It is not clear how Wotanimanu accomplished the crossing. There are
   two possible logical explanations: either he pulled Efate and Erromango
   close together with his spear and strength of mythic proportions; or he
   crossed the sea via the shaft of the spear. The raconteur, however, was
   not troubled to elaborate, feeling perhaps— if I may be forgiven this
   lapse- that how Wotanimanu attained the Efate shore was beside the
   point.

(Reference: Kalo-3. March 23, 1978, Unakapu. Tape 1A, 63-70 & B, 0-31.)

Text No.9:

"Nakainaga Maaga"
pae
Kaltaρ̃au Ñasemata

Doko ragi ni **tuai, tuai, tuai**.
Naatañooli maaga eu doo duñada gani ra, poo duñada ρ̃okati ra.
Goo eu daa duñada atae ra naga eu pei tea sikai maau, nalakena
Namaligo
e doko ragi ni tuai tuai wanogoe.
Goo e peani nawota duua, ero doko Efate ni etano.
Sikai e pei **Roimata** goo sikai e pei **Roimuru**.
Goo nawota sikai e doko elagi, doko taleeva ni Ρ̃au.
Eu soso e ki Marivaleanatañate.
Goo ragi wanogoe ero doo leousiusi naatañooli maaga waina eu doko
    sara navanua maaga,
ñaladigi taliviri Nyu Hebrides [Nguna, Ρ̃ele, Emau, Efate].
Goo eu masau mari naleoana warua sikai
goo ero pitua ki navasaana paki sara naureure
naga
nakuρ̃a **waia**
sara **naatañooli**
eu ga woo pakilina doko ñalala,
ñalala ni Ρ̃au, nagisana e pei **Ñalatañate**.
Goo ñalala wanogoe e doko paapaa paki masoso, goo sara naleo maaga
    waina eu dape a, e doko paapaa paki masoso doko ñalala wanogoe,
    Ñalatañate.
Goo naaleatia wanogoe umai goo tea **laapa** eu pakilina
goo eu dape sara naleo maaga.
Eu dape sara naleo maaga ni natasi, goo eu dape sara naleo maaga ni

117

navanua, kite nakau maaga, waina e[u] pei nakapu.
Goo eu dape a, poo paki m̃alala goo nawota toolu wanogoe eu doko
    m̃aleoputoni m̃alala.
Goo ragi waina tea waina e dape naadi.
Ero pe ruua, kite doolu, eu pe vakilina kii da eu noa, "Nimu ku ga va pei
    taua tokora waina."
Goo tea waina eu dape naika
eu pe laapa kiiki, e naga, "Nimu ku ga va pei taua tokora waina."
Kite vaatu goo sara naleo mamauputi, goo eu doo pei tautaua maaga, tea
    maaga waina eu dape navatuuna maaga wanogoe.
Goo ragi waina eu rumai paapaa eu noopu, goo e noa kii da, e naga, "Ragi
    waia a ga woo noa ki mu navasap̃otaeana sikai.
Nimu maaga waina ku pei naika.
Ku pei famli sikai maau, goo ku ga woo daa moro dum̃amu p̃okati mu.
Kite nimu maaga waina ku dape vaatu
ku pei tea sikai maau, ku ga woo daa moro dum̃amu p̃okati mu poo daa
    moro dum̃amu gani mu.
Kite tea maaga [waina] ku dape napaga
kite tea maaga [waina] ku dape napetau
kite tea maaga [waina] ku dape nawii maaga,
sara naleo maaga,
ku pei tea sikai maau."
Goo ragi waina eu doko, eu moro liliu paki navanua adeada maaga.
Eu liliu paki navanua adeada maaga,
goo eu pano poo noa ki tea adeada maaga asa eu naga, "Nigida,
tu ga mamau."
Tea maaga waina eu madoko navanua waina eu daa paki m̃alala
    wanogoe,
eu naga, "Nigida, tu ga vei nakainaga sikai maau."
Goo eu mari a poo piragi tea mamauputi maaga ni navanua ni Nguna,
    Efate, m̃aladigi Nyu Hebrides mamau, waina
eu mari nakainaga maaga wanogoe.
Goo masoso, nakainaga [maaga] wanogoe e[u] doko, pae ragi ni tuai
    wanogoe e pei nawota— doolu— waina eu mari natam̃ate wanogoe.
Goo line, nakainaga maaga wanogoe, eu doko masoso.
Stori kiik[i] waia e noopu.

"Matriclans"
by
Kaltap̃au M̃asemata

Long, long, long ago.
People used to eat each other and kill each other.
They did not recognize each other as one people, because
The Darkness
reigned in that time long long ago.
And there were two chiefs, who lived down on Efate.
One was **Roimata** and one was **Roimuru**.
And the [third] chief lived further up the coast, toward P̃au.
They called him Marivaleanatam̃ate.
At that time these two [chiefs] thought about the people who lived on the
    various islands,
practically the whole New Hebrides [Nguna, P̃ele, Emau, Efate].
They wanted to make a great feast
so they sent word throughout the islands
that
on a **certain day**
every person
should come to the dancing-ground,
the dancing-ground of P̃au, whose name was **M̃alatam̃ate**.
And that dancing-ground has remained right up to the present day, and
    [likewise] everything that they brought, remains today on that danc-
    ing- ground, M̃alatam̃ate.
So that day **many** people came
and brought every [kind of] thing.
They brought everything from the sea, they brought everything from the

dry land, even trees, for fire-wood.

They took it, and went to the dancing-ground and the three chiefs stood
in the middle of the dancing-ground.

Then to those two or three who brought **bananas**.

Whether there were two, or three, they would appear [before them], and
[the chiefs] would say, "You go and form a group over **there**."

And to those who brought **fish**.

If there were a few more, [one chief] would say, "You go and make a group
over **there**."

[Likewise with] **stones** and **everything** else, they formed groups, those
who had brought each other thing [each formed a separate group].

And when they had finally all come forward, [one of the chiefs] said to
them, "Now I'll explain [this] to you.

You who are **fish**.

You make up a single family [line], and you should no longer kill each
other.

And you who brought **stones**

make up a single group, [and] you should no longer kill each other or eat
each other.

And the people who brought banyan wood

and the people who brought breadfruit

and the people who brought yams,

[and] everything else [likewise],

you are [each] one people."

And after staying there a while, they all went back to their own islands.

They returned to their own islands,

and told their own groups about it, "We

are all one [people]."

The people who had stayed home, who did not go to the dancing-ground,
[then] said, "**Together** we shall be a single clan."

And so they did it, joining together everyone throughout Nguna, Efate,
nearly the entire New Hebrides,

creating clans.

And today, the clan [system] still remains, since that distant time when
the chiefs— [those] three— held that peace ceremony.

And lines, the clans, still exist today.

That is the end of this short story.

(Reference: Kalo-4. March 23, 1978, Unakapu. Tape 1B, 31-40.)

Text No.10:

"Matokoaale, Leilolo goo Tariliu"
pae
Kaltaɓau M̃asemata

A ga woo noa nawosiana sikai waina e pei tea wosiwosikiana doko ragi
ni tuai, waina misi te pei sua umai.

Matokoaale e masau mari naleoana warua doko natokoana aneana doko
M̃alaliu.

Goo e pitautau natokoana **laapa,**

Nguna, goo naure,

eu paki natokoana ni M̃alaliu.

Goo ragi waina eu pano, eu mari nasaleana warua.

Goo Matokoaale, e dum̃ana dekei ki m̃ata ki nia.

Goo ragi wanogoe nasaleana e doko, goo nagoroi ki **Tariliu,** waina nae
maa e pano, nagisana e pei **Leilolo.**

Ragi waina e punusi Matokoaale goo
e midoaki m̃ata ki nia.

Goo ragi waina eu doko paa[paa] nasaleana e noopu, goo nakanikaniana
e noopu, ragi waina eu liliu,

Leilolo te madoko.

Te doko sikoti Matokoaale.

Maa **naara** teu siwo.

Goo ragi wanogoe Tariliu e doo dodomi nagoroi aneana waina Matokoaale te piragi a madoko.

Maa naara teu rumai poo paki Worearu.

Goo eu doko paapaa
o

Tariliu e dodomi ɓarua ki nagoroi aneana.

Goo Matokoaale e dogo navasaana wanogoe goo e noa naga, "Ioro!

Ku ga woo pa raki Leilolo umai maa kinau a pei nawota warua."
Matokoaale e pei nawota warua ni Nguna
waina e pei Tarip̃oaliu.
Goo e naga, "Ku ga woo umai daulua e ki waago rualimaliima.
Edaku
ku ga woo piragi lua e palooti paki Worearu."
Goo naka ni Worearu maaga
eu dape waago maaga.
Eu dape waago maaga paa[paa] maa e daa soko
totowo waina e noa kii da asa, waago rualimaliima wanogoe.
Goo eu naga, "Ee! E ga elagoro pei waago rualimadoolu!
nalakena rualimaliima e p̃arua saa." Goo eu moro noa [totowo]
    rualimadoolu.
Maa rualimadoolu eu tapetape maa e[u] daa paataka na.
Goo waago rualimasikai tamatepaati e [ko] doko.
Goo Tariliu, e sea paki natokoana duua
ni Nguna,
Tikilasoa, goo Unakapu, waina e sea pakii da.
Naseana e dakiusi eu datagovi asa, natokoana duua naga eu ga madeada
    dape waago maaga wanogoe.
Goo natokoana duua
eu poo p̃onoti totowo wanogoe, waago rualimadoolu.
Goo eu noa naga, "Naaleatia waia ku ga toko raki gami." Eu pasa paki
    natokoana duua, Tikilasoa goo Unakapu. "Goo tu ga woo dape waago
    maaga waia sake."
Goo ragi wanogoe eu dapetape poo sake, eu dape waago rualimadoolu.
Goo eu sake, eu sake paapaa
eu ko daa duasai natokoana.
Maa eu duasai tokora sikai waina e pei tea sosoana ki Lake ni natalie ki
    Leisaara, goo nearu e siwo.
Navakalo e pakilina!
Goo tokora wanogoe eu soso e ki Lakenearu, doko masoso.
Goo ragi wanogoe eu nadi ki waago maaga wanogoe!
maa, eu sava!
Tea ni Tikilasoa maaga goo tea ni Unakapu maaga goo tea ni Worearu
    maaga, eu sava!
Maa eu leoatae naka ni Tikilasoa goo Unakap[u].
Maa, eu dipe naatam̃ooli maaga ni Worearu seara, ki natip̃a tapu.
Goo eu p̃okati Tariliu!
waina nae te mate madoko.
Maa teu sava!
Teu sava siwo umai paki elau.
Goo naka ni Worearu maaga eu paluse poo paki naure, paki natokoana
    adeada.

Goo matamai ki nia!
Ragi wanogoe navasaana e umai naga, Tariliu te mate,
maa e madoko.
Goo maliᵽoogi,
naka ni Worearu maaga eu dape naᵽanu, poo umai punusi natokoana
    duua.
Goo eu poo sake.
Eu sake pa raki naᵽatoko mate waina e doko napua.
Goo ragi waina eu pano
maa, te naᵽo nalakena e doko naᵽogiana mamau.
Goo eu kavuti m̃ata ki nia, paapaa [tea ni] natokoana duua pilake tea ni
    Worearu maaga eu poo dape naᵽatoko mate wanogoe siwo,
umai poo duagoto paki naure.
Maa, eu doni nadaana, eu kilikili pesi m̃oru paki pua poo doni nadaana,
    nadaa ni Tariliu.
Goo masoso tokora wanogoe e pei tea sosoana ki M̃oru ni Tariliu.
Nagisa wanogoe e doko masoso.
Goo ragi waina eu rumai, poo paki Worearu.
Goo eu dagisi nawota wanogoe, natokoana duua.
Goo naure mamau
Nguna mamau
eu dagisi mariki nawota wanogoe, Tariliu.
Goo ragi waina e noopu,
eu moro liliu, maa eu pitua ki navasaana waia paki natokoana duua,
    Tikilasoa goo Unakapu, "Ku ga vano!
Maa,
kuᵽa lima kite nakuᵽa rualimasikai, kite rualimaliima, ku ga woo moro
    umai,
nalakena ku silae gami nalo ni naᵽatoko mate waia."
Goo ragi waina eu doko paa[paa] natuuta wanogoe e umai, goo na-
    tokoana duua eu pano.
Goo ragi waina eu pano,
eu mari navinaga warua.
Eu mari navinaga warua.
Ragi waina navinaga e noopu, goo eu moro dovi
naveinawotaana sikai waina e moro du oli tea mate wanogoe,
Tariliu vaau eu moro dovi a.
Goo nawota wanogoe e piragi tea ni natokoana duua,
Unakap[u], goo Tikilasoa.
Goo e naga, "Ku silae ᵽarua ki gami,
goo au daa liliu a ki nia. E doko paapaa.
Elagoro au daa atae naga au ga woo liliu a ki nia seve ragi.
Maa peea, au ga veea dua mu namarakiana kiiki sikai, waina ku pe umai
    pavagoda, maa ku ga too ganikani asa."

Goo naveinawotaana wanogoe e piragi natokoana duua eu paki P̃auka-
    roa, vaatu sikai waina e doko nawora.
E doko masoso.
Nagisana e pei P̃aukaroa.
Goo e digi,
e naga, "Pae nea paki Worakoto, e pei namarakiana kiiki waina au dua
    mu asa.
Ku pe umai paki namaati, maa ku pe vitolo, ku ga kani naniu, kite ku ga
    munu naosi, kite ku ga kani lesi, kite ku ga kani navare maaga seara.
    Maa naveaniana e pei agi naka ni Worearu doko,
maa, nawaana maaga e pei waina ku pe vitolo, ku ga kani a."
Goo ragi waina e sai nasaiana wanogoe pakii da, goo eu moro liliu umai
    paki natokoana adeada,
Tikilasoa goo Unakap[u].
Goo napuku wanogoe, waina e noa e naga "au daa atae a naga seve ragi
    au ga woo liliu a ki nia",
goo eu daa liliu a ki napuku wanogoe, napuku p̃arua wanogoe
nalo ni waago,
goo nalo ni waina eu madeada dape tea mate p̃oa wanogoe umai paki
    Worearu.
Eu daa paloni
nap̃oaana wanogoe, goo e doko paapaa paki masoso.
Kite napuku wanogoe maa eu daa liliu a ki nia. E doko paapaa paki
    masoso.
    Stori kiiki waia e noopu.

"Matokoaale, Leilolo and Tariliu"
by
Kaltap̃au M̃asemata

I would like to tell of one deed which was done long ago, after [our first]
  missionary had come.
Matokoaale wanted to make a great feast in his village, M̃alaliu.
He invited **many** villages,
[on] Nguna, and "the island" [P̃ele],
to come to the village of M̃alaliu.
And when they went, there was a great dance.
And Matokoaale, decorated himself handsomely.
During the dancing, the wife of **Tariliu**, was there as well, whose name
  was **Leilolo**.
When she saw Matokoaale
she found him very attractive.
They stayed until the dancing was over, and the feasting was done, then
  they returned.
[But] Leilolo stayed behind.
She stayed with Matokoaale.
But the **others** went back **down** [from the hills of M̃alaliu].
Tariliu still loved his wife whom Matokoaale had kept with him.
But they went back to Worearu [without her].
And they remained theeeere
  o
Tariliu missed his wife terribly.
[When] Matokoaale heard of this, he said, "So be it!
Come and get Leilolo; but [remember] I am the great chief."
(Matokoaale was the **paramount** chief of Nguna

125

who[se title] was Tarip̃oaliu.)

So he said, "You shall come and redeem her [in exchange] for fifty pigs. After that

you may take her back to Worearu."

So the people of Worearu

collected pigs.

They collected [their] pigs but the number did not reach

the total that he had demanded, fifty.

So they said, "No! It will be thirty instead!

Fifty is far too much!" So they revised [the figure down to] thirty.

They [tried to assemble the] thirty pigs, but they did not have enough.

They were still fourteen pigs short.

So Tariliu, called on two villages

of Nguna—

[it was] Tikilasoa, and Unakapu, on whom he called.

("Calling on" means that he asked them to help, [asked] the two villages
    to help him collect the [required number of] pigs.)

So the two villages

contributed toward the total, [the figure of] thirty pigs.

Then they told [Matokoaale], "Expect us on this [particular] day." They
    then sent a message to the two villages, Tikilasoa and Unakapu, "Let's
    take the pigs up [to M̃alaliu]."

So when they delivered them, there were thirty altogether.

And they went up, up and up [toward M̃alaliu] untiiil finally

they had yet to reach the village.

They came to a place called "the Stump of Leisara's *natalie* tree", and
    [suddenly] an attack [swept] down [upon them]!

War broke out!

And that place is called the **"the Battle Site"**, still today.

So they dropped the pigs!

and they fled!

The people of Tikilasoa and the people of Unakapu and the people of
    Worearu, they [all] fled!

And [the M̃alaliu warriors] recognized the Tikilasoa and Unakap[u]
    people [and did not shoot them],

But they did shoot some of the Worearu men, with sacred [poison]
    arrows.

And they killed Tariliu!

and he lay dead.

And **they ran!**

They ran down to the shore.

The Worearu people paddled across to the island [P̃ele], back to their
    village.

Then **the next day!**

The news came, that Tariliu was dead,
and still lay there [where he had fallen].
So in the **morning,**
the people of Worearu gathered mats, and came to see [those of] the two
      villages.
So [it was] they who went up.
They went [back] up for the **corpse** that remained on the path.
And when they went [to retrieve it],
it stank, having been out all night.
So they wrapped it up well and finally, along with the people of Worearu,
      the people of the two villages brought the corpse down,
and [took it] across to the island [P̌ele].
And there they buried his blood, they dug a deep hole and buried the
      blood, Tariliu's blood.
Today that place is called the "Grave of Tariliu".
That name remains to this very day.
Then they came, to **Worearu.**
The two villages came to mourn the chief.
The **whole** island [P̌ele]
and **all** of **Nguna**
mourned the honoured chief, Tariliu.
When [the period of mourning] was **over,**
they returned [home], but [Worearu] sent word to the two villages, to
      Tikilasoa and Unakapu: "Go now!
But,
whether it be in five or ten or fifty days, [we will send for you to] come
      back,
because you helped us with [the retrieval of] the corpse."
So they waited until the set date came, and then the two villages
      returned [to Worearu].
When they went,
there was a **great** feast.
[Worearu] put on a great feast [for them].
And when the food was gone, they ordained
a [new chief] to replace the late chief,
the new Tariliu was ordained.
And that chief then welcomed the people of the two villages,
Unakap[u], and Tikilasoa.
He said, "You helped us enormously,
and we have not yet repaid [your help]. It is still outstanding.
Perhaps it will remain a very long time, for we do not know how or when
      we might be able to repay it.
But for now, we will give you a small piece of property, whose food you
      may use when you come to gather seafood [on the reef adjacent to it]."

Then the chief led the people of the two villages to **wukaroa**, a stone that
   lay on the shore.
It is still there today.
Its name is P̃aukaroa.
And he **pointed**,
and said, "From here to Worakoto, is the small holding that we are giving
   to you.
If you should come to the reef, and are hungry, you may eat ripe coconut
   or drink coconut water, eat papayas, or the fruit of ripe coconuts. The
   land and its first fruits will still belong to the people of Worearu,
but, if you are hungry, its fruits are yours to eat."
When he had delivered that speech to them, they returned to their
   villages,
Tikilasoa and Unakap[u].
But the **debt**, [what he meant] when he said, "We don't know when we
   might ever be able to repay it",
that debt, they never did repay that heavy debt,
for the pigs,
and for bringing the stinking corpse back to Worearu for them.
They never **washed away**
the stench, and it remains to this very day.
Nor was the favour ever returned. So it too remains until this very day.
   That is the end of the story.

(Reference: Kalo-5. March 23, 1985, Unakapu. Tape 1B, 40-61.)

Text No.11:

"Matanaatamate"
pae
Kaltaɸau Ñasemata

A ga woo noa
stori sikai ni noai sikai doko Unakapu, nagisana Matanaatamate.
Goo noai wanogoe doko ragi ni tuai, e doo sara umai paki elau pae
naɸaloa, umai paki natasi.
Goo nagoroi maaga kite naanoai maaga ni Unakap[u] eu doo ɸasi goo eu
doo loloso asa.
Maa ragi sikai
naatamate wanogoe e peani natuna sikai.
Goo ɸilana e noa ki nia asa naga, "Natasi anigida te daɸa. ɸa woo paki
elau ɸa vautui natas[i]."
Goo ragi waina e siwo umai paki elau, e dape loopu naga e ga vautui
natasi asa.
Goo ragi waina e umai, goo tea ni natokoana eu ɸokati natuna.
Goo nae e doo leogoro natuna paa[paa] maa te daa paki elagi,
doko noai wanogoe.
Goo e naga, "A ga woo leo natugu, a ga woo siwo poo leo natugu."
Goo ragi waina e umai e punusi naga, eu ɸokatipunue natuna e doko.
Goo ragi wanogoe e dape nakau maaga seara goo e punue wootu maaga
waina eu ɸokati a
paapaa e noopu goo e moro mauri goo e poo ova e e poo sake,
paki Matanaatamate.
Goo ragi waina ero madoko,
goo ɸilana e noa naga, "Io!
A ko dua mu noai waia, e umai paki elau, maa ku poo ɸokati natugu.
Maa noai waia e ga woo daa moro sara paki elau, maa e ga woo noopu,
doko taava.

Maa waina nimu ku pe masau naga ku ga vautui noai, ku masau munu,
    ku ga woo umai paki taava."
Goo tero madoko, ero doko paapaa
    o

Ragi waina ero masau naga ero ga woo pavagoda.
Maa ero peani p̃alua sikai ni naika waina e doko euta wanogoe.
E pei p̃alua duua e doko vaatu.
Nagisana e pei, sikai e pei p̃alua ni malasiviri,
goo sikai e pei p̃alua ni mavatu.
Goo ragi waina ero midoaki nia naga ero ga umai paki elau, poo
    pavagoda, ragi waina ero umai ero dape naika duua wanogoe.
Goo ero sake paki taava.
Goo ero mari e pei navinaga adeada sara ragi.
Paapaa e noopu, goo e noa ki naatam̃ooli maaga asa, e naga, "Io!
Ku pe masau noai waia ku ga woo doo umai paki taava."
Maa e moro peani p̃alua kiiki sikai e moro doko etano kakana e pei p̃alua
    ni loluavilosi, nae maa e doko vaatu, e doko etano kakana.
Goo ragi waina naatam̃ooli maaga eu sake,
eu dape nawaanoai maaga.
Goo ragi waina eu rumai paa[paa] eu pautu sua goo eu siwo paki
    m̃aladigi ki p̃alua wanogoe naga eu ga maromaaro.
Goo p̃alua wanogoe e pakulua puti navinoso adeada.
Goo e doo daki p̃olo adeada maaga waina eu pai nawaanoai adeada
    maaga asa. E dap̃a.
Goo eu moro liliu paki noai.
Goo eu moro pautu sala kerua kite ketolu.
Goo ragi waina eu mari a paa[paa] eu leoatae a goo eu naga, "O, io! E
    lagoro pei p̃alua waia, waina nagisana e pei Loluavilosi."
Goo teu poo atae a e pe ragi waina eu pautui noai doko taava, eu siwo poo
    daa moro maromaaro doko tokora wanogoe maa eu dualele umai paki
    esum̃a.
Goo noai wanogoe waina eu soso e ki Matanaatamate, e doko paapaa
    paki masoso waia.
Goo tea ni Unakapu maaga, kite tea ni euta maaga, ragi waina elo e dara
    kasua, goo eu doo umai pautui noai wanogoe.
E noopu.

"The Pool of Matanaatamate"
by
Kaltaṗau Ṁasemata

I shall tell
a story about the pool at Unakapu, whose name is Matanaatamate.
The spring has been there since long ago, and it still flows into a creek,
and down to the sea.
And the women and men of Unakap[u] used to wash and swim in it.
Once upon a time...
the spirit of the pool had a child.
And its mother said to him, "Our pool is empty. Go to the beach and draw
sea-water."
He went down to the beach, taking lengths of bamboo to put the water
into.
But when her child got there, the villagers attacked and killed him.
And she was watching out for her child but he did not come up,
to the pool.
So she said, "I must look for my child. I will go down and look for my
child."
And when she arrived she saw that, they had killed her child and he still
lay there.
So then she took some leaves and squeezed them over her child's wounds
where they had hit him,
and when she was finished he came back to life and she put him on her
back and went back up
to Matanaatamate.
Once there,
his mother said, "Alright!
I have always given you this water, running to the shore, but you killed
my child.

131

So this water will no longer run to the shore, from now on, it will stay
up on the hillside.
So if you want to draw water, if you want to drink, you will have to come
   up the hill."
Then the two of them remained, remained living there, untiiil,
°
One time they decided to gather shellfish.
They had a hole for fish just offshore near there.
There were two holes in the rock.
Their names were, one was the hole of *malasiviri*. [*sp. of fish*]
and the other was the hole of *mavatu*. [*sp. of fish*]
Having decided to come down to the shore, to gather shellfish, they did
   so, and caught two of those fish.
Then they went back up the hill.
And they prepared a meal of them as they normally did.
When it was done, she said to the people, "Alright!
If you want this water, you must come up the hillside."
But she had another little hole in the rock down below the first one, the
   hole of the "Garden of Hate", in the rock, below the [other] one.
And when the people came up the hill,
they took coconut-shell water containers.
When they had finished drawing water they went down and stopped to
   rest by that hole.
And the hole pulled out all their corks.
And it emptied out the baskets that they had filled with the coconut-shell
   containers. Emptied them out **completely**.
So they went back to the pool.
And they drew water a **second** time [and the same thing happened, when
   they rested by the hole of the "Garden of Hate"] and yet a **third** time.
This went on until finally they realized what was happening, "Aha! The
   trouble must be this hole, named the 'Garden of Hate'."
So having figured out what was going on, when they [went back yet again
   to] draw water on the hillside, on the way down they didn't stop to rest
   in that place; instead they kept going straight down to their houses
   without stopping.
And the pool they call Matanaatamate, remains until this **very day**.
And when the sun shines fiercely, the people of **Unakapu** and [all] the
   people from **inland**, still go there to draw water.
That is the end.

(Reference: Kalo-8. April 11, 1978, Unakapu. Tape 3A, 19-28.)

Text No. 12:

"Munuai Vaau"
pae
Kaltap̌au M̃asemata

Io, a poo masau atuusi
naatuusiana ni munuai vaau.
Goo naatam̃ooli waina nagisana e pei P̌akae.
Goo ragi waina e doo midodoa naga e ga, e masau pei munuai.
Goo e paki elau,
elau ni **Farealapa**.
Goo ragi waina e pano, e dasake doko masua ni vaatu.
Goo e doo punusi naika malakesa maaga waina natavara e doo p̌ori elau.
E naga, "O! Naika wanae sikai a masau gani a!
E pei malakesa."
Goo ragi waina e doko kiiki, e punusi
natavara.
E maneana dape naika malakesa sikai umai, paki euta, poo sili lake ni
  vaatu sikai.
Goo ragi waina e masau naga e ga vunusi naika wanogoe waina e sili lake
  ni vaatu wanogoe ragi waina e pano, e pei nagoroi taareare wia sikai
  e doko valea wanogoe.
Goo ragi wanogoe,
e puati nagoroi taare wanogoe, goo ero umai paapaa e doropusi a doko
  looga ni waago aneana.
Maa, P̌akae waia e peani narup̌a **laapa**.
E peani nagoroi laapa.
Goo ragi waina e pa punusi narup̌a aneana maaga, goo eu doo mari
  navinaga.
Eu doo mari navinaga, paapaa

133

e naga, "Io! A ga woo pa dua waago navilalu."
Goo ragi waina eu doo marisokisoki navinaga,
navinaga aneana, eu kokoti a goo eu lulu ki nia e lulugoro paki navilalu.
Goo e doo dape a paki looga, goo ragi waina e dape a paki looga, goo e doo
    pa dua nagoroi taare wanogoe asa. E doo gani a.
Goo e doo mari a paapaa narupa aneana maaga eu leoatae a.
Eu naga, "O! Navatuuna sikai waia mariki waia e doo mari a.
Tu daa punusi e mari dapala nea sala veea.
Goo e pei navatuuna sikai."
Maa e noa ki sua e asa naga, ragi waina eu ga too mari nakoau, maa eu
    ga taa mari nakoau ni nawii miala.
Goo e pano
teu doo mari nakoau taare mau, nawii taare mau eu doo mari nakoau
    asa.
Paapaa
ragi waina e moro pano, ragi sikai naga e ga vagavaga,
goo nagoroi wanogoe sikai e dausi a.
E dausi a maa e pa sili madoko.
Goo e punusi a kite ragi waina e nadi ki navilalu paki looga, dua waago
    maa,e dape kalukalu wanogoe goo e dua nagoroi taare wanogoe asa.
Goo eu noa ki nia asa, eu naga, "E! Nagoroi waina ku doo dua e navinaga,
    pa viragi a umai paki esuma. Au ga mamau doko. Au marisaa maeto
    ki nia."
Goo eu piragi a umai paki esuma.
Eu piragi a umai paki esuma goo eu mamau doko.
Eu doo mari nakoau.
Paapaa goo ragi sikai narupa aneana maaga eu noa ki nia asa, eu naga,
eu noa naga, "Masoso tu ga mari nakoau miala mau.
Tu ga taa mari nakoau taare."
Goo ragi wanogoe eu paki roara adeada maaga goo eu dape nawii miala
    mau, goo eu rumai poo mani nakoau asa.
Maa nagoroi wanogoe e doo punusi a, nagoroi taare wanogoe e doo
    punusi waina eu doo mari nawosiana wanogoe.
Goo ragi waina naanoai aneana e pano, e noa ki nia asa, e naga, "Ragi
    waia,
nagoroi maaga waia teu marisaa ki nau. Ta ga melu tua kiigo."
Paapaa eu puke ragimelu.
Goo nae e marisaa gani nawii miala wanogoe.
Ragi waina e ga kani a te ga melu.
Goo e gani a.
Goo ragi wanogoe te siwo
naga te ga moro pano.
Maa naanoai aneana e dausi a. Pakae.
E dausi a pano paapaa e noa ki nia asa, e naga,

"Ioro! Ti p̃a valooti, maa ti p̃a **kasaa** ki nau?"

Goo e noa naga, "**Nakasuaana aginau** ta dua ko asa. Te navatuuna waina
  ku pe masau na,

p̃a woo laaga asa poo pap̃ai a. Maa kinau ta ga vano."

Goo **nae** te pano.

Maa namidodoaana aneana e masau na naga e ga woo pei munuai.

Goo ragi waina e umai paki esum̃a e doko, paapaa e midoaki nia naga e
  ga va punusi M̃asekaau.

Goo ragi wanogoe e duleana poo pa punusi M̃asekaau.

Ragi waina e paki natokoana ni **Raetoa** goo e punusi M̃asekaau e doko
  varea aneana, Matakudaalo.

Goo ragi waina e doko ekopu,

goo P̃akae e sili, e sili paki ekopu.

E naga, "Ku masau nasava?"

E naga, "Eee, a masau naga a ga vei munuai."

Goo e piragi a paki malo tapu aneana.

E piragi a paki malo tapu aneana goo

e punusi vaatu kiiki sikai waina e doko asa doko e pei vaatu m̃olim̃oli.

Goo e noa ki nia asa e naga,

"P̃a tape vaatu wanae."

Goo ragi waina e dape vaatu wanogoe,

te daa dape a e pei vaatu, maa

te pei p̃ilikaroa **warua.**

Maa e daa matau ki nia, e dapesoki a doko.

Paapaa e moro doropusi a goo te pei **vaatu.**

E naga, "P̃a moro dape a sala **kerua.**"

Goo naatam̃ooli wanogoe e moro dape a sala kerua,

goo ragi waina e dape a sala kerua,

maa e pei m̃**aata warua.**

Maa naatam̃ooli wanogoe e daa matau ki nia. E dape a doko.

Paapaa naga ragi waina e doropusi a, te moro pei vaatu.

E naga, "P̃a vano!

Natapuana te liko ako.

Natapuana ni munuai te liko ako. Maa p̃a moro liliu paki natokoana
  anigo."

Goo ragi waina e pano, e doo mari nawosiana **seara.**

E doo mari nawosiana kirikiri seara waina e pei nawosiana ki munuai.

Maa eu ko **daa** leoatae a

paapaa e noa kii da asa, e naga, "A masau naga nakapu.

Ku ga maripunue puti nakapu mamauputi!"

Nalakena tuai wanogoe e pei ragi waina eu masau naga eu ga vuasoki
  nakapu eu mari nakapu warua naga e pavaga.

E pei nakapu teele.

Goo eu punue puti nakapu maaga wanogoe, daliviri Nguna.

Goo nae, e masau na naga e ga soso nakapu.

Goo e pagi paki elagi.

E pagi paki elagi poo soso nakapu.

Goo naseati sikai e pei tea tiɓakiana pae elagi umai poo nadi natano.

Ragi waina e nadi natano, goo tea laapa eu moro puati nakapu wanogoe,
     poo moro sui a pae natokoana adeada maaga.

Goo e dogorogo nasaleana sikai e doko Emau.

Goo e pano.

E pano, goo eu mamau madoo sale.

Maa eu daa atae tokora waina e pae asa pano.

Maa e pae epua, ni natasi.

Goo eu madoo sale paapaaa e moro liliu umai paki natokoana aneana, e
     doko Farealapa.

Goo m̃alala waina e umai duasai asa eu soso ki Wowolapa.

M̃alala wanogoe e doko masoso.

Paapaa goo ragi sikai

eu doo mari nam̃audu maaga, tea ni Utanilagi goo tea ni Farealapa.

Eu mari nam̃audu, warua.

Goo te ragi seara naka ni Farealapa eu magi naka ni Utanilagi lalawo.

Goo te ragi seara tea ni Utanilagi eu ga umai magi naka ni Farealapa
     lalawo.

Goo ragi sikai

eu moro pitautau naka ni Utanilagi naga eu ga umai madeada lalawo.

Maa naatam̃ooli wanogoe e peani natuna naanoai sikai,

waina e doo pasa ki nia.

Goo tea ni Utanilagi maaga eu pano puti.

Eu rumai madeada mari lawo nawii adeada maaga pae nam̃audu
     adeada wanogoe.

Goo eu lalawo paaa, te pei m̃aladigi "dinner", navinaga ni aleati.

Maa navinaga e diika.

Goo natuna, eu mamau madoo lalawo, goo e umai paki sum̃a e naga,

"Mama,

tau lalawo paa[paa] te ga vei ragi ni nakaniana ni aleati, maa au daa
     punusi navinaga **seara**! Au ga kani **nasava?**"

Goo e noa ki nia asa, e naga,

"Ɓa veea palooti, maa kinau a ga woo palooti."

Maa ragi waina e pano paa[paa] e duasai.

Goo, e noa ki natuna,

e noa naga, "Ɓa soso ra eu ga umai paki melu." "Maa navinaga e diika!

Eu ga umai paki melu eu ga kani **nasava?**

Navinaga e diika."

Goo ragi waina natuna e soso tea laapa ni Utanilagi waina eu doo lalawo,
e naga, "Ku ga umai paki melu."

Goo ragi waina eu rumai paki melu,

goo e noa ki tea laapa **mamauputi**, e noa naga,
"Ku ga p̃ili!
Sagamu sikai e ga **taa** leleo.
E pe rogo te navatuuna waina e pe doo mari duki,
maa, ku ga **taa** leleo."
Goo ragi wanogoe
eu rumai paki melu paapaa eu p̃ili, tea mamauputi.
Maa eu doko melu napaga sikai.
Goo ragi waina eu dogo e kite woosa maaga, eu doo nadi paki natano,
    tokora e doo duki asa.
Maa tea maaga wanogoe seara eu **daa** leleo.
Eu mamauputi p̃ili poo dakidorogo, navatuuna maaga waina e doo duki
    paapaaa goo e noa kii da asa, e naga,
"Ku ga leleo!"
Goo ragi waina eu leleo, eu punusi **woosa maaga** waina e pei tea
    tip̃akiana umai paki melu ni napaga wanogoe.
Goo e naga, "Ku ga vuati m̃ata ki woosa maaga wanae poo pukesi a."
Goo ragi waina eu puati m̃ata ki nia paa[paa] e noopu, e **pivitinu** doko!
Goo e naga eu ga vukesi a. Eu puke.
Maa, eu mataku gani a.
Nalakena eu daa atae naga woosa maaga wanogoe eu pae esava umai.
Goo **nae** e duleana
goo eu maneana kokoti tokora sikai e gani a,
pilake nap̃okasi.
Woosa maaga wanogoe eu pei nap̃okasi mau.
Goo e **doo** suui!
Ragi waina e ganikani peea e naga, "Ku ga **taa** mataku. Ku ga kani a."
    Goo tea laapa eu poo ganikani.
Naatuusiana waia e noopu tokora waia.

"The New Diviner"
by
Kaltap̃au M̃asemata

I have been wanting to tell
the story of the new diviner,
a person named P̃akae.
It was at this time that he decided that, he would like to become a diviner.
He went down to the seaside,
by Farealapa.
When he got there, he sat down on the crown of a rock,
and where the waves were breaking on the shore he could see bluefish.
He thought, "Oh, how I'd love to eat one of those!
They're bluefish."
So he stayed a little while, and, as he watched,
a wave
brought one of the bluefish up, toward the shore, and cast it up at the foot
    of a rock.
So he went over to see the fish that had been cast up there, but what he
    saw instead, hidden at the foot of the rock, was a woman, a beautiful
    fair-skinned woman.
Then
the two of them returned together, and when they had reached his pig
    pen, he deposited her there.
For, P̃akae had many women.
He had a great many wives.
When he [reached home], he saw that his wives were making a meal.
When they had finished preparing it,
he said, "Well, I'll go and give the pigs the rubbish."

When they prepared food,
and cut it into pieces, he would wrap up the peelings in the dirty leaves
    [on which the food had been prepared].
This time, when he took [the rubbish], he gave one [parcel] to the white
    woman, and she ate it.
This went on until eventually his wives took notice.
They said, "This fellow is up to something!
He never used to do this.
There must be something going on."
He had also said, that when they made coconut pudding, they must not
    use red yams.
So that's how it went
they only used white yams, only made pudding with white yams.
Until
one day, he went to do the feeding,
and one of the women followed him.
She followed him, then hid.
She saw him throw the rubbish, to the pigs, but then she saw him take
    the parcel of food and give it to the white woman.
And so afterwards, [his wives] said to him, "Listen! This woman that
    you've been feeding- you go and bring her up to the house and we'll all
    live together. We won't be angry with her."
So they brought her home.
They brought her home and they all lived together.
They went on making coconut pudding.
But finally one day his wives said to her, [in a low, threatening voice]
"Today we're going to make red pudding.
We're not making any white pudding."
Then they went to their gardens and got all red yams, then they came
    back and grated them for the pudding.
And the woman, the white woman, watched them do it.
And when her husband came along, she told him, "Now
these wives of yours are trying to destroy me. I must leave you."
Later that afternoon they took out the baking.
And she was unable to eat the red yams,
If he ate it, she would leave.
And he did.
So then she descended [to the shore]
to return [from whence she had come].
Her husband, P̌akae, followed her.
He kept following her, until finally he said,
"Alright, then! Go! How can you do this to me?"
She replied, "I give you my power. Whatever you want,
seek and you will find it. But I must go."

Then she left.

But his great desire was to become a diviner.

So when he went home, he decided to go and see M̃asekaau [the chief and diviner].

So he rose up and went to see M̃asekaau.

He went to Raetoa and saw M̃asekaau who was in his meeting-house, Matakudaalo.

He was inside,

so P̃akae went in,

and [the chief] said, "What do you want?"

He replied, "Well... I would like to become a diviner."

So [M̃asekaau] took him to his sacred place.

He took him to his sacred place and,

seeing a small stone- a very round, smooth stone,

[the chief] commanded him,

"Pick up that stone."

When he picked [it] up,

suddenly it was no longer a stone, instead

it turned into a large lizard.

But he was not afraid, and held onto it,

and after a time he put it down again and it turned back into a stone.

[M̃asekaau] said, "Pick it up again."

So the man picked it up a second time,

and when he did,

suddenly it turned into a huge snake.

But he was not afraid, and held onto it,

and, when finally he put it down again, it turned back into a stone.

And [M̃asekaau] said, "Go!

The sacredness is upon you.

The sacredness of the diviner is upon you. Go back to your village."

He did so, and thereafter, he did certain deeds,

some of the minor feats that are performed by diviners.

But people had yet to recognize what he was,

until... he told them, "I shall make fire.

Put out your fires- put them all out!"

(For, long ago, they used to keep a big fire going all the time, a perpetual fire from which they could light others at any time.)

[They called it] *nakapu teele*.

So all around Nguna, they put out all the fires.

For he wanted to summon fire.

He climbed up high in a tree.

He climbed up high and summoned fire.

And a fire-brand from on high fell down and struck the earth.

When it hit the ground, people took it up, and used it to re-light the fires in all their villages.

[On another occasion] he heard that there was a dance on **Emau**.

So he went.

He arrived and there they all were dancing.

But no-one knew how he had gotten there.

In fact, he had travelled by the deep, under the sea.

And he stayed there and danced, and eventually returned in the same
way to his village, Farealapa.

The dancing-ground on which they danced was [called] Wowolapa

and it is still there today.

Another time,

the people of Utanilagi and the people of Farealapa were cultivating,
cultivating **huge fields**.

In those days sometimes the people of Farealapa planted for the people
of Utanilagi;

and sometimes the people of Utanilagi came to plant for the people of
Farealapa.

This particular time

[it was Farealapa's turn] to invite the people of Utanilagi to plant for
them.

(And that fellow [P̃akae] had a son

who used to talk back to him [1].)

So the entire village of Utanilagi went.

They came to plant the yam fields for them.

They planted and planted, until it was almost lunch-time.

But there was no food.

All of [P̃akae's] sons, too, were planting; then [this one] came home and
said [*irritably*],

"**Father**,

we have been planting and planting and it's almost time for lunch, but
we have yet to see any **food**! What are we going to **eat**?"

And he said to him,

"You go on back and I'll be there shortly."

And no sooner had he gone than [P̃akae] arrived.

He said to his son,

"Go and call them to come into the shade." [*hotly*] "But there's no **food**!

If they come into the shade, what will they **eat**?

There's no food."

So his son called to all the people of Utanilagi who were planting,

"Come into the shade."

And when they were assembled in the shade,

[P̃akae] said to all of those people,

"Close your eyes!

No-one may open his eyes.

If you hear something, if you hear anything making a noise,
don't look."
So
everyone closed their eyes.
They were beneath a banyan tree.
Then they heard thumping, the noise of packages of baked coconut
    puddings falling to the ground.
But not one of them opened his eyes.
They all had their eyes closed, listening to the thumping sounds, until at
    last he said,
"Open your eyes!"
And when they looked, they saw the puddings lying there in the shade
    of the banyan.
He said, "Take hold of those puddings carefully and open them up."
So they gathered them all up- they were still hot!
Then he told them to open them. They opened them.
But then, they were afraid to eat any,
because they had no idea where the puddings had come from.
So he stood up
and they cut a piece for him,
one with meat in it-
all the puddings had meat fillings[2].
And they were still steaming hot!
So he ate first, then said, "Don't be afraid. Eat." Then everyone ate.
That is the end of the story.

Footnotes

1. The literal phrase to "speak to (someone)" suggests that the speaker
    is being verbally rather aggressive, possibly harassing or reprimand-
    ing. The implication here is that the diviner's son tended to or, at least
    in this instance, was behaving disrespectfully toward his father.
    Hence the English translation: "talk back to".
2. The new diviner vindicates himself and establishes his reputation by
    supplying coconut puddings, literally, out of thin air, for large num-
    bers of people on an occasion wherein there is considerable at stake–
    Farealapa's village pride. Moreover, he provides the most highly
    valued kind of pudding: those with meat baked inside.

(Reference: Kalo-12. April 19, 1978, Unakapu. Tape 4A, 28-50.)

Text No.13:

"Nadue Dua"
pae
Kaltap̃au M̃asemata

Io, a ga woo atuusi natukunoa sikai doko ragi ni **tuai tuai**, tuai saa.
E pei ragi ni navitoloana warua sikai e pakiliina.
Goo nagoroi sikai,
nae e doko paapaa e masau naga e ga kani noopa.
Goo e p̃akuti lau nakau maaga waina eu pei lau nakau mami waina eu
    doo gani [r]a.
Goo e pano paapaa e paki uvea, e surata paki uvea
poo pagi naita sikai.
Maa nagoroi wanogoe e diena doko.
Ragi waina e madoko elagi
goo e dape p̃asi araa ni naita wanogoe, doko dowo.
Ragi waina e dowo, te mate.
Maa natuna waina e doko nap̃alauna e p̃ia doko.
Ero pei **nadue**, ero pei naanoai duua.
Ero doko paapaa p̃ilada e mate, e p̃oa
goo
ero doko paapaa ero pakiliina pae p̃ilada waina te p̃oa.
Goo ero doko asa goo ero paki katama.
Poo doo menae lau nakau maaga waina e pei nameura maaga e dakiusi,
    e pei susu adeada.
Waina uusa e p̃owo lau nakau maaga e pura goo ero doo munugi a.
Paapaa goo ero liliu paki tokora waina p̃ilada e dowo asa.
Ero doo mari a paapaa tero p̃arua.
Goo ragi sikai,
ero surata kiiki paki uvea kiiki,

143

poo paῤai roara **warua** sikai waina e doko.
Eu lawo naadi goo sara naleo maaga.
Maa ero daa atae naga loriki maaga waia eu pei navinaga.
Maa ero punusi manu maaga waina eu doo dae naadi maaga waina eu
    mami.
Ero noa naga, "E! Loriki waia elagoro pei navinaga- lowia sikai."
Goo takalapa e doo save naadi, goo e doo dua takariki goo ero doo gani
    a.
Ero gani sikai paapaa e noopu goo tero paki lake ῤota.
Maa tero ῤarua, ero doko tokora wanogoe doko tero ῤarua.
Ero doko paapaa goo talakea ni roara wanogoe **e** umai.
Ragi waina e umai
  °

goo e naga,
e dogo e kite tea rua ero doo pasa, roara aneana.
Goo e sai kii da, goo ragi waina e punusi ra e noa naga, "Koro pae esa[v]a
    umai?"
Goo e naga, "Aro umai paaa
teete, e pagi nakau waia doko dowo.
Goo kinami aro doko paapaa teete e ῤoa goo aro sulagai a poo umai doko
    tokora waia doko tuai."
Maa mariki wanogoe e daa pei naataᵐooli!
Nae e pei **naatamate** sikai.
Goo e naga,
"Io! E ῤia. Tu ga vaki esuᵐa."
Mariki wanogoe e midoaki naga e ga woo gani tea rua wanogoe.
Goo ragi waina eu paki esuᵐa,
goo te noa kii da asa naga,
"Tu ga va leleo natale, goo tu ga tape nakapu
naga
tu ga woo paki esuᵐa pano poo mari a e ga vei navinaga anigida."
Maa, te pei waina e soro ra, maa te pei tero ga tape nakapu goo navinaga
    maaga wanogoe e ga vei napalala ni **naara** waina e ga woo gani ra.
Goo e noa ki tea matua naga, "Nigida, toro ga va dape nakapu.
Maa, tea kiiki nae e ga too kili natale."
Goo ragi waina tea kiiki e doo kili natale, e daa atae naga navinaga ni
    natale e dapale sava.
Goo nae e doo kili nakoana naga e pei navinagana.
Goo ero pano paa[paa] ero liliu, maa kanao kiiki e daa kili natale seara.
    E doko.
E doo kili nakoana naga e pei navinagana.
Goo taina e noa ki nia asa, e naga, "Ῥa ῤili!"
Goo ragi waina e ῤili,
goo e kurati natano goo vuuti natale maaga paa[paa] e pei taua maduu.

Goo ragi wanogoe tero pai [r]a.

Ero pai [r]a poo paki esuṁa, maa ero pei naataṁooli manumatua,
    piakiiki dua wanogoe.

Ragi waina eu naga eu ga vaki esuṁa, **naara** ero daep̃orae naniu sikai
    waina e p̃oa.

E madoko namalasi.

Goo teu paki esuṁa pano.

Eu pano paaa[paa] pa punusi nagoroi aneana, nae e madoko esuṁa.

Goo ero doko paa[paa] ragimelu, e naga, "Tetu ga kanikani. Koro ga vaki
    esava?" Ero naga, "Eee,

aro ga ko p̃arowaro."

Ero pano poo dae loopu, kolopu ni loopu dua.

Ero dae a poo pa pai laago maaga laago vuvuaa, waina e[u] liko naniu
    wanogoe.

Ero pai [r]a paki loopu wanogoe paa[paa] e noopu, doko pinisomi a, poo
    dape a paki esuṁa.

Goo ero pilokisai malo kirikiri maaga ki namena ni masimasi.

Goo ero dape a paki esuṁa pano.

Goo eu ganikani sua ragimelu goo nae e midoaki nia naga p̃oogi e ga woo
    p̃okati ra.

Goo e sui nakapu tokora sikai waina nakapu e asua asa, e pei waina e pe
    vaki ekopu maa ero ga taa punusi a.

Maa ero dape namata ni naniu, e paati, waina ero asilua e.

Goo ragi waina p̃oogi nae e sui nakapu, e asua,

e maridogo sai kii da naga e ga **p̃okati** ra.

Maa ragi waina e pano,

kite **laago maaga wanogoe** eu doo kai dapala e pei tea rogoṁatakiana
    dapala waina eu doo ple.

Goo ero doropusi namata ni naniu wanogoe e paati, sikai e paki namata
    ni e dua, sikai e paki namata ni e dua, **maa** naara tero doo maturu.

E naga, "E! Naara waia ero leleo doko." Maa e punusi naniu wanogoe
    e daare doko.

Maa **naara** tero doo gora, tero maturu sua.

Paapaa paki malip̃oogi.

Goo mariki e noa kii da asa, e naga, "A midoaki naga a ga valoti saisai
    ki mu. A paloti maa, koro doo ple.

Ta moro liliu."

Maa e **sorosoro.** E naga e ga p̃okati ra.

Matamai ki nia

e moro maridogo ra,

kite naara ero pei naataṁooli manumatua, piakiiki dua wanogoe.

Ero doko naaleatia **doolu.**

Maa e marisara ara paki **tea** saa.

Goo ero noa ki nia asa naga, "Taro midoaki nia naga taro ga liliu,

maa aro masau munu naniu."
Goo mariki e noa kii da asa, e naga,
"Tu ga vaki napua.
Sagamu sikai e ga woo lei naniu."
Goo ragi waina eu pano eu punusi naniu sikai waina e dau p̃arua, goo e
    noa kii da asa, e naga,
"Ita! Sagamu sikai e ga vagi."
Go piakiiki dua ero noa ki nia asa, ero naga,
"Eee.
Kinami aro pei piakiiki.
Goo aro daa atae naniu kasua, goo aro daa atae tea waina e paataka
    naosi, kite nam̃o. Aro daa atae a.
Maa e p̃ia niigo p̃a vagi, nalakena niigo ku pei tea matua."
E naga, "Io, a ga woo pagi."
Goo mariki wanogoe e pagi,
e pagi paaa[paa] e lei naniu,
maa naara ero doko nalake naniu doko.
Ragi waina e lei sua e, naga e poo siwo,
goo ero noa ki nia asa, ero lega, doko naga,
"Ito, ito, taaroa ito!"
Goo te doko dorogo ragi waina e atulake siwo goo e noa kii da naga, "Koro
    noa nasava?"
"Ee, aro laelae a waina ku siwo umai, tetu ga munu naniu."
Goo e moro umai paaa[paa] e disu kiiki, goo ero moro lega,
"Ito, ito, taaroa ito!"
E naga, "Koro noa n[a]sava?"
Ero noa, "Ee, aro laelae a
naga ti p̃a umai, tetu ga munu naniu."
Maa e doo umai goo ero doo lega- paapaa ragi waina te ga vaasi natano.
Goo ero noa naga, "Ito, ito, taaro a ito!", doko p̃okati a.
Ero p̃okati a ragi sikai maau
nalakena tea rua ero peani naap̃e doko.
Ero p̃okati a doko p̃okapunue a.
Te madoko.
Maa naara tero munu naniu.
Ragi waina ero munu sua naniu,
tero paki esum̃a.
Ero paki esum̃a pano doko moro p̃okatipunue nagoroi aneana
doko dokoni nasum̃a.
Ero dokoni a, te madoko.
Ero moro umai, doko moro paki naliada tokora waina ero doko asa.
Tero moro doo gani naadi maaga wanogoe.
Ero doko paapaaa, e pei tuai, tero matua.
Goo ero naga,

"Toro ga moro paki tokora waina
toro dap̃ara ki vitariki waina asa."
Goo ragi waina, ero pano ero punusi a kite
nakau sikai e pisou asa waina te p̃arua.
E pei nakau **warua** te pisou asa.
E pei **namaloku**.
Goo ragi waina ero pano ero punusi nalakena maaga e pei p̃alua.
Ero naga, "Navatuuna sikai waia
e dakiusi e doo gani nakoa ni nakau waia."
Goo ragi waina ero madoo daliepu asa, goo kusue maaga eu dave.
Ero punusi a kite
kusue maaga eu madoo daratara pano.
Ero naga, "Loriki waia
toro ga woo umai dape a.
E pei lowia sikai."
Maa ero moro liliu, ero liliu poo maridogo naga ero ga vaki natokoana
nalakena ero **daa** atae napua ni natokoana.
Ero maridogo poo doo siwo paraki natokoana adeada.
Ragi waina ero doo siwo pano paapaa ero duasai,
goo naatam̃ooli ni natokoana maaga eu punusi ra.
Goo eu noa naga, "Koro pae esa[v]a umai?"
Goo ero noa kii da asa naga,
"Teete aginami,
ragi waina e naga e ga p̃aku, ragi waina e pano e dowo, goo kinami aro
    madoko paapaaa
  o
taro p̃arua namalasi, goo waia taro poo umai."
Goo mama adeada e doko
waina e laelaea p̃arua asa.
Goo eu doko kiiki goo ero paraki loriki wanogoe waina e pisou doko
    matigo ni vitariki wanogoe.
Goo ero moro pano.
Ero pano poo pa kili a.
Ero kili a, ero punusi kusue maaga eu kati nakoana.
Goo ragi waina eu dave, eu madoo daratara pano.
Goo ero dape a umai paki esum̃a.
Ragi waina ero dape a umai paki esum̃a,
goo ero dape a pilake araana.
Goo eu lawo araa ni namaloku wanogoe poo munu nap̃atokona.
Goo
ragi waia waina naatam̃ooli e munu namaloku, e marisaa moro naga e
    ga doropusi a nalakena, vitariki wanogoe
nasei kakana e pei **nasei** waina te liko namaloku wanogoe.
Goo tea laapa eu masau munu namaloku masoso, pae vitariki wanogoe.
Natukunoa waia e noopu.

"The Twins"
by
Kaltaɓau Ñasemata

Alright, I will tell a tale from **long long**, long ago.
It was during a terrible famine.
There was a woman,
and one time she wanted to eat native cabbage.
So she broke off the edible tree leaves they used to eat.
And she went on and on, until she had walked very far away.
and then she climbed up a sycamore tree.
And the woman was pregnant.
While she was up high
she stepped on a branch of the sycamore, breaking it, and she fell.
She fell and **she** was killed.
But her child inside her survived.
In fact, it was **twins**, two boys.
They stayed there until their mother['s body] began to rot
and
they stayed inside for a long time and finally they were born.
Then they stayed there, living outside of her.
And they licked the tree leaves for the dew, which was the breast for
   them.
When it rained and the leaves filled [with moisture] they would drink it.
Then they would go back to where their mother had fallen.
They went on this way until they grew **big**.
And one particular time

they journeyed a little distance
and discovered a **large** garden.
There had been bananas and every other kind of thing planted.
But they didn't know that these things were food.
Then they saw birds pecking at the ripe bananas.
They said, "Hey! Maybe this thing is food–something good."
So the elder brother picked a banana and gave some to the younger one
    and they both ate it.
They finished off one [tree's fruit] and went to the foot of another.
So they stayed there, and as they did, they grew **bigger**.
They lived there until... eventually the **owner** of the garden came.
As he approached
he thought
he heard the two talking, in his garden.
When he appeared he saw them and said, "**Where** did you come from?"
And [one of them] said, "We came when
Mother climbed that tree and fell.
We stayed there until Mother['s body] began to smell and we broke out
    from her and so we have been living here for some time."
But the old man was not a human!
He was a **spirit of the dead**.
He said,
"Alright, then! We'll go to the house."
(The old man intended to eat the two of them.)
So when they reached the house,
he told them,
"We shall look for taro and gather firewood
so
we can go home and prepare it for our meal."
But, he was tricking them, so that they would gather the firewood and
    the food, but they were just to go with the rest of the meal, because it
    was [the **boys**] who would be **his** food.
And he said to the older one, "You and I will go for firewood.
But the little one will stay and dig taro."
The little one started digging taro; but he didn't know what the edible
    part looked like.
So he dug up the **roots**, thinking that was the food.
The others went off and eventually returned, but the little boy still had
    not dug any taro. They were all still [in the ground].
He had dug up only the roots as if they were the food.
So his brother said to him, "Close your eyes!"
When he closed his eyes,
[his brother] kicked at the dirt, and clumps of taro came flying out all over
    the ground.
So then they loaded up [their baskets] with them.

Once they had finished loading them, they went home; but these two
    children were very clever.
When they were about to go home they cut open one rotting coconut.
[Then they left it] there in the bush.
Then they went back to the house
and saw his wife.
They stayed there until finally, in the afternoon, she said, "We're about
    to eat. **Where** are you two going?" "Nowhere.
We're just going for a walk."
They went off and cut bamboo, two lengths of bamboo.
They cut it and filled it with flies, blueflies that had been on the coconut.
They filled the bamboo, then stopped up the ends and took it to the house.
They also drilled small holes in [the coconut] with the point of a knife.
Then they took [these] to the house.
When they had finished their meal that evening, [the spirit man] decided
    that he would kill them later that night.
So he started a fire in a certain spot where it would be smoky and he
    might get inside without their seeing him.
But they cut out the eyes of the coconut, all four.
Then, in the night, he fanned the fire, until it was smoking,
and he went after them to kill them.
But when he went,
the flies were buzzing and it sounded just as if [the boys] were playing.
They also put on the four eyes of the coconut, two on the one [boy's] eyes
    and two on the other's, but **they** slept.
He thought, "Oh! They're still awake!" But what he saw shining were
    the eyes of the coconut.
So the two of **them** kept on snoring, sound asleep
right through untiiil morning.
And the old man said to them, "I was going to come and chat with you.
    I came but you were playing.
So I went away again."
But he was **lying**. He intended to kill them.
The following day
he tried again,
but they were very clever, those two children.
They stayed for **three** days.
And he tried to get them over and over, but in **vain**.
Then they told him, "We've decided to go back,
but we would like to drink a coconut (first)."
So the old man said to them,
"We'll go to the path.
One of you can pick a coconut."
So off they went until they saw [a tree] that was loaded with fruit, and

he said to them,
"Alright then! One of you climb up."
And the two children said to him,
"No, [we can't];
we're just children.
We don't know which one is dried up and which one is just right for water
    or which one is too young. We don't know,
so you should climb up because you're an adult [and do know]."
He replied, "Alright, I'll climb up."
So the old man climbed up,
climbing up until he picked a coconut,
while they waited at the foot of the tree.
When he had picked it and was about to descend,
they sang, like this,
"Oh yes, oh yes, oh yes, throw it!"
And he stopped to listen as he was starting to come down, and said,
    "What did you say?"
"Nothing. We're just glad that you're coming down, so that we can drink
    the coconut."
So he started down, and when he had gone a little way, they sang again,
"Oh yes, oh yes, oh yes, throw it!"
He said, "What did you say?"
They replied, "Nothing. We're glad
you're coming, so we can drink the coconut."
He kept coming, and they kept singing, until finally he touched foot on
    the ground.
And they said, "Oh yes, oh yes, oh yes, throw it!" and attacked him.
They each had a club,
so they both hit him at the same time.
They attacked and killed him.
He lay there [dead].
But they drank the coconut.
When they had finished drinking it,
they went to the house.
They went and killed his wife as well.
and burned down the house.
They burned it, and there it lay [in ruins].
Then they went back, back to the place where they lived,
and returned to eating bananas.
They lived there a looong time, until they were full-grown.
And they said,
"Let's go back to the place
where we burned the old woman [in the house]."
When they got there, they saw

a tree that had taken seed there and had grown.
A **huge** tree had grown up there.
It was **kava**.
When they went up and looked they saw that the base of its trunk was
    full of holes.
They said, "Something
seems to be eating the roots of this tree."
And as they were walking around [the trunk], rats started coming out
    [of it].
They saw that
the rats were staggering.
They said, "Let's come back
for this. It must be something good."
Then they went back, and began trying to find the village,
but they **didn't know** how to get to [it].
They **kept** searching, going downhill toward the village.
They kept on going down and down until finally they emerged [at it],
and the people of the village spotted them.
They said, "**Where** have you two come from?"
So they told them,
"Our mother
was gathering leaves, then she fell; and we lived there in the bush [for
    the looongest time]
    ∘
until finally we grew up and now here we are—we've arrived."
And their father was there;
he was overjoyed.
So they stayed a little while, then they went back for the thing that had
    grown up on the old woman's grave.
They went back.
They went back and **dug** it **up**.
The two of them dug it up.
As they did, they noticed that the rats were chewing on its roots.
And when they came out [from the holes in the trunk], they staggered.
So [the twins] took it home.
When they did,
they brought it branches and all.
Then they planted the kava branches and prepared the trunk for
    drinking.
So now
once someone starts drinking kava, he will never be able to quit because
    of that old woman,

[because of the old woman's] spell—her **spell** still clings to the kava. Today many people like drinking kava, on account of this old woman. That is the end of this tale.

(Reference: Kalo-16. May 7, 1978, Unakapu. Tape 5A, 48-70.)

Text No. 14:

"Takana Waina eu Paρai Nakρea" pae Kaltaρau M̃asemata

Io, a ga woo atulake
natukunoa ni nakρea, takana waina eu paρai nakρea.
Goo tuai ragi waina eu doko,
eu daa atae naga nalaelaeana ni nasaleana e **dapale sava**.
Goo teu doko **sarapaa** doko.
Maa, mariki sikai
nae e mari roara **warua** doko **taava**
tokora wanogoe eu soso e ki Lakenitaρesu.
Goo nae e mari roara warua asa.
Goo e lawo naρarae goo sara naleo maaga.
E solisoli naρarae warua maaga doko roara aneana.
Goo ragi sikai
e midoaki nia naga e ga vaki taava, paki roara aneana.
Goo ragi waina e pano,
e dogo taρesu maaga, eu doo dae, eu doo sari naρarae aneana.
Goo e naga, "E! Navatuuna sikai wanogoe!"
Goo ragi waina e leo e punusi naga taρesu maaga eu daliviria ki soli
    naρarae aneana maaga eu doo dae a,
dakiusi eu doo ρokati nakρea.
Goo **nae** e doo **sale**.
E doo sale natagoto.
Maa taρesu maaga wanogoe eu doo sari naρarae aneana doko naρaunako.
Goo ragi waina **naara** eu maromaaro, goo **nae** maa te maromaaro.
Paapaa eu moro atulake sarisari, goo **nae** maa e **doo** sale.
Paapaa ragi waina taρesu naara teu maromaaro maa nae te doo sale goo

154

tap̃esu eu dogo e.
Ragi waina eu dogo e naga natano e doo duki, naara teu diri.
Maa te ko pa maturu
nalakena e sale p̃arua, e dorotoro.
Goo e paki melu ni nagai sikai poo maturu tokora wanogoe.
E maturu paa[paa] e malaadi goo e naga, "A ga ko punusi navatuuna
    waina tap̃esu maaga waina eu doo p̃osiwosi ki nia."
Goo e pano e punusi eu sari nap̃arae aneana maaga eu dakiusi nakp̃ea.
Goo e puati nakau kiiki sikai goo e p̃okati dogo e asa.
E naga, "O, loriki waia au ga woo lagoro p̃osiwosi ki nia naga e ga vei
nakp̃ea naga a ga woo doo sale asa."
o

Goo e moro paki esum̃a pano, paapaa ragi sikai goo e moro pano.
Goo e **paataka sikai** dapala nogoe.
Goo e naga, "**Masoso**.
A ga vano,
a ga tae nap̃arae maaga waina tap̃esu eu sari a e pei nakp̃ea.
A ga tape a umai paki varea."
Goo ragi waina e pano,
goo e dae nap̃arae maaga wanogoe,
e dae lua tea maaga waina tap̃esu e[u] dae [r]a, dakiusi nakp̃ea.
Goo e dape [r]a umai, goo eu dogo e kite e doo lega siwo.
E pei nalegaana ni **natapetapeana**, waina e kau nap̃arae maaga wanogoe
    poo doo lega:
"Tap̃esu mara, tap̃esu mara.
Io wee tap̃esu mara.
Iero paki roara, iero paki roara.
Io wee tap̃esu mara.
Ieru saari sari, ieru saari sari.
Io wee tap̃esu mara.
Ieru sari nap̃arae, ieru sari nap̃arae,
Io wee tap̃esu mara.
Io! Swa lele! **We!**"
Ragi wanogoe te duasai varea.
Goo te nadi ki nap̃arae maaga wanogoe!
Goo tea laapa eu dogo e waina e doo lega siwo, paki varea.
Goo eu **sava** paki varea.
Goo ragi waina eu pano eu punusi
nap̃arae maaga wanogoe.
Goo eu dape nakau kirikiri goo eu p̃oka dogo e asa!
Goo eu naga, "O, ragi waia tu ga p̃osiwosi ki nakp̃ea."
Maa **tuai** e pei **sara** naleo maaga e[u] diika.
Marikini e diika
kite sara naleo maaga e[u] diika.

Goo eu paki namalasi poo punusi nakau wia maaga paataka ni eu ga
  mari a e ga vei nakρ̃ea.
Goo eu dokoni a.
Eu dokoni nalakena.
Eu dokoni a daliviri nalakena paapaa ragi waina e pavaga paapaa e doko
  goo teu punue a goo teu ρ̃oka lua nam̃elevara kakana.
Paapaa e noopu goo teu dokoni a.
Eu mari a paapaa e soki.
Goo, eu moro dokoni nadom̃ona.
Eu moro dokoni nadom̃ona, e pavaga goo teu ρ̃oka lua nam̃elevara
  maaga paaa[paa]
naga e noopu goo teu dokoni a, mari a paapaa goo nadom̃ona e moro
  makoto.
Goo teu poo doa m̃ata ki nia tokora waina e ga vei nakρ̃ea,
tokora waina eu ga woo sari nakau wanogoe asa naga eu ga woo doo
  ρ̃okati a.
Goo eu moro dokoni a.
Goo eu peani vaatu seara waina eu doo duki lua nam̃elevara maaga
  wanogoe asa.
Paapaa e noopu.
Eu mari m̃ata ki nia.
Eu leo vaatu maaga pae natasi.
Eu soso e ki vaatuvaro.
Poo soroa ki nia asa, mari a e momoaa.
Paapaa e noopu, goo eu atulake poo sike a.
E pei nakρ̃ea vativaati maaga
waina eu sike [r]a poo doo ρ̃okati [r]a raki nasaleana.
Goo masoso
nakρ̃ea maaga tu dogo e pae ragi ni tuai naga e pei tea mariana, maa
  waia, e pei tea vaρ̃aiana pae taρ̃esu
waina nae e madeada paρ̃ai nalo ni nakρ̃ea peea.
Natukunoa waia e noopu.

"How the Slit-Drum was Discovered"
by
Kaltaρ̃au M̃asemata

Alright, I will start with
the tale about slit-drums, how they discovered the slit-drum.
Long ago,
they had no idea what the joy of dancing was.
Theirs was an empty existence.
But [there was] one fellow
who made a big garden up in the hills
in a place they call Lakenitaρ̃esu.
He made a big garden there.
And he planted sugarcane and everything else.
He staked up the big sugarcane stalks in his garden.
And this particular time
he decided to go into the hills, to his garden.
When he got there,
he heard the *taρ̃esu* birds, pecking at his sugarcane.
And he said, "Hey! There's something [going on]!"
And when he looked he saw the *taρ̃esu* in amongst his cane pecking at
    it
as if they were beating a slit-drum.
So he danced.
He danced on the lower side of the garden;
while the *taρ̃esu* pecked at his cane on the upper side of the garden.
And when they stopped, he stopped, too.
Then when they started pecking again, he went on dancing,
until, finally, they stopped but he kept on dancing so that the *taρ̃esu*

heard him.

When they heard the earth resounding, they flew off.

And he needed to rest

because he had danced so much, he was sweating.

So he went into the shade of a *nagai* tree and slept.

He sleeept, until he had cooled off and he said, "I must have a look at what the *tap̃esu* were working away at."

So he went and saw how they had pecked at the sugarcane as if they were slit-drums.

Then he picked up a small stick and tried beating with it.

He said, "Well, perhaps we should make this thing into a

slit-drum so that we could dance to it."

o

So he went home again until... eventually he returned.

And [everything happened] **just** as it had the time before.

So he said, "Today

I'll go

and cut the sugarcane that the *tap̃esu* were pecking on for slit-drums.

I'll take them to the meeting-house."

So then he went

and cut the cane,

cut out the ones that the *tap̃esu* had pecked just like slit-drums.

He carried them off, and as he descended they heard him singing.

As he carried the cane on his shoulder, he sang this song for [that kind of] **carrying** a load:

"*Tap̃esu* leading, *tap̃esu* leading.

Oh, **off** the *tap̃esu* lead.

They go to the gardens, they go to the gardens.

Oh, **off** the *tap̃esu* lead.

On they go pecking, on they go pecking.

Oh, **off** the *tap̃esu* lead.

On they go pecking sugarcane, on they go pecking sugarcane,

Oh, **off** the *tap̃esu* lead.

Io! Swa lele! **We!**"

At that moment he emerged at the meeting-house.

He threw down the sugarcane!

Many people had heard him singing as he descended to the meeting-house.

So they **ran** [there].

When they got there they saw

the sugarcane.

Then they took small sticks and tried beating on it!

They said, "Oh, now we must make slit-drums."

But in the olden days they had **nothing at all**.

No [steel] axe
and **nothing** else.
So they went to the bush and picked out good trees, ones that were just right for making into slit-drums.
Then they would set **fire** to [one].
They fired it around the bottom,
around the base of the trunk until it caught fire and after a little while they extinguished it and knocked out the coals.
When that was done, they set **fire** to it again.
They continued doing this until finally [the whole tree] **fell**.
Then in the same way they burned the **top end** of it.
They set fire to the top until it caught fire then they knocked off the coals.
They continued doing this until the top also broke off.
Then they carefully turned it over [to expose] the part that would become the drum,
the part of the log that they would carve so that it could be beaten.
Then they set **fire** to it once again.
And they had certain **stones** they would use for knocking out the coals.
When this was all done,
they would then properly finish it.
They went looking for stones along the seaside,
called *vaatuvaro*,
with which they sanded it down, making it smooth.
Once that was done, they could pull it **upright**.
There were **four kinds** of slit-drum that they erected and beat for dancing.
And **today**
we know of how slit-drums were made in the past, but they were originally discovered by the *tapesu*.
It was **they** who actually made the first slit-drum.
That is the end of this tale.

(Reference: Kalo-17. May 20, 1978, Unakapu. Tape 5B, 0-21.)

Text No. 15:

"Namataruana ni Namarisaakiana paki Ñalasoro"
pae
Kaltañau Ñasemata

Io, a ga woo atulake naatuusiana waia. Naatuusiana waia e daa pei
naatuusiana ñooli, maa e pei lomau waina e pei tea mariana.
Ragi sikai
naka ni Ñalasoro maaga
ñoogi e pei ragi ni namasu, goo eu daoni nañañe paa[paa] eu doo gani a
varea ñoogi.
Goo, ragi waina eu doko goo naka ni Utanilagi maaga
eu midoaki nia naga eu ga mari naleoana.
Maa waago adeada eu daa paataka.
Goo eu rumai
poo dalivirigoro natokoana ni Ñalasoro.
Goo eu paki varea!
goo eu ñokati naatañooli seara.
Eu ñokati naatañooli ni Ñalasoro seara ñoogi wanogoe.
Goo eu dape [r]a poo paki natokoana adeada,
paki Vareanirogovai, rogovainañau.
Goo naara eu sava pae malo laapa, goo eu daa duñada atae ra naga eu
ñokati seei maaga.
Goo ragi waina maliñoogi
nakñea adeada e kai, e soso ra naga eu ga vaki varea naga eu ga woo atae
naga eu ñokati seei maaga, seei maaga eu puoli.
Goo ragi waina eu paki varea eu punusi naga eu laapa kiiki, paki
rualimasikai tamate waina eu puoli, naanoai kasua maaga.
Goo Makauliu, nawota ni Ñalasoro, e doo midodoa naga, "Ai!
Sara ragi, tu doko tokora waia, tu dogo kite saa nalo ni Utanilagi waina

160

eu doo umai p̃okati gida.
Eu doo gani gida.
Goo e p̃ia tu ga m̃elu tokora waia.
Maa seei? A midoaki nia naga tu ga va punusi Marip̃op̃ogi doko
    M̃alamea.
E ga ko moro piragisoki gida natau seara, goo edaku tu ga woo moro liliu
    umai."
Goo e naga, "Seei e ga vano?
A daa atae naatam̃ooli waina e ga vano
pa punusi Marip̃op̃ogi."
Goo naatam̃ooli sikai eu soso e ki Makauloova.
E p̃asilua lau ni nam̃ele sikai e doko namata ni varea adeada e doko lake
    ni napaga.
E naga, "Kinau, a ga vano."
Goo ragi waina e m̃elu, doko sava!
E sava doliu Vanuatapu.
Lau nam̃ele wanogoe e pei waina e puati a, e pei waina namarisaakiana
    e marisaa pakiliina ki nia.
E sava doliu Vanuatapu poo umai sava doliu P̃ogimao
paki M̃alanaruru, Komali.
Goo ragi waina e umai, e duasai m̃alala ni varea ki M̃asemata.
E pei kinau, waina a peani varea wanogoe doko masoso.
Goo ragi waina e umai, goo mariki wanogoe nae e pei naatam̃ooli waina
    e paki natoga poo dape suisui veea mau umai paki Nguna.
Goo e dosadusugi suisui aneana. E soso e ki Nakaulootu.
Goo e punusi a kite e panop̃ota.
Goo e naga, "Io, p̃a maturu,
nalakena ku sava p̃arua p̃a ko gaegae sua. Goo p̃a woo noa navatuuna
    waina ku paraki nia."
Goo ragi waina e dogo kite p̃ia goo e pasa paki nia, e naga, "Io, p̃a toko,
    maa kinau a ga vaki varea warua,
doko Vareanimatawola."
Goo e pa punusi a, pa punusi nawota warua, Marip̃op̃ogi.
Goo e noa, "Io, e p̃ia. Eu ga woo umai!
o
Goo tu ga woo pa rakii da pano."
Goo e noa kii da asa, e naga, "Io! Ku ga toko,
maa, waina a ga vano,
naaleatia sikai waina au ga vitautau mu goo ku ga woo umai pa raki gami
    au ga woo umai paki tokora waia."
Goo ragi wanogoe naara eu doo dakidorogo
paapaa
eu pioso, eu naga "Ku ga woo umai".
Goo M̃asemata wanogoe nae e kau nakaulootu aneana poo paki

Komalip̃okasi, punusi Atugialiu,
poo noa ki nia asa naga, "**Masoso**,
tu ga viragi naka ni M̃alasoro umai poo doropusi ra navanua ki tap̃esu
    anigida
waina e doko tokora waia."
Atugialiu e suasua, e naga, "Io! E p̃ia!"
Goo naara eu mamauputi poo pa piragi naka ni M̃alasoro.
Goo eu rumai paaa[paa], maa eu ko daa mari nasum̃a.
Goo eu madeada dae weede doko lake ni napaga maaga waina eu maturu
    asa waina eu soso e ki Lake ni Napaga ki Weede.
Goo eu doo maturu lake ni napaga wanogoe. E pei nasum̃a adeada.
Maa eu poo doo mari nasum̃a maaga.
Paapaa, nasum̃a maaga eu noopu, goo eu m̃elu dua ki lake ni napaga poo
    maturu nasum̃a maaga wanogoe.
Goo eu doko ragi varau, natau seara eu doko.
Eu doo p̃osiwosi namarakiana ki tap̃esu waina e doko taava.
Goo eu doko paapaa goo eu midoaki nia naga eu ga moro liliu.
Goo ragi waina naka ni M̃alasoro maaga eu rumai duu tokora wanogoe,
    eu midoaki nia naga, "O! Tokora waia
e p̃ia ki namataruana ni soogi."
Namataruana ni soogi e pei dakiusi eu sili p̃ia doko tokora wanogoe.
Goo wora wanogoe, wora sikai maa e pei tea sosoana ki Matarusoogi, pae
    nagisa ni mariki ni M̃alasoro wanogoe
waina e noa navasaana wanogoe waina eu noa naga e pei Matarusoogi.
Goo **teu doko**.
Paapaa eu midoaki nia naga eu ga moro liliu, natau laapa kiiki.
M̃aladigi e ga vei natau rualima
goo eu naga, "Eee, tau midoaki nia naga tau ga moro liliu."
Maa tea ni M̃alamea eu naga, "Ku ga ko doko kiiki."
Goo eu dip̃a ki M̃asemata naga, "P̃a ko pa punusi M̃asekaau. Nae e pei
    munuai sikai
waina e doko
varea aneana, Matakudaalo.
P̃a ko pa punusi a naga tea ni Utanilagi eu doo mari dapale sava ragi
    waia."
Goo ragi waina e pano, goo e naga, "Ragi waia eu doko p̃arap̃aaro. Eu daa
    midoaki dogo navakalo."
Goo e naga, "E p̃ia!
M̃alamea
goo
narei ki Atugialiu au ga woo pano.
Au ga woo pa kelugoro ra."
Goo naaleatia wanogoe eu pano p̃oogi
pilake tea ni Tokolau goo tea ni Komali maaga.

Teu marisokisoki navinaga maaga p̃oogi eu pano
poo pa **kelugoro varea adeada**.
Goo navasaana e diika, waina eu duu, eu duu paapaa tokora e aleati,
goo nagoroi maaga eu midoaki nia naga eu ga vaki roara.
Eu piragi naala adeada maaga poo naga eu ga vaki roara goo ragi waina
    eu pano goo eu sua naatam̃ooli, waina eu sua ra goo eu **darasa**.
Goo naatam̃ooli **mamauputi**
teu **paki varea**!
Goo naka ni M̃alamea maaga eu dusugi ra paki m̃aladigi varea
naga eu ga dokoni varea adeada poo p̃okati ra!
Goo **Mariwota**, e duleana poo savelua naulu ni nam̃ele sikai waina e doko
    namata ni varea.
E pisei ki natam̃ateana, naga eu ga **taa** p̃okati ra.
Goo nawota ni M̃alamea e pasa pakii da,
e noa kii da asa, e naga, "**E** noopu!
Ku ga **taa** moro p̃okati naka ni M̃alasoro!
Maa tau ga moro liliu. Maa au ga woo dakidorogo.
Goo ku pe moro p̃okati ra,
au ga woo umai dap̃araki varea animu."
Goo **naara** teu liliu.
Teu liliu umai, paki M̃alamea.
Goo eu doko asa, eu poo piragi lua naka ni M̃alasoro liliu paki natokoana
    adeada.
Goo eu madeada mari **navinaga warua**.
Naka ni M̃alasoro eu magi **naka ni M̃alamea** goo naka ni **Komalip̃okasi**
    goo **Tokolau–Komali**–
eu madeada mari navinaga warua.
Eu **sale**!
paapaa e aleati.
Goo naka ni M̃alamea maaga eu moro madeada mari navinaga.
Eu mari naleoana warua. Eu **sale**, paapaa e aleati.
Doko asa, goo eu poo piragi ra liliu paki natokoana adeada.
Poo moro madeada marisokisoki nasum̃a adeada goo sara naleo adeada
    maaga paa[paa] eu noopu,
goo eu moro liliu paki natokoana adeada.
Goo naka ni M̃alasoro maaga eu daa moro sua namarisaakiana warua
    nogoe pae ragi wanogoe, paapaaa paki masoso, waina natokoana e poo
    dum̃ana malaadi ki naatam̃ooli eu daa moro paki asa.
Naatuusiana waia e noopu.

"How the Destruction of Ñalasoro was Ended"
by
Kaltap̃au Ñasemata

Alright, I will tell the beginning of this story. It is not just a story, but
    it is **true** and actually happened.
On this particular occasion,
the people of Ñalasoro,
during the peak of the fruit season, were cooking and eating chestnuts
    in the meeting-house one night.
And, while they were there the people of Utanilagi
decided to have a feast.
But they did not have enough pigs.
So they came
and surrounded the village of Ñalasoro.
And they went to the meeting-house!
and killed a number of people.
They killed several Ñalasoro people that night.
Then they took them home to their village,
to Vareanirogovai, rogovainap̃au.
And the [Ñalasoro] people had fled, and were scattered **all over**, so that
    they could not tell **who** among them had been killed.
So when morning came
their slit-drums cried out, calling them to the meeting-house in order to
    find out who had been killed, who all were **missing**.
When they arrived at the meeting-house, they saw that there were quite
    a few—over ten—men in their prime missing.
And **Makauliu**, the chief of Ñalasoro, was worried: "**Ai!**
All the time we have lived here, we have suffered from the people of

164

Utanilagi coming and attacking us.
They are devouring us.
So it would be best if we left this place.
But who [would be willing to help us]? I think we should go visit
    Maripoᵽogi in M̃alamea.
He could look after us for a few years, and after that we'll return."
So he said, "Who will go?
I can't say what man should go
to see Maripoᵽogi."
But there was a man called Makauloova.
He broke off a leaf of the *nam̃ele* tree that stood by the door of the
    meeting-house under the banyan tree.
He said, "I will. I'll go."
So then he left, and he ran!
He ran past Vanuatapu.
(The *nam̃ele* leaf that he took was to prevent harm from befalling him.)
So he ran past Vanuatapu and on beyond Ᵽogimao
to M̃alanaruru, Komali.
When he got there he went to the dancing-ground of M̃asemata's
    meeting-house.
(Today it is I, [M̃asemata], who have this meeting-house.)
And when he arrived, [there was a man there]–this fellow had been
    overseas and had brought back the very first gun to Nguna–
who pulled his gun close to him. (He called it *Nakaulootu*.)
He could see that something was wrong.
So he said, "Now then, you rest,
for you've run a long way and you're all out of breath. Then you can tell
    [us] what you've come about."
So when he felt better, he told him, and he replied, "Alright. Stay here
    and I will go to the main meeting-house,
Vareanimatawola."
So he went to see him, [to speak to] the high chief, Maripoᵽogi.
And [the latter] said, "Yes, fine. Let them come!
°
And we will go and get them."
So [the M̃alasoro man] said to them, "Alright–you stay [here],
and, I'll go [ahead],
and one day we will send word asking you to come and move us all here."
So then they waited,
until...
finally they sent the message, "Come."
So M̃asemata shouldered his gun and went to
Komaliᵽokasi, to see Atugialiu,
and told him, "Today,

we shall bring out the people of M̃alasoro and put them here
on the land of the *tap̃esu* bird."
Atugialiu agreed [to this]: "Yes! That's good!"
So they all went and led out the people of M̃alasoro.
They kept coming and coming, but they had yet to build any houses.
So they carved beds for them that they called Beds in the Foot of the
    Banyan.
And so they slept at the foot of the banyan. It was their home.
In the meantime they built houses for them,
and when at last they were all finished, they left the foot of the banyan
    and slept in [their own] homes.
And they stayed a long time, some years.
They worked the dominion of the *tap̃esu* in the hills.
They lived there until... finally they decided that they would go back
    again.
When the people of M̃alasoro [first] came and stood on that spot, they
    thought, "Oh, this is a good place!–
it will spell the end of the violence."
(By saying 'spell the end of the violence' they meant that they [felt they]
    were safely hidden there.)
And there is a spot there called "The End of Violence", which is so named
    after the M̃alasoro man
who said that this would spell the end of the violence.
So they stayed there.
They remained until they began thinking they might go back again, after
    a few years [had passed].
It had been almost ten years
when they said, "Well, we think we should go back."
But the people of M̃alamea said, "Wait just a little longer."
And they sent off M̃asemata, saying, "Go and see M̃asekaau. He is a
    diviner
and he lives in
his meeting-house, Matakudaalo.
Go and find out what the people of Utanilagi are up to now."
So he went to see him and [M̃asekaau] said, "They're not doing anything
    right now. They aren't considering making war."
So he said, "Good!
We of M̃alamea
and
Atugialiu's people will go.
We'll go and surround them."
So that day, by night, they went,
accompanied by the people of Tokolau and those of Komali.
They prepared food and at night they went

and **surrounded the meeting-house** [of Utanilagi].
And there was not a word spoken, as they stood, until daybreak
when the [Utanilagi] women were getting ready to go to their gardens.
They picked up their baskets to go to the gardens and as they started out
    they came upon the men, who came after them **yelling out.**
So all the **people**
made for the **meeting-house!**
And the people of M̃alamea chased them towards the meeting-house
so they might set fire to it and kill them!
And **Mariwota** [the chief of Utanilagi], stood up and broke off a leaf of a
    nam̃ele tree that stood by the door of the meeting-house.
It was a gesture of peace, meaning that they should **not** kill them.
Then the chief of M̃alamea spoke to them,
he said, "It's **all** over!
You must **not** kill any more of the people of **M̃alasoro!**
We will go back. But we will wait, listening.
If you attack them again,
we will come back and burn your meeting-house down to the ground."
Then **they** left.
They went back to M̃alamea.
And they began returning the people of M̃alasoro to their own village.
And they staged a **great feast** for them.
The people of M̃alasoro put it on for the **people of M̃alamea** and the people
    of **Komalip̃okasi** and **Tokolau–Komali.**
They made a great feast for them.
And **danced!**
until daybreak.
And the people of M̃alamea in turn put on a great feast for them.
They made a huge feast, they **danced,** until daybreak.
Then they took them back to their village.
They prepared their houses and everything for them and once it was all
    ready
they returned again to their own village.
The people of M̃alasoro never again met great violence from that time
    right up until today when the village stands empty, devoid of people.
That is the end of this account.

(Reference: Kalo-18. May 20, 1978, Unakapu. Tape 5B, 21-40.)

Text No.16:

"Marikori goo Leilega"
pae
Kaltap̃au M̃asemata

A ga woo atuusi naatuusiana sikai waina e pei lomau.

Naatam̃ooli sikai e doko P̃au, waina e pei m̃aau [nagisana e pei Marikori].

Goo sara ragi waina e ganikani sua malip̃oogi, nagoroi aneana e mari
navinaga sua, e ganikani sua, goo e puati naap̃e aneana goo e paki
taleeva ni Eton.

Goo vaatu sikai e doko namaati ni Eton, maa e daa doko elau, e doko
m̃aladigi euta.

Goo sara ragi e doko pa maturu tokora wanogoe.

Goo ragi waina e punusi naga naatam̃ooli eu liu pae napua

goo e sava paki euta goo e p̃okati ra! e p̃okapunue ra!

Goo tea ni Eton goo tea ni P̃agop̃ago maaga, goo tea ni P̃au eu daa atae
naga nasava e doo maripunue naatam̃ooli tokora wanogoe.

Goo talakeada maaga eu pa leoatae naatam̃ooli adeada maaga waina eu
mate goo teu dape ra pa ova kii da.

E dapala nogoe e pei ragi varau.
°

Goo ragi sikai naatam̃ooli dua ni Eton,

ero naga, "Eee! Naatam̃ooli anigida maaga teu ga mate puti.

Goo nigida

toro ga va pap̃ai navatuuna waina e doo marisaa ki naatam̃ooli anigida
maaga!"

Goo sikai e noa naga, "Kinau,

kinau, a ga vano; maa niigo, p̃a sili doko."

E naga, "Maa ku suasua ragi waina naatam̃ooli wanogoe e umai e
mariatae maripunue te pe maripunue ko?"

168

Goo e naga, "Io! A suasua."
"Maa kinau a ga sili doko."
Goo ero pano, ero paki tokora wanogoe.
Napua kiiki sikai e siwo pae tokora wanogoe poo paki elau, paki vaatu
    wanogoe.
Goo naataṁooli kerua kakana e sili doko.
Maa, tea waina e duṁana suasua ki nia naga e ga mate, e pano paapaa
    e doko p̃ai napua kiiki wanogoe goo naataṁooli wanogoe e sake.
E sake umai doko p̃okati a.
E p̃okati naataṁooli wanogoe goo ero moro pile!
Maa tea wanogoe e sili doko.
Ero doko paapaa
goo e marimatua ki naataṁooli wanogoe goo e p̃okati a,
e p̃okapunue a.
Goo e moro sava pa maturu vaatu wanogoe, goo nae e moro paki
    natokoana, ni Eton.
E naga, "A poo pap̃ai loriki waina e doo maripunue naataṁooli."
Goo e sava umai paki P̃au
poo punusi nawota ni P̃au, Marivaleawia.
Poo noa ki nia, "E pei ṁaau aniigo waina e doo mari nawosiana saa waia
    waina e doo p̃okati naataṁooli, doko taleeva ni Eton.
Goo masoso a poo pap̃ai a.
Naataṁooli sikai waina aro dua pano e p̃okapunue a, ragi waia teu dape
    a pano naga eu ga ova ki nia.
Goo kinau a umai naga a ga noa ki sai ko asa."
Maa nae e ko pueli,
e ko pueli vaatu wanogoe.
Maa anagoroi e doko.
Anagoroi e doko goo nawota e pano poo pusuusu ki nia.
Goo e naga, "E pueli."
Goo e nadi ki naap̃e, e madoko nasuṁa aneana, nasuṁa ki ṁaau
    wanogoe.
E nadi ki naap̃e e pisei ki naga nae e ga woo pei tea maripunueana.
Goo nagoroi aneana,
e punusi a,
goo e naga, "O, io... a manaunau nawosiana waia.
E lagoro pei nae waina e doo mari nawosiana saa waina."
Ragi waina e ko pueli maa vitariki e doo pauria, e marisokisoki navinaga.
E pano paa[paa] goo e pakiliina.
Te maligo goo e pakiliina.
Goo e noa ki nia asa e naga,
"Naap̃e wanae one.
Ragi waia eu pap̃ai ko naga ku doo mari nawosiana saa sikai."
Goo navasaana e daliviri Efate ragi sasaṁooliwia wanogoe.

Naga naatam̃ooli wanogoe eu ga woo p̃okati a.

Goo naara ero doo marisokisoki p̃oogi, ero doo pauria.

Ero mari navinaga, napuuri.

Goo ero p̃okati waago sikai, poo dao nia doko navinaga adeada.

Malip̃oogi saa tero ga sava!

○

Goo ragi wanogoe

ero marisokisoki paapaa ero marisokisoki sara naleo adeada goo ero pai
    sugoro adeada maaga, paapaa e noopu.

P̃oogi goo ero puke.

Ero puke goo ero paisokisoki navinaga adeada goo ero sava p̃oogi, waina
    naata sikai e daa atae a.

Goo ero sava umai paapaa paki nawora **matua**.

E pei nawora ki **Esno**.

Goo ragi waina ero umai doko asa doko, paa[paa] goo e poo aleati goo
    naatam̃ooli ni Nguna eu doolu eu naga eu ga vaki namaati.

Naara eu dape rarua.

Goo eu pano.

○

Goo eu leo kite naara ero doko.

Goo eu dum̃ada "Malip̃oogi wia!" kii da.

Ero naga, "Nimu ku ga vaki esava?" Eu naga, "Au ga vaki namaati."

Eu naga, "Maa nimu koro ga vaki esava?" Goo ero naga, "Aro ga vaki
    Nguna.

Io, ku ga ko paki namaati, maa aro ga ko doko raki mu doko.

Maa waina elau e ga mua ku ga woo umai musagi gami, tetu ga woo
    pano."

Naara ero doko.

Maa **naara** eu paki namaati, eu dape sara naleo maaga, lolo maaga pano
    paa[paa] e noopu, goo elau e mua.

Goo eu rumai punusi ra nawora.

Goo e soso ra naga, "Ku ga ko umai ganikani!"–naara e[u] doolu–
"Ku ga ko umai ganikani!"

Goo eu ganikani.

Eu ganikani paapaa e noopu goo eu naga, "Iita! Koro ga tape sara naleo
    animu paki rarua."

Goo ero dua naala adeada paki rarua.

Paapaa e noopu.

Goo tea doolu wanogoe, **sikai** e madoko kivea, goo **sikai** e dape nawose,
    goo **sikai** e dasake kiedaku poo puasoki natali ni nalae.

Maa, tea waina e madoko kivea, nae maa e dape naasu.

Tuai eu marisaa masale ki sara naleo maaga ni navakalo.

Goo mariki wanogoe nae maa e puati **naap̃e**, poo lawoduu katea.

Goo tea waina e p̃owolau, nae maa e peani aneana **naasu** e doko.

Goo tea waina e puati natali, aneana **naasu** e doko.
Goo ragi wanogoe, e pei nalagi wia, eu purasa doo sava umai
paraki nagisu ni naure kiiki,
P̃ele.
Goo eu rumai paki m̃aladigi [ki] euta, goo tea ni kivea e dipe a!
E dipe naatam̃ooli wanogoe, m̃aau wanogoe.
E dipe a goo e p̃okalua nalua aneana paki natasi pano.
Maa tea waina e puasoki natali nae e solisoki natali paki rarua.
Goo nae maa a dipe a!
Goo ero dua ero dipe a, maa tea waina e p̃owolau nae e doko dorogo,
    nalakena nae e dape nawose.
Goo ero dipe a paa[paa] sikai e dipe p̃ai a.
Goo e pei natip̃a **tapu** waina ero dum̃ada dipe a asa.
E pei kup̃a latolu, naaleatia latolu, p̃a woo mate.
Goo eu pano poo paki euta goo e naga, "Ei!
Tekoro poo **marisaa** ki nau!"
Goo eu pano poo paki euta nagisu.
Goo nagisu wanogoe masoso nagisana e pei Nagisu ni M̃aau Rarua.
E pei mariki wanogoe waina e mari nagisa wanogoe.
M̃aau e pasalea ki rarua tokora wanogoe.
E naga, "Ku ga vae elau, maa kinau, a ga vae euta."
Eu musagi vitariki aneana.
Goo naara eu doolu, eu paati poo pae rarua pae elau.
"Maa ku ga leo waina a ga dai naone, ku ga woo moro paraki nau nagisu,
    Nagisu ni Koroi Lolo."
Goo teu pae elau umai paaa paki euta lau ni Tikilasoa.
Goo eu leo kite te dai naone.
Goo rarua e moro paraki nia, e pa musagi a umai.
E doko kiiki naaleatia latolu, goo **te** mate.
Maa vitariki kakana **te** doko, nagoroi aneana.
E pei nakainaga ni **naika**, vitariki wanogoe.
Goo nagisa ni vitariki wanogoe e pei **Leilega**.
∘
Goo e doko paa[paa] mariki aneana wanogoe e mate,
goo teu ova ki nia, eu ova ki nia doko matigo ni Tikilasoa.
Goo ragi wanogoe Marogoe nae e **doko**, maa Mariwota e ko daa umai.
Goo Marogoe e moro piragi nagoroi wanogoe e pei narup̃a aneana.
E pei nagoroi **kerua** aneana.
Goo teu doko, eu doko paapaa e moro maneana dape natuna nagoroi
    duua.
Goo ero doko paaa sikai e laki paki Meere.
E pei tuai
goo sikai e moro laki paki Farealapa.
Goo doko nawora ni tea rua wanogoe, tamadawota wanogoe waina ero

pae P̃au umai, **naara** eu doko masoso.
Sikai e umai paapaa e moro pa pei **Willie Bertie** waina te mate.
Maa natuna maaga eu doko.
Goo e moro pa dape nagisana, e pei Leilega.
Willie Bertie p̃ilana nagisana e pei Leilega, waina
e moro dape Willie Bertie.
Goo sikai e laki paki Meere.
Goo *laen* [namatarau] ni Meere wanogoe **naara** eu doko masoso.
Goo eu peani nagoroi maaga seara waina eu doko.
E pei **Irene**, goo e pei **Norsi** waina eu pei *famli* [namatarau] ni naika
wanogoe, waina naara eu doko masoso.
Goo naatuusiana waia e noopu.

"Marikori and Leilega"
by
Kaltap̃au M̃asemata

I will tell a **true** story.

There was a man who lived in P̃au, who was a *m̃aau*. [His name was Marikori.]

Every morning when his wife had made his meal, and he had finished eating, he took his club and went to the coast near Eton.

There was a rock on the reef at Eton, not down at the beach, but back up on the shore.

And it was **there** that he used to go and sleep.

And whenever he saw people passing by along the path

he ran to the beach and **attacked** them! killed them!

And the people of Eton and the people of P̃agop̃ago did not know **what** it was that was killing people there.

Their leaders[1] would go and identify the dead and take them away to bury them.

It went on that way for a long **time**.

o

Then one particular time two Eton men

said [to each other], "*Eee*! Soon all of our people will be dead.
You and I

must go and find out what this thing is that is harming our people!"

And the one said, "I,

I will go; but you must stay hidden."

The other replied, "But are you still willing even though whoever it is might attack you and you might be killed?"

He answered, "Yes! I am."

173

"Then I will hide."

So off they went, to that place.

A small path went down by the spot toward the beach, toward that rock.

So the second man hid there.

Meanwhile, the one who was willing to die, went on until he struck the
    path and the man [Marikori] came up [along it toward him].

He came up and attacked him.

So the two of them fought!

But the other one remained in hiding.

They kept on...

until finally [the m̃aau] defeated the man, and beat him,

beat him to death.

Then he ran back to the rock and went to sleep, while the other man came
    back to the village of Eton,

and said, "I have discovered the thing that has been killing people."

Then he ran to P̃au

and saw P̃au's chief, Marivaleawia.

And he told him: "It is your m̃aau who has been doing this evil business,
    killing people along the coast near Eton.

Today I saw him.

Another man and I went together and he killed him, and right now they
    are carrying him away to be buried.

So I came on here to inform you of it."

But that man was still gone,

still out at the rock.

But his wife was at home.

So the chief went and asked for him.

She replied, "He's out."

So [the chief] took his club and threw it so that it landed in the [wall of
    the] m̃aau's house.

(His throwing the club like that meant that the m̃aau was to be killed.)

His wife

looked at it,

and said, "Oh, I am appalled by this business.

Perhaps he is the one who has been doing this evil deed."

He was still away, yet the old woman started baking and began making
    a meal.

She kept at it until... eventually he appeared.

It was already getting dark when [finally] he appeared.

So she told him,

"[You see] the club lying there—

this time they've found you out, found out that you've committed this evil
    deed."

And even at that very moment the word was going all around Efate.

They would kill that man.
So by night the two of them made ready, baked.
They cooked food-slices [2].
And they killed a pig, and cooked it with their food.
In the wee hours of the morning they would flee!
o

In the meantime
they got ready, gathering up all their belongings and packing their
    clothes until... finally it was all done.
During the night they opened the oven.
They packed up their food and the two of them escaped in the dark
    without anyone knowing.
Then they fled until they came to the main landing-place,
Esno's[3] passage.
When they got there they stopped, until... day broke... and there were
    three Nguna men who decided to collect shellfish on the reef.
They took a canoe
and off they went.
o

Then they noticed the two [people standing] there.
And they said "Good Morning!" to each other.
[The couple] said, "Where are you going?" They replied, "We're going to
    the reef."
They asked [in turn], "And you—where are you two going?" They
    answered, "We're going to Nguna.
You go to the reef and we'll wait for you.
When the tide comes in, come and pick us up and we'll all paddle over
    together."
The two of them waited there
while the others went on to the reef, and collected shellfish, shellfish of
    all kinds, until... eventually they were all done and the tide was
    coming in.
Then they came [back] to see [the other two] at the landing-place.
[Marikori] called to them, "Come and eat!"–[to] the three [men–
"Come and eat!"
So they ate.
They ate... and when they had finished, they said, "O.K.! Take all your
    things to the canoe."
So the two loaded all of their things into the canoe.
When it was done,
the three [men got in], one in the bow, one taking the paddle, and one
    sitting in the stern to hold the line for the sail.
And, the one sitting forward had a bow.
(In the old days they could never be without all the weapons of war.)

[Marikori] took his **club** and stood on the side opposite the outrigger.
The one who was steering had his bow.
And the one who held the line had his bow as well.
Then, there being a good breeze up, they ran smoothly
toward the point of the small island,
P̃ele.
And [as] they came close to shore, the one in the front shot him!
shot the m̃aau.
But he pulled out the arrow and threw it into the sea.
Then the one holding the line tied it to the canoe
and then **he** shot him!
They both shot at him, but the one who was steering stayed still, because
    [all] he had [was] a paddle.
And they kept shooting at him until... one hit him squarely.
And they were **sacred** arrows[4] with which they were shooting at him.
(The ones that will kill you in eight days; eight days, then you die.)
Then they went to shore, and [Marikori] cried out [*his voice rising very
    high, in agony*], "Ei!
You've **destroyed** me!"
Then they went ashore at the point.
Today they call it "Point of the M̃aau's Canoe".
It was that fellow for whom it is named.
There the champion shoved off the canoe with his foot.
He said, "You go via the shallows, but I am going by land."
They took his wife,
and they four went by canoe through the shallows.
"But keep watch—when I throw sand up into the air, come back to the
    point for me, to Sweet Girl Point."
So they kept going along until they came ashore at Tikilasoa.
And then they saw him throwing up sand into the air.
So the canoe returned, to pick him up.
He lived for a short time—eight days—then he died.
But the woman, his **wife**, remained.
She was a member of the **fish** clan.
Her name was **Leilega**.
o
She stayed until her husband died
and they buried him, in the graveyard at Tikilasoa.
Now at that time [chief] Marogoe **was** there, but [chief] Mariwota had not
    yet come.
So Marogoe took the woman as his lover,
as his **second** wife.
So they lived on there... and, eventually, she bore him two daughters.
And in time one of them married into Meere.

Some time later
the other also married into Farealapa.
So the descendants of those two, the couple from P̃au, **are** alive today.
One [line of descent] comes down until it becomes **Willie Bertie**, who is
   now dead.
But his children are still living.
Willie Bertie's mother also took her name, Leilega.
So Willie Bertie's mother's name was Leilega.
And the other married into Meere.
So [some of those of] the Meere branch of the clan **are** alive today.
They still have some female [members].
It is **Irene**, and **Norsi** who are the descendants of that branch of the fish
   clan, and they are still alive today.
And that is the end of this story.

Footnotes

1. Literally "their owners", this refers to those who were entrusted with
   the villagers' safety: their chiefs and/or family group heads.
2. The term, *napuuri,* translated here as "baked slices", refers to large
   cross-sectional slices of whatever vegetable tuber is used. It stands in
   contrast to the usually preferred pudding, *nakoau*, which is made by
   first grating the tuber then mixing it with coconut milk. *Napuuri* can
   be prepared for baking in considerably less time than can *nakoau*, a
   small culinary detail that lends a sense of urgency to the narrative
   moment.
3. At the moment this story was recounted, a man named Esno was the
   current owner of the spot under discussion.
4. *Natip̃a tapu,* literally the "holy or sacred arrow", was one which was
   magically treated with a type of poison that was inevitably fatal, but
   which did not take full effect for eight days.

(Reference: Kalo-19. May 20, 1978, Unakapu. Tape 5B, 40-61.)

Text No.17:

"Roimata, Roimuru goo Leimaarona"
pae
Lui Taatalele

Roimata, Roimuru, Leimaarona–
naara eu pei tamataida maaga goreda e pei Leimaarona.
Tamataida dua wanogoe goreda e pei Leimaarona.
Ragi waina eu doko [Retoka], paa[paa] goo p̃ilada e mate
goo naara ero pei nawota.
Ero naga ero ga mari natapua sikai doko natokoana adeada.
Goo eu mari naniu e dapu.
Eu ga mari a raki natam̃ate ni p̃ilada waina [e mate] goo eu ga woo mari
    a nakup̃a rualimaliima.
Ragi wanogoe naniu e dapu.
Goreda wanogoe, Leimaarona, e doko goo nae e peani nakaroa seara.
E doko goo ragi waina nawota e doo leo punusi naniu waina e dapugoro
    e.
E doo pueli, e punusi pueli e doko asa.
Ragi wanogoe e maridogo laaga asa.
Maa e daa mariatae pap̃ai a.
Goo e peani namidoakiana sikai e dapala nea naga,
"Elagoro
a ga mari napua waia naga a ga woo pap̃ai a naga seei waina e dapiri
    natapua aginau."
Ragi sikai e noa nawosiana sikai.
Ragi waina
woli e dagi e noa nawosiana sikai naga eu ga um̃a.
Tea laapa eu paki namalasi.
Maa nae e ga woo edaku pano.

Ragi waina e edaku dausi ra pano, te daa dausi tea maaga waina e naga eu ga va uma; maa nae e poo sili namalasi tua pagi nakau.
E pagi nakau sikai [paapaa te] paki palo, poo moro doo leo liliu paki esuma.
Ragi waina e leo liliu pano, e pagi one palo one e doo leo paki ekopu paki nasuma adeada pano paa[paa] e punusi naga koroi wanogoe, e paki katama!
E paki katama goo e purasa sole pano, pano paapaa doko pa dape naniu maaga wanogoe, doko moro sili paki ekopu.
Ragi wanogoe e naga, "Ragi waia ta poo papai a.
E pei **kusue napoolo**, maa **kinau** ta doo laaga asa.
Kusue napoolo ni suma ni kiagu."
o

Ragi wanogoe
teu doko.
Eu doko panopano e midoaki naga e ga mari natamate ni naaleatia ki pilada
te pei rualimaliima.
Goo e naga, e noa ki narei aneana maaga, e naga, "Ku ga tuti naniu maaga!"
Eu tuti naniu maaga paapaa e noopu.
E naga, "Ku ga vuati a paki elau!"
Eu puati a paki elau ni nagole ni natasi.
Ragi wanogoe gorena wanogoe eu soso e ki Leimaarona, eu puati a poo doropusi a, elagi ni puripuri ni naniu maaga wanogoe.
Ragi wanogoe eu doropusi a natasi poo doo sai ki nia eu salea ki nia.
Eu salea ki nia, e sale tua pano.
Eu daa atae naga e ga woo **paki** esava.
Eu midoaki nia naga e ga woo mate elagoro.
E sale sale sale sale paaaa e paki euta
elau ni Rewokaninapua [Fareafau].
Doko nawora wanogoe e paki euta e pei Valeatainimele, tokora wanogoe e paki euta asa eu soso e ki Valeatainimele, nawora wanogoe.
E paki euta asa, tua sili doko valea sikai.
Natasi e doo paki ekopu kakana, maa e daa mariatae marisaa ki nia nalakena e pei valea warua.
Ragi wanogoe nawota ni natokoana wanogoe eu soso e ki Uusamooli.
E pei **ragi ni napetau sikai** goo nae e peni napetau paapaa e midoaki naga e ga va dipe naika.
E dape napetau aneana siwo, doropusi naala aneana doko, maa e ditipe paaa ragi waina e umai e midoaki naga e ga kani napetau.
Goo ragi waina e gani napetau, e nadi ki nawilina paki natasi, doko valea wanogoe, maa
nae e doko taleeva–

vitariki wanogoe e doko taleeva–maa nawota **nae** e doko taleeva.
E doo gani sapura ki nia natasi dapala nea, e punusi naga
natavara waina e pei paki ekopu, e dape nawili ni napetau pano paaaa
  naga natavara e liliu dapala nea. Nawili ni napetau wanogoe e daa
  moro lop̃ai naga eu **pae** esava.
Maa koroi wanogoe ragi wanogoe e dape nawili ni napetau wanogoe, te
  gani a.
"E! Nawili ni napetau waia a nadi ki nia goo te pueli **dapal[a]** esava?"
Ragi waina e poo dakimata paki taleeva kerua e punusi kite koroi
  wanogoe e doko.
E lop̃ai kite e doo lop̃ai dapala nea namatana e doko lop̃ai.
Ragi wanogoe e midoaki nia naga e pei saatana sikai.
E p̃ili, e p̃ili doko pano paaaa naga ragi waina e leleo,
kite koroi wanogoe e doo lop̃ai.
E naga, e doko asa doko pasa ki nia:
"E! Ku pae esava pei?"
Ragi wanogoe, koroi e naga, "Eee!".
Te noa napua aneana, naga e sale pae.
E pano paapaa mariki wanogoe nawota wanogoe e daa saralomau naga
  e pei naatam̃ooli.
E naga, "Io, toro ga vaki esum̃a."
Ragi wanogoe ma nawota wanogoe e mari looga sikai e doko erasa,
  m̃aladigi.
E doropusi waago asa.
Ragi wanogoe ero poo atulake sake maa nalakena e daa saralomau naga
  e pei naatam̃ooli,
e naga e pei **saatana** sikai,
ragi waina ero poo atulake sake pano goo e maridogo e.
E noa ki nia naga, "Lau ni nakau waia, kinami au gani a."
E noa lau ni napilelu.
Maa Leimaarona e noa naga, "Ee! Lau ni napilelu waia kinami au daa
  doko gani a."
Maa e noa ki nia asa,
"Lau namelesi, loriki waina eu soso e ki napuraru, waina e doko
  nam̃asua ni vaatu?" e naga, "Loriki waia kinami au **daa** gani a."
Maa Leimaarona e naga,
"Ee! Loriki waia **kinami** au gani a."
Ero sake, ero sake paraki looga wanogoe waina nasum̃a e doko asa waina
  e magi waago mari a e doko asa.
Ero pano paapaa ero doko asa doko noa ki nia, "Lau nakara?"
E noa ki nia, "Ee, loriki waia e pei 'lo saa. Au daa gani a."
Ragi wanogoe e saralomau naga e pei naatam̃ooli. Ero pano paapaa e noa
  ki nia naga, "P̃a doko nea doko!"
Te doropusi a doko nasum̃a ki waago wanogoe doko, nalakena e matau

ki narupa aneana maaga.

Naga e doropusi a doko, maa te paki suma. E daa noa kii da. E doko pano pano paapaa

ragi waina eu dao nawii–naara eu pagavaga nawii tuai–eu magi waago dao nawii.

E maneana lopai tea dapala, te maneana dape lua e.

Ragi waina e dape a naga e siwo pano, doko mari dapala nogoe sara ragi.

E pagani waago maa te dua e tea wia.

E pano paapaa

narupa aneana maaga eu leoatae a naga navatuuna sikai e doko waina e peani a e doko.

Ragi wanogoe tea waina e pei napauda te poo sai ki nia.

Ragi waina nae e moro dape navinaga pano napura ki waago, goo narupa aneana napauda e dausi a. E dausi a pano pano pano paa[paa] te sili duu.

Ragi waina e sili duu, e lopai waina e dua waago maa te maneana doropusi na e pagani waago, maa te maneana dape tea wia doko pa dua e.

Goo koroi e dave goo e poo dua e, poo doo pasa ki nia.

Paa[paa] e dapala nea, goo e naga, "Ah! A poo papai mu!

Takana waina ku dasuru ki nagoroi wanae doko e pei nalakena ku doo mari dapala na.

Ekasaa ku daa naga pa viragi a pei?"

E naga,"Ee! A naga a ga viragi a paloti maa a matau ki mu asa."

Pae ragi wanogoe ero piragi a paki suma.

E daa midoaki saa ki nia maa tero piragi a paki suma.

E doko suma doko paapaaaa doko peani natuna duua, naanoai duua.

(Maa naanoai duua wanogoe a daa atae nagisada; maa e peani natuna duua wanogoe ero doko.)

Ero doko, ragi wanogoe ku atae piakiiki eu mariatae pakitaku doko lina.

Ragi waina ero pakitaku maa narupa maaga wanogoe eu mari navasaana seara naga ero pei natu ni tea saa.

Ragi wanogoe pilada e dogo e, te dogo kite saa navasaana waina eu noa e.

E doko noa kii da asa ragi wanogoe tea rua ero doko asa naga, "Koro ga vaki punusi aloamu maaga."

Tea rua wanogoe ero doko asa doko mari rarua sikai.

Ero mari rarua sikai pano paaa naga e noopu.

Tero pano–pano pano paapaa poo pakiliina,

paki Retoka naga teu puasoki ra.

Eu puasoki ra doko soli ra.

Eu soli ra doko, maa teu pa dape navinaga rakii da naga eu ga woo gani ra. Eu pano paapaa eu dape navinaga liliu, maa ero doko.

Ragi wanogoe teu ga maripunue ra maa eu daa dovai ra ki masimasi maa eu dovai ra piiti, loopu.

Eu peea puati tea veea doko naga teu ga tovai a.

Eu poo dovai namanuna dapala nea,

goo e noa navasaana sikai,

e naga, "Keekee! Teete Leimaarona, O!"

Ragi wanogoe teu moro peresi natali asa, nalakena teu midoaki p̃ai koroi
waina eu peea salea ki nia.

Goo eu moro puasoki **kerua**.

Eu puasoki **kerua** goo eu moro dovai namanuna, goo e moro noa
navasaana sikai maau.

Ero pei tea veresiana.

Teu doko, eu madeada pauri paapaa e noopu.

Eu ganikani paapaa e noopu, tero ga liliu.

Tero noa kii da naga, "Kup̃a lima, ku ga moro punusi gami."

Ero pei tero atuusi napua maaga panopano paapaa paki p̃ilada naga e
noopu.

Ero noa ki nia naga aloa maaga eu pe vakiliina teu ga mate.

Goo e naga, "Ee! Koro ga taa marisaa kii da!"

"Ee! Maa wootu e ko **pavaga** doko."

Goo naaleatia lima

ero paki elau pano, duu madoko rakii da.

Aloada maaga eu pei, eu pei paapaa naga ero kooro ero dae kup̃e ni
napuka tau.

Paka sikai kooro e paapaa dua doko goo rarua e poo sava pano paapaa
paki nawaritau dapala nea.

Goo tero kup̃e m̃orua ki rarua.

Rarua te diro.

Aloada maaga teu mate.

Tea maaga wanogoe teu mate.

Te noopu.

"Roimata, Roimuru and Leimaarona"
by
Lui Taatalele

Roimata, Roimuru, Leimaarona—
two brothers, and their sister, Leimaarona.
The two brothers' sister was [named] Leimaarona.
They were living in Retoka ("Hat Island"), and [one day] their mother
    died
and the two [brothers] became chief[1].
They decided to put a restriction on their village.
So they declared coconuts prohibited.
They did this for the peace ceremony on behalf of their dead mother, to
    be held on the fiftieth day [after her death].
So from then on [using] coconuts was prohibited.
Their sister, Leimaarona, had some itching sores.
And when the chief was checking the coconut trees on which he had put
    the restriction, he noticed that a few coconuts were missing.
And they kept disappearing.
So he tried to find out why.
But he could not discover [what was happening to them].
Then he had an idea,
"Perhaps
I should take this way of finding out who has been violating my
    prohibition."
So one day he announced a task [that was to be done].
When
the shell-trumpet sounded he announced the task: they should clear
    bush for gardens.

Everybody went to the bush.

But **he** would follow later.

When he went, he did not follow the people he had told to clear the bush; rather, he went into the bush and climbed a tree.

He climbed a tree until he was up high, and could look back toward the houses.

He stretched out along a limb, and stayed there looking back and inside their house... until finally he saw the girl [his sister] come out!

She came out, crawling, crawling slowly along, until she [got to the bush], collected some coconuts, then went back again inside.

At that point he said, "Now I've found out.

It's the **rat** in the **house wall**, and here I was looking [elsewhere] for it.

The rat is in the walls of my [own] house."

Then

they remained [as they were].

They kept on until he decided to make the peace ceremony as it was the fiftieth day of [mourning for] their mother.

So he said to his people, "Tie the coconuts together!"

They set about tying them... and finally it was done.

He said, "Take them to the shore!"

They took them to the shore [and put them down at] the water's edge.

Then they took his sister whom they called Leimaarona, and set her on it, up atop the bundle of coconuts.

Then they put it into the sea and shoved it off, set it afloat.

They set it afloat, and out it drifted.

They had no idea **where** it might go.

They thought that she would probably die.

It drifted, drifted, drifted, and drifted... until eventually it came ashore [below] Rewokaninapua [Fareafau].

And its landing-place, the place where it went ashore, was called Valeatainimele.

She went ashore there, and took shelter in a cave.

The sea washed up inside it, but it could not harm her as it was a large cave.

At that time the chief of that village was named Uusamooli.

It was the season for a certain [kind of] **breadfruit** and after having roasted a breadfruit he decided to go and catch fish [by shooting them with his bow and arrow].

Taking his breadfruit, he set his bag down, then started catching fish until he decided to eat the breadfruit.

When he had eaten [it], he tossed the skin into the sea, into that [same] cave; but

she was [inside] off to one side—

the woman was on the one side—and the **chief** was on the other.

As he went on eating, throwing the skins into the sea like that *[with a tossing hand gesture]*, he watched
the wave go inside *[gesture of the open hand sweeping in front of and across the body]* and carry off the breadfruit skin, then after a time the wave would come back out again like this *[gesture of the hand sweeping in the reverse direction]*. But he could not see **where** the skins of the breadfruit had gotten to.
For the girl was plucking out the skins, and eating them.
"Hey! I threw the breadfuit skins away, now **where** have they gotten to?"
Then he glanced around toward the other side and caught sight of the girl.
When he saw her, she was looking at him [at the same moment].
He thought she must be a spirit of the dead.
He shut his eyes, and kept them clooosed... finally he opened them again, but she was still looking at him.
[This went on, until...] he felt that he had to speak to her:
"Hey! Where did you come from?"
Then the girl replied [*with both sadness and relief*], "Oooh!".
She told him of her route, from where she had drifted.
She went on [with her story]... but in the end the old chief still did not believe that she was a human.
He said, "Alright then, let's go home."
He had built a sty just back from the shore, closeby on the cliff.
He kept pigs in it.
So then they started up; but because he did not believe she was a human, and thought she was a spirit of the dead,
once they started up, he tested her.
He said to her, "We eat the leaves of this tree."
He was talking about [inedible] *napilelu* leaves.
But Leimaarona said, "Oh, no! **We** don't eat *napilelu* leaves!"
Then he said,
"*Namelesi* leaves—what they call [edible] *napuraru*—that grows on top of rocks?" He said, "We **never** eat that."
But Leimaarona said,
"No?! **We eat it!**"
They went on up, up and up, toward the pen and the shed that he had built for the pigs.
They went on... until finally they reached it and he said to her, "*Nakara* leaves...?"
The girl replied, "No, it's no good. We don't eat it."
At that point he believed that she was indeed a person. They continued on and presently he said to her, "Wait here!"
He left her there in the pig shed, because he was afraid of his wives [2].
So having left her behind, he went on to the house. He told them nothing.

He waited and waited until
they had baked yams for the pigs—in those days they used to feed the pigs
baked yams.
He spotted a nice one, and kept it aside for her.
Then he took it and went down [to the pig pen], and he did the same every
time [thereafter].
He would feed the pigs and give her the nicest [yam].
It went on [this way]...
until at last his wives realized that he was keeping something there.
So the one who was their head followed him.
The next time he took food for the pigs, the head wife followed him. She
followed and followed and then she hid.
While she was hidden, she saw him feed the pigs, but keep the nice one
to give to [the woman].
Then the girl emerged and he gave it to her, and began to talk with her.
[Seeing] how it was, [his wife] spoke, "Aha! I've found you out!
You've been acting like this because of this woman you've been hiding
here.
Why didn't you bring her [home]?"
He replied, "No, [I couldn't!] I thought about bringing her, but I was
afraid of all of you."
So after that they brought her to the house.
[His head wife] didn't wish to harm her, so they brought her home.
She lived theeere... and eventually she bore two children, two boys.
(I don't know their names, but she did have two sons.)
You know, in those days children could defecate anywhere.
When the [two boys] did, the wives started talking, saying that they were
sons of a bad person.
When their mother heard this, she was upset over what they were
saying.
So she told the two of them, "You should go and visit your uncles."
So they set about building a canoe.
They worked on it... until at last it was finished.
They left—they went on and on until they arrived,
at Retoka and were captured.
[The Retoka people] caught them and tied them up.
They tied them up, then went to get food to eat [along with the boys].
They went ahead [and ate], then they took the [remains of the] food away,
and just the two [boys] were left.
Then they were going to kill them; but rather than stabbing them with
a knife, they would slit [their throats] with a blade, [of] bamboo.
They took hold of the first one to cut him.
They cut his neck like this [*horizontal slashing motion of the hand*] ,
and he uttered these words:

"It hurts! Oh, mother, Leimaarona!"

Then they untied the ropes from about him, because they immediately
  recognized [the name of] the girl whom they had set adrift before.

Then they took hold of the other [boy].

They held the other one and cut his neck, too; then he uttered the very
  same words.

Both of them were released.

They stayed [with them], and baked [food] for them... until eventually it
  was ready.

They ate... and, when that was done, the two were about to return.

They said to [the Retoka people], "Five days from now, you should come
  and visit us in return."

[The boys] came back and recounted their journey to their mother from
  beginning to end.

They told her that if [their] uncles showed up they would die.

And she said, "No! You mustn't harm them!"

"What! [Our] wounds are still raw!"

So five days later

they went to the shore, and stood there waiting for them.

Their uncles came; and as they came along, the [boys] cut and cast spells
  on [a few] blocks of wood from the white canoe tree.

They cast the spell then stood ready, as the canoe ran up and reached the
  reef's edge, like here [gesture indicating the reef behind the narrator].

Then they heaved the pieces of wood smashing open the [hull of the]
  canoe.

The canoe sank.

Their uncles were killed.

They were dead.

That's it.

Footnotes

1. Though very understated, here is an example of a female chief, one of
   very high status. For other examples of female chiefs, see the texts by
   Kaltap̄au M̃asemata and Lui Taatalele, #3 and #4 respectively, in this
   volume.

2. Readers interested in common narrative themes might compare the
   narrative sequence, or sub-plot, which begins at this point with the
   initial portions of Kaltap̄au M̃asemata's text, "Munuai Vaau/The New
   Diviner" (#12), as the two interludes bear strong resemblance to each
   other.

(Reference: Lui-3. May 7, 1978, Fareafau. Tape 3B, 42-end.)

Text No. 18

"Namateana ni Mariameara"
pae
Lui Taatalele

Naatuusiana sikai ni navakalo e dapala nea.
E doko ragi ni tuai.
Naatam̃ooli seara maaga eu doko natokoana sikai ni Taava,
natokoana ki Mariatugia.
°
Ragi waina eu m̃elu raki navakalo
eu rumai paki taava sikai ni M̃atoa poo doo pioso paki natokoana ki
    Mariameara, naga,
"Ku ga vei **naanoai**, ku ga umai paki nea.
Tu ga tum̃agida mari gida."
Ragi wanogoe naatam̃ooli maaga wanogoe eu **daa** mariatae sake pano.
Maa eu peani naleo sikai waina eu soso e ki natip̃atapu.
Goo **naara** eu doko dorogo natokoana adeada.
Goo eu dape naasu adeada goo
nalua
poo dipe ki nia paki p̃alo.
Maa nalua wanogoe e pei natip̃a tapu.
E sale pae elagi, pano pano paapaaaa, goo e lawo namata ni nawota
    adeada,waina e pei Mariatugia.
Ragi wanogoe naatam̃ooli maaga
eu puati nawota adeada
poo paki natokoana adeada.
Edaku ki tea wanogoe,
e moro pei ragi p̃ota sikai,
maa eu moro sokari navakalo adeada.

Goo

naataṁooli maaga ki Mariameara, goo tea p̃ota ni te natokoana seara
    waina eu duṁada silae ra,

eu sake paki Taava poo moro mari navakalo.

Maa sara naataṁooli maaga eu pei taatapera nalakena navakalo, goo eu
    marisasaa ki natokoana wanogoe.

Maa

eu peani ṁaau seara waina eu doko.

Goo

eu peani napua seara waina naataṁōoli eu doo usi asa.

E pei nawosaia.

Ragi wanogoe

naataṁooli ṁaau sikai, nagisana e pei Manasogosogo.

E **atae** naga napua waia e pei nawosaia goo naataṁooli seara eu ga woo
    usi asa.

Ragi wanogoe e moro dape aneana natip̃a.

Goo e doko raki te naata seara waina e pe vano e ga woo dipe a.

Goo ragi wanogoe

nawota ni Ṁatoa waina e pei Mariameara e usi napua wanogoe.

E sava usi a napua wanogoe;

goo ragi wanogoe, Manasogosogo e punusi a, goo e dipe a ki natip̃a.

Maa

e moro sokari nasurataana aneana, e daa doko.

E moro sava siwo paki natokoana ni etano.

Goo e pap̃ai mariki sikai e doko asa doko.

Mariki wanogoe e pei nakainaga ni **naika**.

Goo ṁaau aneana ero sava pano,

goo Marianeara wanogoe e dapesoki a poo soso ki ṁaau aneana naga nae
    e ga atugi a.

Ragi waina ṁaau aneana e punusi a goo e atae naga e pei nakainaga ni
    naika.

Ragi wanogoe

e daa mariatae atugi a nalakena e pei nadaana, goo te pei tea veresiana.

Ero doko asa goo ero moro siwo paki Meere,

ero paki Meere,

goo ero pap̃ai mariki sikai e doko.

E pei atavi ni Mariṁasoe,

Taivakalo.

Goo

e pei tea ataeana paki nia naga nawota wanogoe e pano, maa e ova
    natip̃a.

Ragi wanogoe e dape lua naap̃e aneana poo nadi ki nia dua e asa.

Goo e naga,

"Naataṁooli maaga seara

eu sava raki namauriana, eu duu valea wanae, valea ni vaatu."
Ragi wanogoe
o

Mariameara wanogoe
e puati naaρe wanogoe
pilake naatam̃ooli aneana ero sava pano poo atugi nagoroi maaga goo
     piakirikiri maaga.
E noopu.
Edaku ki nia ero poo sake paki natokoana adeada, M̃atoa.
Goo ragi wanogoe
nawota wanogoe e mate
nalakena eu dipe a ki natiρa tapu.
o

E noopu.

"The Death of Mariameara"
by
Lui Taatalele

[There's] one war story that goes like this.
It took place long ago.
There were some people who lived in the village of Taava,
[chief] Mariatugia's village.
°
They left [Taava] to wage war
and proceeded to one of the hills around [the village of] M̃atoa; and they
    started calling [up] to [chief] Mariameara's village [M̃atoa]:
"You should act like men, and come [down] here.
We will do battle."
For [the Taava] people could not mount the hill [in the face of opposition
    from the village above].
But the [others, the people of M̃atoa,] had something they called a sacred
    arrow.
So the latter remained [where they were] in their village.
And they took their bow and
arrow
and shot [straight up] into the air.
But it was the sacred arrow [not just any arrow].
It sailed up high, on and on it fleeeew, until finally it [came down],
    piercing the eye of the [attacking party's] chief, Mariatugia.
Then those people
carried their chief away
and went [back] to their village [Taava].
After that,

on yet a different occasion,
they added [another episode] to their [ongoing] war.
And
Mariameara's people [of M̃atoa], along with others from an allied village,
went up to Taava to launch a return attack.
But all the people had scattered, [fleeing] from the attack [into the bush],
    so they laid waste to the village.
But
some of [Taava's] m̃aau were still there, alive.
and
there is a certain path that people would use-
a narrow trail.
At that time
there was a certain person, a m̃aau [of Taava], whose name was
    Manasogosogo.
He knew
of this trail and knew that someone would take it.
So then he, too, took up his sacred arrow.
And he waited for someone to go by and he would shoot him.
Meanwhile,
the chief of M̃atoa, Mariameara, was coming along the path.
He came running, along that same path;
and Manasogosogo saw him, and shot him with the arrow.
But
[Mariameara] kept going; he never paused.
He ran on down to the village below.
And there he found an old fellow.
The old man belonged to the clan of the fish.
[Mariameara] and [one of] his [own] m̃aau ran;
and he—Mariameara—seized [the old man], calling to his m̃aau to come
    and kill [the old man].
But when the m̃aau saw him, he recognized him as a member of the fish
    clan.
So then
he couldn't kill him because he was of his own blood, [a fellow clansman];
    and so [the old man] was released.
Then [Mariameara and his m̃aau] went on their way, going on down to
    Meere.
They went to Meere,
and there they found an[other] old man.
It was [chief] Marim̃asoe's assistant,
Taivakalo.
And
he realized that, even though the chief was still going, still he bore a

sacred arrow [in his body].
So then he took out his club, and threw it to [Mariameara].
And he said,
"Some people,
[went by] running for their lives; they're [hiding] in the cave over there,
    [in] the cave in the rock."
Then
    o

Mariameara
grasped the club and
he and his aide ran there and [started] killing women and children.
[Then] it was [all] over.
Afterwards they went [back] up to their village, M̃atoa.
And it was [only] then that
the chief died,
for they had shot him with the sacred arrow.
    o

That's it.

Footnotes

1. *Goo nawota wanogoe, Mariameara wanogoe, nagisa kiiki aneana e pei
   Manaatamate.* The personal name of the man who at this time bore
   the title, Mariameara, was Manaatamate.

(Reference: Lui-4. June 7, 1978, M̃atoa. Tape 6A, 0-20)

Text No. 19:

"Naworearu ni M̃atoa"
(Namagovai Veea)
pae
Ronneth Manutukituki

A masau atuusi nariwota ni naveinawotaana ni M̃atoa.

Nariwota ni naveinawotaana ni M̃atoa waina eu doko M̃atoa eu pei
   nagoroi **mau**, nagoroi maaga wanogoe eu pei nagoroi rualimasikai.

Nagisada pae navanua eu pei **naworearu**.

Goo naworearu maaga wanogoe eu pei nagoroi rualimasikai.

Goo eu peani m̃alala sikai waina eu doo sale asa.

Goo m̃alala wanogoe, e pei **Sakedoko**.

Eu doo sale paapaaa p̃oogi sikai

goo mariki sikai e doko, nae e doko aneana natokoana.

Natokoana aneana e pei **Manukakau**.

Mariki wanogoe nagisana e pei **Tariwiawia**.

E doko paa e dogo wa[ina] nagoroi maaga eu doo sale.

Ragi waina e dogo dapala nogoe e naga, "O! Nawaa ni natukutukumena
   sikai waina a dogo. A ga ko paki m̃aladigi poo pa atae naga e pei
   nasava."

E pano kite e pei nagoroi maaga eu doo sale m̃alala adeada.

E pagi doko nakau kiiki sikai eu soso e ki nadamami.

E doko asa lop̃ai ra paapaa eu sale paapaa e noopu; e daa pasa kii da maa
   e moro liliu paki natokoana aneana.

E madoko paa[paa] matamai, e moro dogo eu doo sale, e moro umai
   punusi ra, matamai ki nia.

Ragi waina e umai punusi a,

"O! E p̃ia a ga vaki m̃aladigi ki nia, a ga vano, a ga vunusi a. Au ga
   tum̃agami punusi gami."

Ragi waina e paki m̃aladigi, e siwo paki etano pa punusi ra, eu noa ki nia asa, eu naga, "E! Maa niigo ku doko esava?"

E naga, "Ee! Kinau natokoana aginau e doko elagi waia."

Ragi wanogoe nagoroi maaga wanogoe takalapa adeada e noa naga, "E!
Matamai p̃a moro umai! Tu ga moro sale.

P̃a umai punusi gami tu ga moro sale."

Maa ragi waina nasaleana e noopu, te moro liliu paki natokoana aneana.
Matamai ki nia

te moro umai teu doo sale. Eu doo sale paapaa e moro noa ki nia asa naga,
    "Matamai p̃a moro umai ragi waina nasaleana e noopu."

Natuuta wanogoe, ragi waina vitariki wanogoe e noa ki nia asa naga eu
    ga woo sale,

maa te pei waina e ga umai tero ga vitawiri, e ga viragi a, e ga vei nagoroi
    aneana.

    o

P̃oogi eu dogo e kite teu doo dagi.

Tariwiawia te mate.

Ragi waina eu doo sale, eu naga, "Ee! Nadagiana sikai waina e doo [e]lagi
    waia tu ga ko pa punusi a."

Ragi waina eu pano,

kite te pei Tariwiawia te mate.

Nagoroi **wanogoe** nagisana e pei **Konamsese**, nagoroi takalapa, nawore-
    aru wanogoe takalapa adeada e pei Konamsese.

E noa ki taina maaga asa, e naga,

"Waina tu ga vano niimu ku ga **taa** dagi, maa kinau a ga masikigu dagi."

E ga tagi, e pei waina te ga mari a e ga vei nadagidagiana ni nalegaana
    waina eu ga tape a asa.

(Nalegaana wanogoe ta malioki nia, a daa mariatae lega asa.)

Ragi waina eu dape a,

te doo **peea**,

e peea, te doo dagi **peea**, maa taina maaga, tanari maaga,

eu dape a, teu doo dausi a.

Ragi wanogoe teu ga atulake kokoi adeada.

Eu ga atulake pae kokoi.

(Pae navasaana ni navanua eu noa naga kokoi maa pae navasaana ni
    English eu noa naga boundary.)

Eu rumai paapaaa doko siwo wora waina e pei kokoi adeada doko siwo,
    doko siwo siwo siwo, maa nalegaana e doko paapaa elau.

Ragi waina eu paki elau pano,

e doko noa ki taina maaga asa, e noa naga, "Wora waia tu ga woo doropusi
    mariki tagida asa.

Maa tu ga woo pa tiroa ki nia elau."

Goo ragi waina eu dape a duu,

goo vitariki, Konamsese e noa kii da e naga, "E! Tai maaga, nasum̃a
    anigida te sooro!"

Ragi waina e noa dapala nogoe,
eu leo sake dapala nea, doko dapepele Tariwiawia. Goo Tariwiawia te
   dowo paki natasi.
E dowo paki natasi doko pei vaatu varau.
Vaatu wanogoe e doko natasi epua ni natasi. E doko paapaa paki masoso
   waia.
Goo naara maa
nagoroi maaga wanogoe ragi waina eu paki euta eu duu nawoka ni valea
   sikai.
Goo nawoka ni valea ni vaatu wanogoe eu doko asa paapaa paki masoso.
Stori aginau e noopu tokora wanogoe.

"The Family of M̃atoa"
(Part I)
by
Ronneth Manutukituki

I want to recount the ancestry of the M̃atoa [village] chiefship.
The ancestry of the chiefship of M̃atoa were all women—ten women.
The name for them in our native language is **naworearu**.
So the founding family [naworearu] was composed of these ten women.
And they had a dancing-ground on which they used to dance.
[It] was [called] **Sakedoko**.
They were always dancing there aand, on this particular night,
there was an old fellow, who lived in another village.
His village was **Manukakau**.
The old fellow's name was **Tariwiawia**.
There he was when he heard the [sound of] the women dancing.
When he heard it he said, "Oh, that sounds like the fruits of the
  natukutukumena tree! I must go closer and find out what it is."
He went along and [saw that] it was actually the women dancing on their
  dancing-ground.
He climbed up into a little tree that they call a nadamam̃i.
He stayed there waaatching, until finally they finished dancing; then he
  went back to his village without speaking to them.
He remained there until the next day when, hearing them dancing once
  again, he went back to see them.
When he got there, [he thought],
"Oh, I must go up close to see—I'll go and see. [Then] they'll see me. We'll
  see each other."
When he climbed down to the ground, and went close to see them,
they said, "Hey! Where did you come from?!"

He said, "Oh, [nowhere special!] My village is just up over there."
Then the eldest of the women said, "Well, then!
Come back tomorrow. Dance with us.
Come and see us and we'll dance some more."
So when the dance was over, he returned to his village.
The following day
he came back again and they [all] danced. They danced and danced, until
    at last she spoke to him again, "Come back again tomorrow after the
    dance is over."
This date—when the woman made that date with him that they would
    dance together—
what it meant was that when he came they would get married, he might
    take her to be his wife.
  o

[That] night [the women] heard them wailing.
Tariwiawia had died.
While they were dancing, they said, "Hey! We should go and see [who]
    the wailing up there [is for]."
When they went,
[they discovered that in fact] it was Tariwiawia who had died.
The woman, the eldest of the group of sisters, was named Konamsese.
She said to her sisters,
"When we go, you aren't to wail; I alone shall wail."
She would wail, that is, she would sing the song of mourning to
    accompany it as they bore [the corpse] along.
(I've forgotten how the song goes, so I can't sing it [for you].)
When they picked it up,
she went first,
she went ahead, wailing in front, while her sisters, [and] his friends,
carried him along, following after her.
They started at their boundary.
They began [following] along their boundary.
(In our language we say kokoi, but in English they say "boundary").
They moved along until they reached the spot where their boundary
    begins to descend, and from there they went down, down, down, with
    the singing continuing all the way down to the shore.
When they reached the shore,
she said to her sisters, "This is the spot where we will leave our dear
    friend.
But we must sink [the body] offshore."
And as they stood there holding it,
the woman, Konamsese, said to them, "Oh, sisters! Our house is on fire!"
When she said that,
they looked up in that direction, and let go of Tariwiawia. And

Tariwiawia['s body] fell into the sea.

It fell into the sea and turned into a long rock.

The rock lay deep in the sea. It is has been there ever since, right up to this very day.

Then they,

the women, went ashore and stood in the mouth of a cave.

And they have been there ever since, in the mouth of the cave where they stood, right up to this very day.

That is the end of my story.

(Reference: Ronneth-1. May 5, 1978, Mere. Tape 4B, 4-30.)

Text No.20:

"Soogi ki Mariwota ni Utanilagi"
pae
Ronneth Manutukituki

Naataṁooli maaga ni Makura rualimadoolu eu rumai paki euta Utanilagi.
Eu rumai, doko punusi nagoroi maaga seara ki Mariwota [ni] Utanilagi.
Naataṁooli maaga wanogoe eu pei rualimadoolu.
Ragi waina eu punusi nagoroi maaga ni Utanilagi,
teu dua ra nakau maaga naga eu ga taa peani pipia.
Maa **naara**, eu rumai raki eu ga woo pa kili taumako, Siviri.
Ragi waina eu rumai, teu punusi nagoroi maaga wanogoe paapaa e
  noopu, teu rumai pano poo madoko Tikilasoa poo duagoto paki Efate.
Ragi waina Mariwota e liliu, goo nagoroi maaga teu pitua ki navasaana
  paki nia, eu noa naga, "Tea ni Makura maaga eu rumai, punusi gami
  paapaa e noopu, doko dua gami nataputea naga au ga taa peani pipia."
Ragi wanogoe Mariwota e dape navago, navago e pei navinaga **saa**.
Navago wanogoe te ragi seara e pei **namatai**, eu karopuludoa e pilake
  natai, poo pitua ki nia.
E dape namatai wanogoe pilake natai seara poo karopuludoa e asa
  paapaa e noopu doko umai dua Manasogosogo asa.
Manasogosogo e dape navago wanogoe, doko sake paki Mariatugia, poo
  doko pa dua e asa goo e noa naga, "Ṗa woo dua ṁaau aniigo asa. E pe
  vei naanoai, e ga woo dape navago waia, poo dape a paki Tikilasoa,
  punusi Mariwota ni Tikilasoa."
Ṁaau aneana duua, ero dape a siwo poo pa dua Mariwota asa, Tikilasoa.
  Poo noa ki nia asa, naga, "Waia e pei navago ni naataṁooli rualima-
  doolu ni Makura waina eu rumai punusi nagoroi ki Mariwota ni
  Utanilagi.
Goo e dua ko navago waia, e naga, 'Naataṁooli aniigo maaga eu ga kani

a poo doo leogoro naataᵐooli rualimadoolu wanogoe waina eu ga woo umai eu ga woo [maginau] ᵽokati [r]a.'"

Paapaa ragi waina naara teu duu sua napua, navago nae te peea pano sua paki elau.

Ragi waina eu rumai naka ni Tikilasoa, teu leogoro sua ara naga eu ga woo pakiliina, ᵐaau aneana maaga.

Eu pakiliina.

Teu mari navasaana maaga ni nasorosoroana seara pakii da naga ragi e pe woo saa.

Goo eu madeada marisokisoki sara naleo adeada–nelikau adeada maaga.

Ragi waina eu marisokisoki sara naleo adeada maaga nelikau adeada maaga paapaa e noopu, teu duᵐada noa kii da asa naga, "Ragi waina tu ga madoko elau kiiki, goo tu ga woo ᵽokati ra ragi wanogoe". Maa naataᵐooli ᵽota nae e dape wooli doko duu euta.

Ragi waina e duu euta, naara eu pano paa[paa] teu doo ᵐaleoputo wia ni natasi.

Goo teu sui wooli.

Ragi waina eu sui wooli, eu atulake ᵽokati ra.

Ero puati nawose adeada maaga–**naara** eu musagi ra. Maa tea ni Makura maaga wanogoe, **naara** eu daa paluse; maa ᵐaau duua ni Taloa **naara** ero paluse.

Ragi waina ero paluse, sikai e doko kiveea goo sikai e doko kiedaku.

Goo ragi waina wooli e poo tagi dapala nea tea waina e doko kiveea e ᵽokawoka goo tea waina e doko kiedaku e ᵽokawoka. Eu ᵽokati naataᵐooli rualimadoolu wanogoe eu ᵽokati **puti** ra.

Eu maraka mate duu.

Teu poo loloso kii da paki euta.

Eu musagi ra paki euta goo tea seara eu loloso parakii da goo tea wa[ina] teu loloso paki natasi teu lawo ra ki naio adeada maaga.

Eu piragi ra paki euta, paa e noopu.

ᵐaau adeada e moro sava paki Taava poo noa ki sai Mariatugia, e naga, "Naataᵐooli aniigo maaga waina ku dua gami ara, tau maripunue puti ra."

Maa navasaana waina Mariwota e pasa asa pusi a pilake navago aneana e naga, "Waina ku pe ᵽokati ra, ku ga maginau kili nawii na**ᵽeka**, naᵽeka **maau** napu rualimadoolu. E ga vaataka naataᵐooli rualima-doolu."

Nawii wanogoe, navasaana wanogoe, e pei tea vakavuroana.

Eu kili naᵽeka **maau** napu **rualimadoolu,** eu solisoki a eu pei guᵐa maaga dapala waina naataᵐooli maaga eu mate, ragi waina eu dape ra umai eu solisoki ra paa[paa] teu maraka pei guᵐa.

Poo dape ra sake paki Komaliᵽokasi.

Eu dape ra sake paki Komaliᵽokasi pano, kite nawii maaga teu maraka pei tea ovarakisuaana raki natuturiana paki tokora maaga waina eu ga woo sakesake paki a[sa].

Eu dape naatamooli rualimadoolu wanogoe doko doropusi a paki natu-
tuuriana, navasua maaga waina teu doropusi sua ra, doropusi ra
paapaa paataka paa[paa] e noopu.

Mariwota maaga, narei aneana maaga, teu rumai raki nia seara eu
pakiliina.

Eu punusi sua e goo teu poo sale.

Natamate ni tea wanogoe te poo pei tea mariana. Eu sale paapaa e
noopu, goo nasakesakeana te poo pa.

Goo Mariwota nae maa te pei tea ataesuaana naga navasua waia e pei
navasua aneana.

Ragi waina eu sakesake paki natokoana maaga paapaa e noopu, paki
varea maaga paapaa e noopu, eu sakesake agi Mariwota.

Goo

nasaleana maa te noopu, eu dapetape doko paki natokoana adeada
maaga.

Wanogoe e pei namatapago ni navusumakiana kakana.

"The Vengeance of Mariwota of Utanilagi"
by
Ronneth Manutukituki

Thirty people from Makura came ashore at Utanilagi.

They came, and "saw"[1] some women [belonging] to Mariwota of Utanilagi.

There were thirty of these [men].

When they "saw" the Utanilagi women,

they gave them [certain] leaves so that they would not get pregnant.

But [the **Makurans**] had come in order to dig *taumako*[2], at Siviri.

So when they had finished with the women, [the Makurans] went on to Tikilasoa [from which] they crossed [the bay] to Efate.

When Mariwota returned, his wives told him about it, "Men from Makura came and saw us, and when they were finished [with us], they fed us leaf-medicine so that we wouldn't get pregnant."

Then Mariwota took *navago*, which is [a sort of] bad food.

Navago is **breadfruit**, that is mixed with **faeces**, and then given to [someone].

He took some breadfruit and some faeces and mixed it together, and when it was done, he went and gave it to Manasogosogo.

Manasogosogo, [the chief of Malaliu village], took the *navago* and went up inland to see Mariatugialiu, [the chief of Taava village], about it. And he said, "Give this to your *m̃aau*. If he is a man, let him take this *navago* and deliver it to Tikilasoa, to [chief] Mariwota of Tikilasoa."

Two of [Mariatugialiu's] *m̃aau*, took it and descended [toward the shore village of Tikilasoa] and delivered it to Mariwota. And they told him: "This is the *navago* of thirty men from Makura who came and saw Mariwota of Utanilagi's women.

He is giving this *navago* to you, and says, 'Have your people eat it and then keep watch for those thirty men. When [the Makurans] come [back], have [your people] kill them for [me].'"

So even as the [Makurans] were still on their way [to Siviri], the *navago* had already reached the shore.

When they came [back], the Tikilasoa people—that is, [Mariwota's] *ṁaau*—were already on the lookout for them.

They arrived.

[Then] the [Tikilasoans] gave them some information to mislead them— that there might be bad weather [3].

And, [meanwhile, the Tikilasoans] readied all their equipment—all their weapons.

When they were all ready, had prepared all their weapons, they conferred with each other, "Once we're a little ways out from the beach, we'll attack them." Then one of them got a shell-trumpet and took up a position up on shore.

He remained there, while the others [paddled] off until they were well offshore.

Then the shell-trumpet sounded.

As it sounded, they started the attack.

The two [*ṁaau*] took up the paddles they had been using. For the **Makurans** weren't paddling; **rather** it was the two *ṁaau* from Taloa[4] who were doing the paddling.

They paddled, with the one fore and the other aft.

So when the shell-trumpet wailed the one in the bow struck out and [simultaneously] the one astern struck out. They slew the thirty men, **all** of them.

The entire group was dead.

Then [all of the warriors] brought [the bodies] ashore.

Some retrieved them from their canoes, swimming out, then pushing the canoes ashore, while others swam out and speared those that were floating out to sea.

They went on bringing them ashore, until finally it was all done.

[Then one of the Tikilasoa] *ṁaau* ran to Taava [village] to tell Mariatugia, saying, "We've killed the people you handed over to us—every last one."

But [part of] the message Mariwota had given along with the *navago* was, "Once you've killed them, you are to dig [the] **hard** [type of] yam for me, **only** hard yams, thirty bunches [of them]. It's to be the equivalent of thirty men."

The yams, the request for the yams, was fulfilled.

They dug **thirty** bunches of **only** hard yams, then tied them into bundles just as the dead men were tied and trussed together in bundles.

Then [the bodies] were carried up to Komaliᵽokasi.

They carried them up to Komaliᵽokasi, where the yams had already been laid out [on the ground] to be divided into [separate] piles for [each of] the destinations that would be announced.

They took the thirty men and began placing them on the existing piles, until it was complete, until everything had been properly apportioned.

Mariwota [of Tikilasoa], along with some of his people, came for [the ceremony].

Once they had witnessed [the division of what was to be distributed], they danced.

The peace ceremony for the other [Mariwota, of Utanilagi] was complete. They danced and danced... and when they were done, the distribution took place.

Mariwota [of Tikilasoa] already knew which pile was his [5].

But it was only when they had **finished** calling out the villages [one by one], only after they had **finished** going through all the [names of the various] meeting-houses, that they made the presentation to Mariwota.

Then,

after more dancing, everyone loaded up [what they had been given] and returned to their own villages.

And that is the end of the discussion of this [event].

Footnotes

1. A euphemism for having sexual relations.
2. A large variety of sweet potato.
3. The false warning of coming stormy weather was a means of ensuring that the Makurans would delay their departure long enough to give the Tikilasoa warriors time to prepare their weapons and plan of attack, and to lure the Makurans into accepting help in getting their canoes out to sea through the reef passage—to make them believe that they needed navigational pilots for safety's sake. The seemingly friendly offer was a ploy to get the doomed men out in deep water with two of Nguna's expert killers, the *m̃aau*.
4. Another name for Tikilasoa village.
5. Mariwota of Tikilasoa was able to recognize his own food-gifts because they constituted the largest pile and/or that with the choicest pieces of the slain men (their heads). Having accepted the *navago*, thereby assuming the burden of avenging the offence against Mariwota of Utanilagi, it would be Mariwota of Tikilasoa's right to receive these honours.

(Reference: Ronneth-2. May 5, 1978, Mere. Tape 4B, 38-46.)

Text No.21:

"Mariori goo Masiloa"
pae
Ronneth Manutukituki

Stori waina a ga noa e ragi waia,
e pei stori ni nawota duua. Nawota duua sikai
ero mari nawosiana sikai maau waina Roimata ma Roimuru naara ero
   moro mari a.
Nagisa ni nawota duua waina a ga atuusi ra e pei
Mariori
goo **Masiloa**.
Tuai navakalo e doko usuraki navanua maaga ni Nguna goo ni Efate.
Ero punusi naga naatam̃ooli maaga eu doo dum̃ada p̃okati ra goo eu doo
   dum̃ada **gani** ra.
Goo ragi waina ero doo midodoa asa naga, "Tu ga mari e ga **tapal**[a] **esava**
   naga navakalo waia e ga vei tea maripunueana?"
Ero doo pusum̃aki paa[paa] ero poo midoaki nia naga, "Toro ga pitautau
   naatam̃ooli maaga naga eu ga woo umai paki naleoana sikai nalo ni
   navakalo wanogoe waina e doko usuraki navanua tuai."
Ragi waina ero doko paapaa ero pitautau sara naatam̃ooli pae sara
   natokoana ni navanua ni Efate goo paki Nguna, goo natokoana maaga
   goo naure kiiki.
Ero pitautau naatam̃ooli maaga eu ga rumai poo noa kii da asa naga, "E
   pei m̃oogi **larua,** aro ga woo mari naleoana sikai goo aro masau naga
   waina ku ga umai ku ga tape **sara** navatuuna maaga mamauputi
   waina eu doko navanua, goo doko natas[i]."
Goo waina eu rumai, eu doko paapaa naga e pei natuuta eu rumai.
Eu rumai eu dape **sara** naleo maaga. Seara [eu] dape vaatu,
goo seara dape napetau.

Seara dape nawii, seara dape noopa,
seara dape natale, seara dape naadi.
Waina eu rumai eu pei naatamõoli eu **laapa**. Eu rumai, eu dape dogo puti
    sara naleo maaga wanogoe—
karau, goo naika.
Waina eu dape ra umai, eu rumai paapaa naga ero soso ra naga eu saisai
    ki sara naleo maaga.
Goo ero punusi naga sara naatamõoli maaga mamauputi waina eu
    rumai eu dape puti sara naleo **mamauputi**.
Goo ragi waina eu rumai saisai ki nia tea waina e dape naika, goo tanari
    sikai e dape naika, naara tero pei nakainaga sikai maau. Wanogoe e
    atulake pae nakainaga.
Goo tea waina e dape vaatu, goo tanari sikai e moro doropusi vaatu, goo
    e naga, "Nimu koro pei nakainaga sikai maau."
Goo sikai e moro umai, e doropusi wiita, tanari sikai e umai doropusi
    wiita, goo [e naga], "Nimu koro pei nakainaga sikai maau."
Ragi waina eu doo saisai ki sara navatuuna maaga wanogoe paa[paa] e
    noopu, goo e naga, "Tea maaga waia teu pei nakainaga animu maaga.
Goo ku ga woo daa moro dumãamu marisaa ki mu, goo ku ga woo daa moro
    dumãamu atugi mu.
Ragi waia ku pei tamataida maaga goo ku pei nakainaga maaga sikai
    maau. Ku ga woo daa moro dumãamu marisaa ki mu."
Naara
ragi wanogoe
ero midoaki nia ero marimatua ki navakalo waina e doko **tuai** waina eu
    doo dumãada marisaa kii da doko dumãada p̃okati ra doko doo dumãada
    gani ra.
Goo natamãte e doko. Natamãte e doko doko doko paapaaaa...
paki ragi seara.
Wanogoe stori e noopu.

"Mariori and Masiloa"
by
Ronneth Manutukituki

The story I'm going to tell now,
is the story of two chiefs. [These] two chiefs
performed the same task as Roimata and Roimuru did[1].
The names of the two chiefs of whom I shall tell are
Mariori
aand **Masiloa**.
Long ago there was war throughout the lands of Nguna and Efate.
The two [chiefs] saw that people were killing and **eating** each other.
They worried about it: "**What** can we do to wipe out this warfare?"
They discussed it and decided, "We shall invite the people to come to a
　　feast to deal with the warring that has been [going on] throughout the
　　land for so long."
So in time they invited everyone from all the villages of Efate, including
　　Nguna and the small island [P̃ele].
They asked them to come, telling them, "**Seven** days from now, we will
　　hold a feast and we want you to come and bring **everything** that exists
　　both on the land, and in the sea."
So they went [back home] and waited until the appointed day; and then
　　they arrived.
They came bringing things of **all** kinds. Some brought stones,
and some brought breadfruit.
Some brought yams, some brought native cabbage,
some brought taro, some brought bananas.
When they all assembled there were a great **many** people. They came,
　　bearing every possible kind of thing–

clams, and fish.

They kept coming and coming... until finally the two [chiefs] called out for them to pool everything.

Then the two [chiefs] saw that all the people assembled had brought every possible thing.

When they came forward to pool them if someone brought fish, and a friend of his brought fish, the two of them became [members of] a single matriclan. That was the beginning of clans.

And [to] the one who brought a stone, and a friend of his who also brought a stone, [one of the chiefs] said, "You two are [of] the same clan."

And another came, and presented an octopus, and a friend of his came and presented an octopus, so [the chief] said, "You two are [of] the same clan."

When they had finally finished pooling everything, he said, "These are your clans.

[As clanmates] you are not to harm each other, or to kill each other anymore.

You are now brothers, you are [members of] the same clan. You must not harm each other anymore."

[The two chiefs]

at that point

felt that they had vanquished the warring that had been going on so long in which [people] used to harm each other and kill each other and eat each other.

So there was peace. Peace lasted and lasted and laaasted...

for a considerable time.

That's the end of the story.

Footnotes

1. See Kaltaβau M̃asemata's text #9 in this volume.

(Reference: Ronneth-3. June 29, 1978, Tikilasoa. Tape 9A, 0-4.)

Text No.22:

"Navakalo ni 1874"
pae
Ronneth Manutukituki

Navakalo sikai e moro atulake 1874.

Navakalo wanogoe e doko ragi waina miisi **matua** aginami, Mr. Peter Milne, te doko sua navanua.

Goo navakalo **warua** sikai e moro pakiliina.

Navakalo wanogoe e pakiliina pae naatañooli sikai
e mari nasorosoroana sikai!

E mari nasorosoroana sikai—mariki sikai e piragi nagoroi sikai, e piragi nagoroi wanogoe nagisana Leisoogi.

Goo Leisoogi wanogoe e pei Mariwoota Tikilasoa, **gorena.**

E piragi a.

Goo mariki wanogoe waina e piragi Leisoogi wanogoe nagisana e pei **Mantaura.**

Mantaura wanogoe e pei tea ni **Sauwia.**

E doko napapitaata ni Ñatoa goo Meere—natokoana aneana e pei **Sauwia.**

Mariki sikai nagisana e pei **Maanearu,** Maanearusoogi.

E pano doko poo madoko punusi vitariki wanogoe nagisana Leisoogi waina Mantaura e piragi a, madoko **soro** e,
doko masau mari naga e ga moro piragi lua nagoroi aneana.

Paapaa ero pusuñaki paapaa nagoroi wanogoe e suasua,
e naga, "**Matamai,**
a ga woo moro umai punusi ko.

Waina mariki e ga vaki nalalawoana aneana a ga woo moro umai punusi ko.

Goo a ga tape **suisui** poo pa **sui** a!"

Mantaura wanogoe te paki roara aneana, poo madoko lalawo.

E madoko lalawo paapaaa

mariki Maanearusoogi e pano, e dape suisui,

doko laaga asa. E pano paapaa paki naɓoro ni napatiira sikai, taava,

taava waina e duu Unakapu paki elagi.

E pano paapaa mariki wanogoe e lalawo paapaa e noopu, e dape naɓarae
    doko pa munugi a napatiira, doko malo saa.

E munugi a, mariki e sai pano paapaa paki lolua aneana pano.

E leo doko punusi mariki e doo pagi nakau kiiki sikai e doko pisari erasa.

E dape suisui doko sui a!

Ragi waina e sui a, mariki wanogoe te dowo paki malo saa, doko pa
    magona doko nakau sikai.

Nae e liliu,

Maanearusoogi e liliu, doko dape suisui paapaaaa doko pa moro pa sike
    a doko nasuma ki mariki ɓota sikai.

E mari a e pei nasorosoroana,

naga waina eu pe laaga asa, eu pe vaɓai mariki wanogoe, teu ga noa naga
    mariki wanogoe nae e sui a.

Maa, e pei Maanearusoogi nae e sui a te mari nasorosoroana wanogoe.

E doko asa doko moro dape

loriki sikai eu soso e ki navago.

Te ga va pitua ki navago kakana naga eu ga woo pa mari navakalo paki
    tea ni Tikilasoa,

naga naka ni Tikilasoa naara eu sui Mantaura.

E dape navago wanogoe; navago wanogoe e pei navinaga saa.

E dape a doko pa dua naatamooli sikai eu soso e ki

Matooa, Matooataapunu.

E dape navago wanogoe pa dua e asa, goo nae e moro dape a doko pa laaga
    naatamooli ɓota duua waina naara eu ga woo mari soogi, eu ga woo
    sava paki sara tokora maaga naga naara eu ga woo mari navakalo
    paki tea ni Tikilasoa.

Navasaana kakana e sava, mariki wanogoe e pitua ki navasaana kakana
    e sava paapaaa, paapaa liliu, Utanilagi.

E doko usuraki Nguna,

navakalo wanogoe.

Tea ni euta maaga pae Malaliu doko pano paapaa liliu Utanilagi.

Sara natokoana mamauputi ni euta eu maridiɓa naka ni Tikilasoa.

Ragi waina eu rumai,

eu parakii da ɓoogi, eu maturu goro ra.

Eu doko paapaa naga tooa e daare

goo teu atulake suisui paki natokoana!

Eu suisui paki natokoana,

tea ni Tikilasoa, eu doko noa naga, "O, navakalo te pakiliina!

Ragi waia, Leisoogi waina e mate teu noa naga nigida tu maripunue a.

Tu ga atulake laaga napua anigida."
Eu doko musamusa paki P̃eele!
Seara eu pa sili sum̃a ki miisi!
Tea laapa eu pa!
Ragi waina eu pa suisui dapala nogoe, maa nawota e noa kii da asa naga,
     "Ragi waina ku pe woo pa mari navakalo, ku pe woo suisui maa, ku ga
     leoparaati m̃ata ki varea,
varea nalolu ni nawota e doko asa.
E pei ku ga taa dokoni a!"
Ragi waina eu paki natokoana, eu suisui, naatam̃ooli maaga mamauputi
     ni Tikilasoa seara eu sava paki P̃eele goo seara eu pa sili sum̃a ki miisi!
Naatam̃ooli **rualimaduua** eu sili sum̃a ki miisi, maa tea mamauputi ni
     Tikilasoa eu pano puti paki P̃eele.
Eu suisui pano pano paapaa tokora e poo marama p̃ia eu paki natokoana
     eu dokoni nasum̃a **maaga**, eu maripunue **waago**, eu p̃okati **tooa**, eu
     marisasaa ki sara naleo adeada [maaga] paapaa e diika.
Maa varea sikai maau saa te doko.
Teu liliu.
Ragi waina eu liliu,
eu moro liliu paki natokoana adeada maaga.
Doko paaa naka ni Tikilasoa eu rumai,
pae P̃eele umai, paki natokoana, tokora e malaadi.
Natokoana, nasum̃a adeada, teu **sooro** puti.
Eu doo midoaki nia naga eu ga mari e ga **tapal[a] esava**
naga eu ga vap̃ai navakalo waina e pakiliina natokoana adeada.
Eu laaga,
paapaa doko naga, "E, tu ga vitautau munuai sikai pae **Leleppa**."
Paapaa eu pa vuati munuai sikai pae Leleppa.
Munuai wanogoe nagisana e pei **Munuaikoriia**.
Munuaikoriia e m̃elu Leleppa doko umai paapaa paki naure kiiki, P̃eele.
Ragi waina e umai paki P̃eele,
e pitautau tea ni Tikilasoa maaga umai naga, "Ku pitautau au umai naga
     a ga manimu lop̃ai navakalo waia e dapala esava.
Io, a laelae a. A ga woo manimu mari a.
A ga woo laaga asa."
E noa kii da asa naga, "Ku ga maginau p̃okati waago eu ga latolu. Ku ga
     tua au waago latolu."
Ragi waina eu dua e waago latolu, te poo surata pae waago wanogoe, e
     laaga takana waina navakalo wanogoe e pakiliina,
seei e pei nalakena navakalo wanogoe e pakiliina.
Pae asa e surata pano paapaaaa
doko paki Unakap[u], e doko Unakap[u] doko paki Meere.
Ragi waina e paki **Meere**,
doko moro liliu.

E moro liliu umai paapaa paki P̃eele.
Doko noa naga, "Io.
Ta poo pap̃ai navakalo waina.
Navakalo waina e daa pei navakalo sikai waina e pae **malo** p̃ota,
maaa,
nagoroi sikai
e laki paki Meere.
Nagoroi wanogoe e pei nagoroi ni Tikilasoa, agi **mariki** [na]wota.
E mari navakalo waina.
Nae e naga e ga viragi nagoroi ki mariki Mantaura.
E pei nalakena e sui a, doko puati anagoroi,
te poo puati nagoroi wanogoe."
Ragi waina e noa sua navasaana wanogoe te poo daap̃otae waago
     wanogoe,
waago latolu wanogoe.
E dua ra
e **latesa**.
E dua naka ni Tikilasoa goo P̃eele waago latesa, maa nae te peani duua.
Doko moro liliu paki Leleppa.
Te puati waago aneana [maaga] duagoto liliu paki naure aneana,
     Leleppa.
Wanogoe e moro pei namatap̃ago ni stori aginau waina a doo atuusi a
     nalo ni navakalo,
takana waina navakalo e moro pakiliina 1874.

"The War of 1874"
by
Ronneth Manutukituki

Yet another war occurred in 1874.
The attack took place after our former missionary, Mr. Peter Milne, was
    already on Nguna.
And a **huge** war broke out.
This war was caused by a [certain] person
using trickery!
He used trickery—there was a fellow who married a [certain] woman, he
    married a woman named **Leisoogi**.
And Leisoogi was [chief] Mariwoota of Tikilasoa's **sister**.
He married her.
And this fellow who married Leisoogi was named **Mantaura**.
Mantaura was from **Sauwia**.
It lay between M̃atoa and Meere—his village was **Sauwia**.
[There was] another fellow named **Maanearu**, Maanearusoogi.
He started going to "see" this [married] woman, Leisoogi, Mantaura's
    wife, and **tempting** her,
as he wanted to lure [Mantaura's] wife away.
They talked it over again and again until... finally she consented,
[and] he said, "**Tomorrow**,
I'll come to see you again.
When your husband has gone to do his planting, I'll come to you.
And I'll bring a **gun** and **shoot** him!"
Mantaura went off to his garden, and started planting.
He was still planting wheeen
Maanearusoogi started out, taking his gun,

214

looking for him. He kept going until he reached the edge of a certain cliff, a hill,

the hill that overlooks Unakapu.

As he moved along, the other man, having finally finished planting, got some sugarcane and went off to chew it at the cliff's edge, a [*falling, breathy tone*] **dangerous** spot.

As he chewed, the man tracking him finally reached his garden.

The latter, [Maanearusoogi], looked around and spotted the old fellow just as he was climbing up into a small tree at the edge of the cliff.

He grasped the gun and shot him!

Having been shot, [Mantaura] tumbled down into a precarious spot, and [his body] lay jammed against a tree.

The other went back,

Maanearusoogi went back, taking the gun untiiil he came to **another** [a Tikilasoa] man's house and he left it inside.

He did it to fool them,

so that when they went looking for the old man, and found him, they would [then find the gun there and] think that **he** was the one who shot him.

But [in fact] it was Maanearusoogi who shot him then pulled this trick.

Having done this he went further and got

a [certain] thing called **navago**.

He used *navago* for this so that [Mantaura's group] would launch an attack on the people of Tikilasoa,

thinking that it was the Tikilasoa people who shot Mantaura.

He took the *navago*, *navago* being [a] **bad** [kind of] food[1].

He went to give the *navago* to a man called

Matooa, Matooataapunu.

He gave the *navago* to him, and the latter in turn took it and sought out two other people who would arrange for vengeance, running to each place to get them to launch the attack on the people of Tikilasoa.

The news began to travel, [Maanearusoogi] sent out word and it travelled along [from village to village] until it finally finished up, [at the furthest reaches of the island], in **Utanilagi**.

It involved the whole of Nguna,

that attack.

[All] the inland peoples, from M̃alaliu all the way over to Utanilagi.

Every last one of the inland villages set upon the people of Tikilasoa.

They assembled,

and went after them by **night**, sleeping surrounding [Tikilasoa].

They waited until at last the cocks crew

and they started firing toward the village!

When the firing on the village started,

the people of Tikilasoa cried, "Oh, it's war!

Leisoogi must be dead and they think we murdered her[2].
We have to find a way out of here."
Some piled into canoes and fled across to Ƥeele!
Others took shelter with the **missionary**!
Everybody fled!
When the shooting had started, the [inland peoples'] leader had said [to
    his warriors], "When you attack, go ahead and shoot, but watch out for
    the meeting-house,
the meeting-house is where the chiefs' hair are kept.
You must not burn it!" [3]
When they entered the village, firing their guns, all the Tikilasoa people
    had already either fled to Ƥeele or hidden in the missionary's house!
Twenty people were hiding in the missionary's house, and all the rest
    had gone to Ƥeele.
They kept firing on and on and on and once it was fully light they entered
    the village, they burned down the **houses**, killed the **pigs**, killed the
    chickens, destroyed all of their belongings, until there was absolutely
    nothing left.
The meeting-house was the one and only thing remaining.
They left.
They left,
and returned to their own villages.
When some time later the Tikilasoa people came back,
returned from Ƥeele, to the village, the place was devoid of life.
The village, their homes, everything had **gone up** in flames.
They tried to think of **some** way
of finding out why the attack had been made on their village.
They searched and searched [for a way],
and finally decided, "Alright, we'll call out a diviner from **Leleppa**."
After a time they secured a Leleppa diviner.
The diviner's name was **Munuaikoriia**.
Munuaikoriia left Leleppa and travelled along until he got to the small
    island, Ƥeele.
Having arrived in Ƥeele,
he invited the Tikilasoa people to come, "You asked me to come and
    divine the cause of this attack.
Certainly, I'll be happy to. I'll do it for you.
I'll search out [the cause]."
He told them, "You are to kill eight pigs for me. Give me eight pigs."
Once they had given him the eight pigs, in return for them, he began
    travelling, searching for why the attack had taken place, [for]
who was the reason why the attack had occurred.
In order to do that he walked and walked until eventually
he reached Unakap[u], he stopped in Unakap[u] then went on to Meere.

Once he'd been to [*rising tone*] **Meere,**
he [*falling tone*] returned.
He came back again to P̌eele.
And said, "Alright.
I've found out about the attack.
It's not a war that originated **elsewhere,**
raaather,
[with] a woman
who married into Meere.
That woman is a Tikilasoa woman, related to the **chief.**
She caused the attack.
[**Another** person] wanted to take away old Mantaura's wife.
That's why he shot him, then took away his wife,
took away that woman."
Having uttered that message [the diviner] divided up the pigs, the eight
    pigs.
He gave them
six.
He gave the Tikilasoa and P̌eele people six pigs, and kept two for himself.
Then he went back to Leleppa.
Taking the pigs he made the return crossing to his island, Leleppa.
That's the end of my account of the attack[4],
of how war broke out once more in 1874.

Footnotes

1. *Navago* is "bad food" indeed, being a concoction prepared by mixing
   breadfruit with faeces. For a comparative example of the context of
   its use, see Ronneth Manutukituki's text #20 in this volume.
2. The reader may be tempted to think that this *ought* to be "...Leisoogi's
   husband is dead..." rather than "... Leisoogi's dead..."; but, this
   statement only *appears* to be an error in narrative performance. It
   is, rather, an instance of dramatic irony. While the reader, along with
   the inland peoples, know that it is Leisoogi's husband who is dead, not
   Leisoogi herself, the Tikilasoa people have yet to discover the truth of
   the matter. This statement implies that, on seeing that they are under
   attack by the inland peoples, the Tikilasoans assume (1) that their
   former village member, Mariwoota's sister, Leisoogi, is dead, (2) that
   therefore they and/or their chief are under suspicion of having killed
   her by sorcery, and (3) that it is as a result of this that they find
   themselves under seige.
3. Such relics were traditionally held to be possessed of a most dangerous
   power. It is clear that, even though they have no compunction
   regarding laying waste to the rest of the village, the relics of hair kept

in that building are so powerful that the attackers daren't harm them lest the entire spiritual assembly of past Tikilasoa chiefs attack them in turn.

4. Some interesting comparisons might be made between this account and the one by Peter Milne which is found in Don's biography, *Peter Milne of Nguna* (158-60). Though he places it in 1877 rather than '74, and his account differs in numerous other details from Manutukituki's, it is quite clearly the same incident.

(Reference: Ronneth-4. June 29, 1978, Tikilasoa. Tape 9A, 4-30.)

Text No.23:

"Seiseinai goo Aisei"
pae
Thomas Tavirana

Naataṁooli sikai
ni **Forari**, naara maa anagoroi ero doko **Forari**.
Naaleatia sikai
ero doko maa nagoroi aneana kanao wanogoe nagisana **Aisei**.
Nagoroi aneana nagisana e pei **Seiseinai**.
E noa ki anagoroi,
Seiseinai, e naga, "P̃a doko
aleati waia, maa **kinau**, a ga ko pa dipe **navakalo**.
P̃a doo pau aleati, maa a ga va dipe.
Waina ku pe vunusi
manu sikai, e pei diri duagoto naraeṁa, manu wanogoe e pei manukav-
    ina.
Ti p̃a atae naga teu dipe au navakalo.
Maa waina ku pe taa punusi navaivaiana sikai,
io! eu daa dipe au. A ga woo moro liliu umai."
Ragi waina anagoroi e dogo sua e, e doo doko raki nia.
Maa e pano paapaaa goo teu dipe a.
Eu dipe a ki natip̃a, natip̃a namateana.
Te mate madoko.
Maa **naatana**, e poo moro liliu umai. E dape naasu goo nalua aneana.
Ragi waina Seiseinai anagoroi e punusi a, e pa naga e ga kisi p̃ai a.
Goo te noa ki nia, Aisei anawoota, e noa ki nia,
"Eee! P̃a taa kisi dogo au.
Kinau ta panop̃ota.
P̃a doko, maa ta ga vano."

E dape naasu goo nalua natip̃a aneana doko siwo paki elau.

Elau, e pei nagisu sikai, eu soso e ki nagisu ni **Maniura**.

Ragi waina e lawo siwo paki elau,

e punusi naika seara eu doo ganikani.

Goo naika maaga wanogoe eu pei **malakesa**.

E dipe tea warua sikai, doko puati a, doko nadi ki nia paki euta.

E noa ki Seiseinai, "P̃a vuati a paki sum̃a ni kiagida, poo pa dao nia maa
    kinau ta ga vano."

E pasadara anawoota e naga, "Eee!

A masau naga a ga tausi ko paki tokora waina p̃a vaki asa."

Te poo dausi a, ero **doo** siwo, ero umai paapaa ero umai paki elau ni Eton,
    nagisu kakana.

Goo te moro dipe naika wanogoe sikai, **malakesa**.

E moro nadi ki nia dua e asa, "P̃a vuati a paki sum̃a ni kiagida poo pa dao
    nia poo gani a, maa kinau ta ga vano."

"Eee! A daa masau na, a masau dausi ko paki tokora waina p̃a vaki asa."
Ero **moro** siwo.

Ero umai paapaaa, ero umai paki **Eratap**, nagisu kakana sikai.

Naika wanogoe eu moro doo ganikani goo e moro dipe sikai.

E puati a doko moro nadi ki nia dua Seiseinai asa waina e pei anagoroi,
    "P̃a vuati a pano paki sum̃a pano poo mari a, poo gani a, maa kinau ta
    ga vano."

E karae.

E moro dausi a, ero siwo umai paapaa, ero umai paki
Erakor, nagisu kakana sikai.

E moro puati naika wanogoe eu moro doo ganikani, malakesa.

E moro dipe sikai.

E moro nadi ki nia dua anagoroi asa, "P̃a vuati a paki sum̃a ni kiagida
    pano poo dao nia, poo gani a."

Maa e karae.

E moro dausi a ero siwo umai paapaa, ero umai paki nagisu sikai ni P̃ago.

Goo e moro dipe sikai, e nadi ki nia dua anagoroi asa e ga vuati a liliu poo
    pa **dao** nia,

poo madoo gani a, maa e karae, e moro **dausi** a.

Ero umai paapaa ero umai paki Viila.

Doko nagisu kakana sikai, e moro dipe naika wanogoe sikai, e puati a, e
    nadi ki nia dua anagoroi asa, maa anagoroi e karae, dape a.

E moro dausi a.

Ero siwo umai paapaa ero umai paki M̃eele doko nagisu kakana sikai.

E moro dipe naika wanogoe sikai e moro nadi ki nia dua anagoroi asa,
    naga e ga vuati a pano poo pa mari a e ga maaso, poo gani a.

Maa anagoroi e karae.

"Eee! Maa a masau dausi ko paki tokora waina p̃a vaki asa. Toro ga ruua
    paki asa pano."

Ero umai, ero umai paapaa paki nagisu waina eu soso e ki nagisu ni
Tip̃iniu–"*Devil's Point*".

E moro dipe sikai poo dua e asa, maa e karae.

Ero moro siwo umai paki nagisu **kerua** kakana waina eu soso e ki nagisu
ni **Leimaea**.

E moro dipe sikai e dua e asa, maa e karae puati a.

"Eee! Tokora waina p̃a vaki asa pano a masau dausi ko paki asa."

Ero duua siwo umai paapaa, ero umai paki nagisu ni **Tukituki**.

Tukituki wanogoe, e peani natoto sikai e p̃ora doko vaatu, doko nagisu e
sai ki araana e dau natasi tau.

Naata ni Aisei e dausi araa ni natoto wanogoe paapaa e pa maduu
namatap̃agona, te **dam̃alua**.

Goo vaatu sikai te duleana,

vaatu wanogoe nagisana **Tavitokai**.

E lawo duu asa, e doko raki natavara waina e ga **woo** umai.

Goo natavara kerua e moro umai.

Natavara **kerua** umai, e moro kiiki.

Kedoolu, kevaati, kelima, paki kelatesa, e puka paapa tepa ni venive e
pei valea dau goo e duu araa ni natoto doko **dam̃alua**, paki vuuka
wanogoe waina e doo ni venive.

Ragi wanogoe, te pano.

Eu noa naga te paki navanua p̃ota.

E paki navanua wanogoe eu naga, e paki **P̃okasi**.

Te paki **P̃okasi** pano.

Nagisa wanogoe, **P̃okasi**, e dakiusi e peani nap̃okasi doko asa dapala
maramana anigida **waia**.

Sara navinaga [eu] doko a[s]a–naadi, nawii, sara naleo.

E doko asa naaleatia **liima**.

E doko raki

natano, te ga tap̃olaga.

E mawora, kite e maaga.

Goo ragi wanogoe, te diro paki natano wanogoe.

Goo ragi waina e pano, teu daa atae tokora waina te paki asa pano.

Maa te paki **Maagaseasea**.

Maagaseasea wanogoe, nanoaana ni **seasea**, dapala waina nam̃enau e
doo sooka, goo te **seagoro** natano wanogoe waina e **maaga**.

Goo te noopu, namidoakiparaatikiana ni tea mate adeada, te noopu.

Nae nogo, e liliu tokora wanogoe.

Thank you!

"Seiseinai and Aisei"
by
Thomas Tavirana

A person
from **Forari**, he and his wife lived in **Forari**.
One day
there they were—the man's name was **Aisei**.
His wife's name was **Seiseinai**.
He said to his wife,
Seiseinai, "You stay [home]
this morning, but I, I'm going to fight in the **war**.
You stay home and weave [this] morning, while I go to fight.
But if you should see
a **bird**, if it flies past you, it will be a dove.
Then you'll know that they've shot me in the war.
But if you don't see a sign,
it's alright! they haven't shot me. I'll be coming back."
When his wife had heard that, she waited for him.
And he left... until... they did shoot him.
They shot him with a poison arrow, the death arrow.
He lay dead there.
But his **spirit**, came back again[1]. It was carrying his bow and arrow.
When his wife Seiseinai saw it, she went to touch him.
And [the spirit of] her husband, Aisei, said to her,
"No! Don't touch me.
I've **changed**.
You stay [here], but I'm going."
He took his bow and poison arrows and went down to the shore.
At the shore, there was a point, they call Point **Maniura**.

When he went down and stood on the beach,
he spotted some fish that were feeding.
They were **bluefish**.
He shot a big one, pulled it in, and threw it up on shore.
He said to Seiseinai, "Take it home, and bake it, but I'm going."
She answered her husband, "No!
I want to go with you wherever you're going."
She went after him, and they went on down, until they came to Eton
   beach, to the point there.
And again he shot one of those fish, a **bluefish**.
Again he gave it to her, "Take it home and bake and eat it, but I'm going."
"No! I don't want to. I want to go with you wherever you're going."
They **continued** on down.
They went along until, they reached **Eratap**, one of points there.
The same fish were feeding so once again he shot one.
He pulled it in and threw it to Seiseinai his wife, "Take it home and
   prepare it, and eat it, but I'm going."
She refused.
She kept following him, as they went on down until, they reached
Erakor, a point there.
He caught another one of the fish that were feeding, bluefish.
He shot another.
He again threw it to his wife, "Take it home and bake it, and eat it."
But she refused.
She following him they continued down, until they came to a point at
   P̃ago.
And once again he shot one, threw it to his wife for her to take it back and
   bake it,
and stay there and eat it, but she refused, and kept **following** him.
They came along until they reached Viila.
On one of its points, he shot another of those fish, pulled it out, and threw
   it to his wife, but she refused, to take it.
She kept following him.
They continued down until they reached M̃eele a point there.
He shot another of those fish and threw it to his wife, for her to take it and
   go and cook it, and eat it.
But his wife refused.
"No! I want to go with you wherever you're going. We'll go there
   together."
They came on, until they reached the point called Tip̃iniu–"Devil's
   Point".
He shot another and gave it to her, but she refused.
They continued on down to the **next** point there called Point **Leimaea**.
He shot another and gave it to her, but she refused to take it.

"No! Wherever you're going I want to go there with you."

The two of them continued on down, until they reached point **Tukituki**.

This **Tukituki**, has a *natoto* tree growing out of the rocks, whose branches
    jut out from the point [and] overhang the deep sea.

The **spirit** of Aisei went out along the branch of the *natoto* until he stood
    at the end, then he **jumped**.

And there is a rock sticking up,

a rock named **Tavitokai**.

He stood up on it, waiting for the waves to **come**.

And the next wave came.

A **second** wave came, but it was too small.

And [likewise] a **third**, a **fourth**, a **fifth**, until the sixth, and as it crested
    about to break, it opened up like a cave [and] he stood on the branch of
    the *natoto* and **leaped**, into the wave just as it was breaking.

At that point, he was gone.

They say that he went to another land.

They say that he went to the land, of Ƥokasi.

He has gone to Ƥokasi.

This name, **Ƥokasi**, it means that there is meat there just as in our world
    here.

Every kind of food is there—bananas, yams, everything.

He stayed there for **five** days.

He waited for

the **ground**, to open.

It would split, or gape open.

And then, he fell down into the ground.

And once he was **gone**, they had no idea where he went.

But he went to **Maagaseasea**.

Maagaseasea—*seasea* means when grass takes hold, and **grows over** the
    ground where it has **opened**.

So **that's** all, they² have no further knowledge of their dead, **that's** it.

There, that's the end.

Thank you!

Footnotes

1. Though not explicitly stated, this implies that Seiseinai sees the dove
   and recognizes it as the sign foretold.
2. "They" refers here moreso to the pre-Christian indigenous population
   than to the indefinite contemporary "they/one". The narrator, a
   staunch Presbyterian, is relating a set of notions about the after-life
   that he certainly does not hold nor, probably, does anyone else in the
   Efate area.

(Reference: Tavirana-1. March 26, 1978, Tiki. Tape 2A, 52-70 & B, 0-3.)

Text No.24:

"Tamataida Rualimasikai goo Rovemao"
pae
Jack Taviṁasoe

A masau atuusi nalo ni tamataida rualimasikai maau [goo] nagoroi sikai
nagisana [e pei] Rovemao.

Tamataida rualimasikai wanogoe eu doko P̃agona.

Goo nagoroi wanogoe e doko Vetenirana.

Tamataida maaga wanogoe eu doo punusi naga sara malip̃oogi e doo
loloso goo e duṁana pagarae a doko naworaone.

Sara malip̃oogi ni sara naaleatia e doo mari dapala nogoe.

Goo tamataida rualimasikai wanogoe takalapa kakada, e naga,

"E p̃ia naga sikai kakagida e pe viragi nagoroi waina e pe wia naga e ga
too manigida mari navinaga."

Naaleatia sikai takalapa ni tamataida maaga wanogoe e noa ki taina
maaga, e naga, "Matamai, tu ga maginau lawo roara aginau."

Goo taina maaga, eu naga, "Io! E p̃ia."

Matamai kakana

e p̃okati waago.

E pei mat100aloa.

Napatina e puri [sasama] paka ruua.

Goo e mari navinaga.

E madeada dao ni waago, goo nawii.

E dape naruna goo e sai ki rarua aneana, poo doropusi nap̃okasi ni waago
paki asa goo e atulake poo paluse.

Goo taina maaga eu doo lalawo roara aneana.

Maa e paluse e atulake poo lega, e naga:

"Rovemao, Rovemao, Rove.

Rovemao, ku one rekei.

Rovemao, ku one rekei.
Rekei sili diele ka ta mai.
Rekei sili diele goro e."
E noopu goo te paluse.
E paluse paapaa goo te moro lega:
"Rovemao, Rovemao, Rove.
Rovemao, ku one rekei.
Rovemao, ku one rekei.
Rekei sili diele ka ta mai.
Rekei sili diele goro e."
Goo e pasa paki nagoroi waina e paki m̃aladigi ki euta:
"Pule toko kite pule vano?"
Goo Rovemao e naga, "Pule toko."
"Pule toko?"
E naga, "A ga toko."
Goo te moro liliu.
E **daa** suasua. 'Pule toko' e naga e **daa** suasua.
Goo te moro paluse liliu.
Goo taina maaga eu punusi naga e pano m̃ooli.
Matamai ki nia, goo taina takarausia e naga,
"Matamai, tu ga maginau lalawo roara aginau."
Goo taina maaga eu naga, "Io! E p̃ia."
Matamai ki nia, e moro p̃okati waago, goo madeada mari dao nia pilake
    nawii.
E dape naru ni waago goo e moro paluse.
E doko nam̃ooso goo e moro lega: "Rovemao."
[E moro lega nalegaana sikai maau waina taina takalapa adeada e peea
    lega sua asa.]
Goo e doo dapala nogoe paapaaa
taina maaga eu lofeti.
Maa **sikai** e pei **takariki**.
Goo e noa ki taina maaga, e naga, "Tu ga maginau lalawo."
Goo taina maaga eu naga, "Ee! Niigo ku kiiki. Ku daa peani navinaga."
E noa kii da, e naga, "Io! Maa a peani nawii kiiki piisa."
Goo eu naga, "Ku daa peani waago."
Goo, "A peani waago kiiki."
Goo e noa ki taina maaga, "E p̃ia tu ga maginau lalawo."
Goo ragi waina matamai ki nia eu maneana lalawo.
Nae e p̃okati waago kiiki **saa**.
Goo e madeada mari sua navinaga e dao nia e dao maa e dape naru ni
    waago kiiki aneana, goo sai ki rarua, doropusi a, goo atulake paluse.
Paapaa te moro lega:
"Rovemao, Rovemao, Rove.
Rovemao, ku one rekei.

Rovemao, ku one rekei.
Rekei sili diele ka ta mai.
Rekei sili diele goro e."
E maromaaro, te moro paluse.
Paapaa te moro lega:
"Rovemao, Rovemao, Rove.
Rovemao, ku one rekei.
Rovemao, ku one rekei.
Rekei sili diele ka ta mai.
Rekei sili diele goro e."
E paki ﬁaladigi doko naga, "Pule toko kite pule vano?"
Goo Rovemao, e naga, "Pule vano."
E paki euta, doko musagi Rovemao.
Ero duua moro paluse liliu, paki P̃agona.
Goo taina maaga eu punusi naga taida kiiki wanogoe waina eu midoaki
    naga e kiiki saa,
maa ragi waina e doo lega paraki Rovemao, goo e naga, 'P̃a toko kite p̃a
    vano? P̃a umai!' e naga 'A ga valooti!'.
Goo eu punusi a waina e paluse umai goo nagoroi raewia wanogoe taina
    maaga teu doitoi a.
Goo teu doo duﬁada noa kii da asa, eu naga, "O, nae e kiiki!
E pano goo Rovemao e poo masau na goo ero poo duua umai.
E p̃ia naga tu ga woo maripunue a!"
Goo eu duﬁada noa kii da naga,
"Matamai
tu ga woo piragi taigida kiiki.
Tu ga va musuvi matadoko.
Waina tu ga va musuvi matadoko,
sara naata kakagida tu ga tape naviila,
tu ga tape nakonotina,
goo tu ga woo pa leo matadoko maaga, waina tu ga vunusi sikai waina
    e ga maaga doko.
Goo sikai e ga veea, e ga veea musu paapaa waina e ga umai, paki elagi,
    goo te ga kani naviila.
Goo te ga noa naga, 'Oo! E pei nap̃okasi wia!'
Goo sikai maa te ga vano.
Tu ga mari dapala nogoe paapaa tea mamauputi.
Maa
ragi waina nae e ga naga e ga woo moro pano, goo nae e diika naviila.
E ga vano e ga tape nasuﬁilina. E ga tape nasuﬁilina, nalakena
    nasuﬁili ni matadoko eu gani a e paataka sikai magi naviila."
Goo eu [ga] noa ki nia asa naga, "P̃a vano doko sai ki naruﬁa paki
    matadoko, poo dape nasuﬁilina."
Maa te noa ki nagoroi aneana, e naga,

"P̃a woo doo punusi noai kiiki waia doko laasa.

Goo waina p̃a woo punusi nunu e doko asa, te pisei ki naga ta mate.

Niigo p̃a tuñaña maripunue ko."

Ragi waina eu pa loloso, nagoroi aneana te doo punusi noai wanogoe.

Goo ragi waina nae e musu paapaa naga e doovi nawoka ni matadoko, matadoko te katisoki a.

Goo nagoroi aneana e punusi naga nunu e doko noai wanogoe, maa e pano doko dape natali, poo duñana soli nanoana, poo likoti a paki araa ni nakau, goo e dowo siwo.

Goo namenana te soka goo te mate.

Taina maaga ragi waina eu paki euta eu laelae a naga sikai e masau naga e ga sava peea goo e ga woo puati nagoroi wanogoe.

Goo kerua e masau naga e ga sava peea poo puati nagoroi wanogoe. Tea mamauputi eu sava maraverave raki nagoroi wanogoe.

Ragi waina eu pano, kite nagoroi wanogoe te duñana solipunue a.

Te mate.

Goo tea mamauputi ragi waina eu punusi naga e mate, naara mamauputi eu mamauputi dapepele.

Te wanogoe e pei namatap̃ago ni naatuusiana waia nalo ni tamataida rualimasikai

goo Rovemao.

Te noopu.

"The Ten Brothers and Rovemao"
by
Jack Taviṁasoe

I want to tell about ten brothers and a woman named Rovemao.
The ten brothers lived at Ƥagona.
And the woman lived at Vetenirana.
The brothers used to see her wash and dry herself on the sand every
  morning.
Every morning of every day she did it in the same way.
And the eldest of the ten brothers said,
"One of us should marry that woman; then she would cook for us."
One day the eldest said to his brothers, "Tomorrow let's plant my
  garden."
And his brothers said, "Yes! Fine."
The following day
he killed a pig.
It was one of the [very large type called] *mataloa*.
Its tusks had pierced [the cheek] twice, [making two full circles].
And he prepared food.
He baked the pig, and yams for them [in return for planting for him].
He took the pig's leg, pushed off his canoe, putting the meat into it, then
  started paddling.
And his brothers stayed behind to continue planting his garden.
And as he paddled he began to **sing**:
"Rovemao, Rovemao, Rove.
Rovemao, decorate yourself.
Rovemao, decorate yourself.
Decorated, laugh with joy as you see me coming.

229

Decorated, laugh with joy about what is to come."
When he had finished [his song] he continued paddling.
He paddled on until once more he began to sing:
"Rovemao, Rovemao, Rove.
Rovemao, decorate yourself.
Rovemao, decorate yourself.
Decorated, laugh with joy as you see me coming.
Decorated, laugh with joy about what is to come."
And he addressed the woman as he approached the shore:
"Will you go or will you stay?"
Rovemao answered, "I'll stay."
"You're staying?"
She said, "I'm staying."
So he went back again.
She had **refused** [him]. [When she said] *"Pule toko"* it meant that she
    refused.
So he paddled back again.
And his brothers saw that he had gone in vain.
The following day, the next eldest brother said,
"Tomorrow, let's plant my garden."
And his brothers said, "Yes! Fine."
The next day, he also killed a pig, and baked it for them with yams.
He took the pig's leg and paddled off.
He lay just off the island when he started singing: "Rovemao."
[He sang the same song as the eldest brother had sung before.]
And [as it was with the eldest brother] so it went for each of the brothers
until all nine [had gone].
But there was still **one**, the **youngest**.
And he said to his brothers, "Let's plant for me."
But his brothers said, "What! You're too little. You have no food."
He said to them, "Yes, I do! A have a few little yams."
And they said, "You have no pigs."
And, "I have one little pig."
So he said to his brothers, "Please help me plant."
So the following day they planted for him.
[Meanwhile,] he killed a **very** small pig.
Then when he had prepared the food and it was in baking, he took the
    leg of his little pig, pushed off his canoe, putting it into it, and began
    to paddle.
Eventually he, too, sang:
"Rovemao, Rovemao, Rove.
Rovemao, decorate yourself.
Rovemao, decorate yourself.
Decorated, laugh with joy as you see me coming.

Decorated, laugh with joy about what is to come."
He rested, then continued paddling,
until once more he sang:
"Rovemao, Rovemao, Rove.
Rovemao, decorate yourself.
Rovemao, decorate yourself.
Decorated, laugh with joy as you see me coming.
Decorated, laugh with joy about what is to come."
He went near and said, "Will you stay or will you go?"
And Rovemao replied, "I'll go."
So he went ashore, and picked up Rovemao.
They paddled back together, to P̃agona.
And his brothers saw their little brother, whom they had thought was too little,
when he sang for Rovemao, and said, 'Will you stay or will you go? Come!', she answered 'I'm coming!'
So when he came paddling back with that beautiful woman his brothers were jealous of him.
They began talking amongst themselves, saying, "He's so little!
Off he goes and Rovemao desires him and now here they are returning together.
Let's kill him!"
So they planned it with one another,
"Tomorrow
we'll take along our little brother.
We'll go diving for giant clams.
When we dive for the clam,
each of us will get a *naviila*,
take the nut,
and then we'll look for clams, until we see one that's already open.
And one [of us] will dive first, and when he comes up again, he'll put the nut in his mouth and eat it.
Then he'll say, 'Oh, this meat is so good!'
Then another one [of us] will go.
One after the other each of us will do the same.
But
when it's his turn, he won't have a nut.
He'll go to get the clam's meat. He'll go for it because clam meat looks just like the *naviila* nut."
So then they would tell him to put his hand in[to the giant clam's mouth] and take the meat [so that it would close tight on him and he would drown.]
But [the little brother] said to his wife,
"Go and watch the water in this coconut shell.

If you see an image in it, it means that I'm dead.

Then you must kill yourself."

Then they swam off, [and] his wife went to watch the water.

Then [it went according to their plan and] he dove down and touched the mouth of the giant clam, and it clamped down on [his arm].

Then his wife saw the vision in the water, and she went and got some rope, tied it around her neck, and to a branch of a tree, then [let herself] drop [from the treebranch].

Her tongue **stuck** out and she was **dead.**

His brothers were elated as they came ashore, **each one** trying to run ahead to take the woman.

And every **other** one wanted to run ahead and [be the one to] get her. So they **all** sped **swiftly** towards the woman.

But when they got there, she had hanged herself.

She was [already] **dead.**

When they saw that she was dead, they realized that they had all, every one of them, lost out.

That is the end of the story about the ten brothers

and Rovemao.

That's it.

(Reference: Jack T.-1. April 18, 1978, Nekaap̃a. Tape 3B, 0-31.)

Text No.25:

"Kaidaliki"
pae
Thomas Tanearu

Nakp̃ea wanogoe nagisana e pei **Kaidaliki.**
Tea matua eu dae a, nap̃aloa sikai, e pei malo **saa.**
Eu sua ki m̃aau ni Utanilagi asa naga eu ga madeada puati a umai paki
    m̃alala.
Ragi waina eu paraki nia pano,
eu soli a paapaa e noopu.
Eu **lega** doko naga eu ga vuati a sake.
Eu lega pano pano pano, puati a, puati a pano pano paapaa maa e **daa**
    parivari.
Nakp̃ea wanogoe, e maligo, maa nakp̃ea wanogoe te madoko.
Maa tea ni Utanilagi teu umai paki esum̃a, natokoana ni Meere.
Eu ganikani paa[paa] te noopu, eu liliu paki Utanilagi pano.
Matamai kakana, tea ni Meere naara teu poo dum̃ada puati a.
Eu puati a umai pae nap̃aloa wanogoe,
eu puati a umai pano pano paapaa doko lawo ki nia m̃alala.
M̃alala wa[ina] eu lawo ki nia asa nagisana e pei M̃alaripu.
M̃alaripu.
Eu lawo ki nia asa goo nakp̃ea wanogoe nagisana e pei **Kaidaliki.**
E pei waina eu sua ki naka ni Utanilagi asa, maa eu **daa** madeada puati
    a,
naara teu poo pa dum̃ada puati a.
Teu poo salagisa ni nagisana e pei Kaidaliki.
Nanoap̃otaeana ni nakp̃ea wanogoe.

"Kaidaliki"
by
Thomas Tanearu

The name of [this particular] slit-drum was **Kaidaliki**.

[Our] predecessors carved it, in a creek, a **rough** place.

They asked the *m̃aau* of Utanilagi to come and take it to the dancing-ground for them.

They came for it,

[and] bound it all up with ropes.

[Then] they **chanted** so that they might be able to move it.

They sang on and on and on, and they pulled, and pulled, but it didn't **budge**.

Darkness fell, but the drum still lay there.

So the people of Utanilagi went home, that is, to Meere village.

They ate, and when they had finished, returned to Utanilagi.

The following day the Meere people went and got it themselves.

They carried it up from the creek,

carried it aloooong and eventually put it up on the **dancing-ground**.

The **name** of the dancing-ground where they erected it was M̃alaripu. M̃alaripu.

They erected it and named the slit-drum **Kaidaliki**.

So what happened was that they asked the Utanilagi people, but they **couldn't** move it, so they moved it **themselves**.

[Then] they named the drum Kaidaliki.

That's the explanation of [how] that slit-drum [came to be].

(Reference: Tanearu-1. May 5, 1978, Meere. Tape 4B, 0-4.)

234

Text No.26:

"Vaatu ni M̃aatoa"
pae
Thomas Tanearu

Navarakale
sikai,
eu pei navarakale rualimasikai.
Ragi waina eu doko paa[paa] e pei ragi ni nalalawoana.
Teu naga eu ga va lalawo.
Eu pa lalawo, maa taida kiiki
nae e dape nau sikai.
Teu noa ki nia asa naga nae te ga toko madeada peeni.
Maa naara teu pa madoko madeada lalawo.
Eu madoko lalawo maa taida kiiki wanogoe te doko madeada peeni.
E doko peeni maa e nadi ki veni doko nakapu doko, maa te one sui nau.
Te one kove nau sikai.
Ragi waina e doo kove a,
tivinivinikopai sikai e doko p̃alua napaga.
Ragi waina e dogo kanao kiiki wanogoe e doo kove nau, e umai punusi
  a doko naga, "Tai, p̃a tua au nakapu."
E dua e naseati sikai, e puati a, e sake pano, e surata pano, e daa pei tuai,
  maa te moro umai.
E noa ki nia e naga, "Tai, p̃a tua au nakapu."
E mari a paapaa nakapu aneana e diika.
E moro noa ki nia asa, e naga, "Tai, navatuuna sikai a dogo ku doo kove
  a.
P̃a tua au asa, a ga ko pa kove dogo e."
Ragi waina e kove nau wanogoe,
e daa moro dua kanao kiiki wanogoe asa, maa e dape a

doko pa sili p̃alua ni napaga.

Ragi waina e sili p̃alua ni napaga, kanao kiiki wanogoe te doo kai.

E doko dagisi nau aneana.

E dagisi a, taina maaga eu madoko lolua, eu dogo kite taida e kai.

Seara eu dogo naga e pei nadaleo ni taida,

goo seara eu noa naga, "Ee! [E pei] nawaa natukutukumena nalagi sui
a nogo wanogoe e doo kai."

Goo seara teu naga, "Eee, taigida nogo."

Paapaa eu rumai paki m̃aladigi doko dogoatae naga e pei taida.

Ragi waina eu dogoatae naga e pei taida, eu rumai paki m̃aladigi doko
usiusi a asa naga, "Ku dagisi **nasava?**"

Goo e noa kii da asa naga,

"Tivinivinikopai sikai e dape lua nau aginau, doko pa sili p̃alua napaga
wanana doko."

Ragi waina e noa kii da asa dapala nogoe, teu dae kaali, eu dae kaali
sarasara ra—rualimasikai.

Eu dae ra doko paraki lake ni napaga wanogoe.

Ragi waina eu paraki lake napaga wanogoe, teu lega.

Goo nalegaana e dapala nea:

"Nau, nau, nau, [a] dagisi a.

Nau, nau, nau, [a] dagisi a.

Napaga marierie, napaga marierie."

o

Goo teu pukai, teu pukai napaga wanogoe.

Eu pukai a panopanopanopaapaa napaga e **dowo.**

E dowo,

goo tivinivinikopai wanogoe e doko liina doko.

E doko liina doko, eu moro **savi** naio adeada maaga e makali, takalapa
e noa naga, "Kinau, a ga lawo e."

Ragi waina e lawo e, tivinivinikopai wanogoe e **sorovi**, e lawopele a[sa].

Goo **kerua** e moro noa naga, "Kinau, a ga moro lawo."

Kerua e moro lawo me e **paataka** sikai.

Tivinivinikopai wanogoe e sorovi a, maa e moro lawopele a[sa].

Ketolu!

Paapaapaa e noopu.

Takariki, te moro naga e ga moro lawo.

Goo taina maaga eu noa ki nia asa naga, "Kinami au matua maa au poo
lawopele asa.

Maa niigo, ku **kiiki**, waina p̃a lawopele asa te ga woo gani gida."

Goo takariki e noa kii da asa, e naga, "A kiiki, maa a ga ko maridogo."

E dape naio aneana,

e soro e, goo te taleeva ki nia.

Goo te mari a panopanopanopaapaa e moro soro e, goo te poo daki goo te

    lawo p̃ai a!
E lawo p̃ai a, e **mate**,
te dɔko p̃alua napaga, goo teu maripunue a.
Nae te noopu wora wanogoe.

"The M̃aatoa Rock"[1]
by
Thomas Tanearu

[There were once]
ten brothers,
a family of ten brothers.
They had been living there for some time, and then came the planting
    season.
They decided to go and do the planting.
They went off to plant, but their little brother
took along [his] bamboo flute.
They told him to stay behind to roast [food] for them.
Meanwhile, they were off [in the gardens] planting.
They were planting away and the little brother was behind roasting
    [food] for them.
Once he'd put [the yams] on the fire to roast, he lay down and started
    playing the flute.
He went on playing the flute.
And, as he played,
there was an evil spirit in the opening of a banyan tree.
When he heard the little boy playing the flute, he came to him and said,
    "**Brother**, give me [some of your] fire."
He gave [the evil spirit] a fire-brand, who took it, and went away, but it
    wasn't long, and he was back again.
Once more he said to him, "Brother, give me [some of your] fire."
He kept doing this until eventually [the boy's] fire was all **gone**.
He spoke to him again, "Brother, I heard you playing something.
Give it to me, I'd like to try playing it."

He took the flute,
but then he didn't give it back to the little boy; instead, he took it away
and went into the opening in the banyan.
When he disappeared into the opening, the little boy started to cry.
He was crying for his flute.
As he cried, his brothers, who were off in the gardens, heard their
   brother.
Some of them thought it was their brother's voice,
but the others said, "No! It's only the wind blowing the *natukutukumena*
   fruits and making a sound like crying."
But the others said, "No, that is our brother."
Eventually they came back and when they got up close they realized that
   it was indeed their brother.
Once they realized that it was, they came up to him and asked, "Why are
   you crying?"
So he said,
"An evil spirit came and took my flute away, then he went into the
   opening in the banyan over there."
When he told them that, they cut digging-sticks, one stick for each of
   them—all ten.
They cut them then went over to the foot of the banyan.
As they neared the foot of the banyan, they sang.
The song goes like this:
"The flute, flute, flute, [he is] crying over it.
The flute, flute, flute, [he is] crying over it.
The banyan is falling down, down, the banyan is falling down, down."
o
And they pried up [with their digging-sticks], pried up on the [base of the]
   banyan.
They kept prying prying prying untiiil finally the banyan fell.
It fell,
leaving the evil spirit out in the open.
With him standing there in the open, they sharpened their spears again,
   and the eldest said, "I will, I'll spear him."
As he was throwing his spear, the devil growled, and he missed him.
Then, the second [brother] too said, "I will, I'll spear him."
So the second [brother] also tried to spear him, but the same thing
   happened.
The evil spirit growled at him, and he missed.
[Then] the third [brother]!
[And the fourth, and fifth and on down] until [all nine had tried and
   failed].
[Then] the youngest brother, said that he too would try to spear him.
But his brothers said, "We're big and we missed him.

But you, you're [only] little, and if you miss him, he'll eat us all."
And the little brother replied, "I'm little, but I'm going to try [anyway]."
So he picked up his spear,
and tricked him *[arm gesture of feigning a throw]* , making him turn
   aside *[a gesture with the arms and shoulders to suggest the spirit
   jumping to one side to avoid the feigned throw]*.
He kept on doing this over and over, tricking him, so that he would turn
   aside, until finally he [threw the spear], striking him!
He speared him squarely, he collapsed,
then as he lay there in the opening of the banyan, they killed him.
And that's the end of it.

Footnotes

1. This account was offered in explanation of the origin of a stone
    formation of a distinctive obelisk-like shape. It stands alone on flat
    ground near Meere.

(Reference: Tanearu-2. May 5, 1978, Meere. Tape 4B, 46-52.)

Text No.27:

"Lawomidimiiidi"
pae
John Tarip Mariwota

Naatuusiana ni naveinawotaana ni Farealapa.
Nagisa ni nawota e pei Masenap̃au.
Masenap̃au wanogoe e peani m̃aau e[ro] duua.
M̃aau sikai nagisana e pei
Lawomidimiiidi.
Kerua e pei Lawopoaga.
M̃aau duua wanogoe ki Masenap̃au, ero doo paki natokoana p̃ota, poo
    p̃okati naatam̃ooli,
goo ero panako
nawii, navinaga goo nap̃okas[i], poo dape a umai dua nawota adeada asa-
    Masenap̃au.
Ragi sikai
ero paki Utanilagi
goo ero punusi nawota ni Utanilagi, Mariwota.
E peani lolua warua, ni nawii.
Goo tea ni Utanilagi eu maneana eu kili a goo eu likoti puti ra doko
    paapaa p̃oogi goo tea ruua wanogoe ero pano,
m̃aau duua wanogoe, Lawomidimiiidi goo Lawopoaga.
Ero pano goo ero panako nawii.
Nawii wanogoe e[u] pei agi mariki nawota ni Utanilagi, Mariwota.
Maa ragi waina ero dape [r]a umai dua mariki nawota asa, Masenap̃au,
    nawota adeada.
Goo Masenap̃au e leoatae natano ni Utanilagi.
E daa paataka sikai natano ni Farealapa.
Goo e atae naga e pei natano ni Utanilagi goo nawii wanogoe e[u] pei

241

nawii ni Utanilagi.

Maa

ragi waina m̃aau ki Mariwota, nawota ni Utanilagi, nae e moro paki
    lolua ki nawota aneana.

E pano poo punusi naga

natali waina eu likoti nawii asa te doko, maa nawii seara te[u] pueli.

Ragi wanogoe, m̃aau ki Mariwota, nae e pano doko moro likoti natali
    wanogoe. E likoti a e pei navasaana.

Goo e likoti natali wanogoe nalakena tuai ku mariatae likoti natali sikai
    waina e pei navasaana sikai.

Goo, e noa naga, "Niigo seei waina ku panako nawii ki nawota aginau,
    a likoti natali waia e pei navasaana."

Goo ragi waina m̃aau ni Farealapa ero duua ero moro pano, ero moro
    panako nawii, goo ero punusi natali waina e liko doko.

Goo ero noa naga, "O, io! Ragi waia teu atae naga tea vanako e panako
    nawii ki Mariwota."

Goo naara ero moro dape lua nawii duua p̃ota pae nakau waina eu likoti
    nawii asa

doko moro peresi natali waina eu peea mari navasaana asa,

doko moro likoti a e pei navasaana doko naga, "Kinami, Lawomidimiidi
    goo Lawopoaga aro panako."

Goo ragi waina

tea ni Utanilagi eu pano eu punusi a, eu naga, "O, io!

M̃aau ni Farealapa ero umai panako."

Goo eu moro mari natali sala kerua doko naga,

"P̃a woo moro umai matamai,

poo moro umai matamai poo moro dape nawii."

Ragi wanogoe, m̃aau ni Farealapa e noa kii da asa e naga, "Io.

A ga woo moro umai matamai.

A ga umai matamai waina eelo e sake."

Goo ragi waina eelo e ko daa sake matamai nae te pano

te pano poo madoko sua doko lolua waina agi Mariwota ni Utanilagi.

E doko asa doko, paapaa

ragi waina eelo e sake umai paki elagi goo tea ni Utanilagi eu sake umai
    paki lolua ki Mariwota, nawota adeada.

Goo ragi waina eu noa naga, "Tu ga taliepu sua roara waia!

Tu ga taliepu sua roara waia maa m̃aau wanogoe e ga woo umai."

Goo ragi waina eu doo daliepu roara goo m̃aau wanogoe e doko sua e noa
    naga, "Kinau, ta doko sua tokora waia!"

Goo ragi waina eu darasa, eu naga eu ga p̃okati a, p̃okati m̃aau wanogoe.

E daa pei m̃aau duua maa m̃aau sikai maau waina e pano!

M̃aau wanogoe eu soso e ki Lawomidimiidi.

E pano,

e doko, goo e pioso, e naga, "Ta doko sua".

Goo ragi waina eu naga eu ga p̃okati a, e sava paki taleeva ni roara, paki
    taleeva ni etano!

Goo ragi waina tea laapa eu **sava** paki **etano** goo e sava paki [taleeva ni]
    elagi!

Goo ragi waina tea laapa eu moro sava paki taleeva ni elagi goo ragi
    wanogoe nae e **sava** ki **nakasuaana** mamau aneana!

E sava pano doko dam̃alua kalau nakoro, **poo** sava pano!

Goo ragi waina eu **maridogo** naga eu ga p̃okati a maa eu **marisaa** maa eu
    mariatae dum̃ada p̃okati ra waina m̃aau wanogoe te sili pae melu,
    melu kakada.

Goo e sava paapaa paaa

eu daa p̃okati a maa te **sava liu** ra doko paki esum̃a.

Mariwota ni Utanilagi e peani nagoroi duua ero doko sikoti a sara ragi.

Goo nagoroi duua aneana wanogoe ero doko **sikai** e doko navidina
    taleeva goo **sikai** e doko taleeva.

Mariki nawota e doko m̃aleoputo.

Goo m̃aau ni Farealapa e sava pano poo **dape lua** nagoroi sikai,

doko **sava** paki elau, doko sava pae elau pae vaatu looa ni Utanilagi,

doko **sava** daliepu!

Mariki nawota e marisaa mari te navatuuna seara nalakena m̃aau
    wanogoe te dape lua nagoroi aneana [goo] te pano.

Ragi waina navasaana e pae namalasi umai, eu noa naga,

"M̃aau waina e umai! Te paki [e]**sava** pano?"

Goo eu pa punusi mariki nawota, e noa kii da asa naga, "Te dape lua
    nagoroi aginau doko dape a pano!"

Goo e pano paapaa

e pagi pae vaatu doko pano paa[paa] e sake paki Farealapa.

Goo tea ni Farealapa eu punusi a goo eu noa, "Ai!

Naatam̃ooli sikai wanae e doo umai! E dapala e dape **nakau** kite e dape
    naatam̃ooli sikai."

Goo eu doo punusi a, eu naga, "E!

M̃aau ki mariki nawota!

E dape **nagoroi** sikai!"

Goo e dape a pano paapaa e paki m̃aladigi ki natokoana goo e doropusi
    a doko maa e pitautau mariki nawota naga

e ga noakisai asa naga nae, m̃aau ki mariki nawota ni Farealapa, e
    maneana dape nagoroi ki Mariwota ni Utanilagi.

Goo Masenap̃au e noa ki nia asa e naga, "P̃a viragi a umai!"

Eu piragi a umai goo Masenap̃au e poo piragisoki a.

Mariki **nawota** ni **Farealapa** e piragisoki a pei nagoroi aneana sikai.

Paapaa

ragi waina navasaana e paki Utanilagi pano paki mariki Mariwota,

goo

Mariwota e noa ki nia asa, e naga, "Io, e p̃ia naga

nagoroi aginau e ga moro liliu umai paki namarakiana aginau, Utanilagi."

Goo Masenap̃au e noa ki naatam̃ooli aneana maaga asa, e naga, "Ragi
waia tu ga viragi nagoroi ki Mariwota ni Utanilagi pa doropusi a
kiana, namarakiana aneana."

Goo ragi waina eu piragi a pano paapaaa, eu pa doropusi a,

Leimaara, lake ni nearu sikai doko taava.

Eu doropusi nagoroi ki mariki nawota asa.

Goo

eu noa dapala nea,

"Tokora waia, te pei kokoi ni Farealapa goo Utanilagi.

Nagoroi ki Mariwota ni Utanilagi e ga moro liliu paki Mariwota."

Masenap̃au e ga moro liliu paki nagoroi aneana maaga waina eu doko
asa doko tuai.

Ragi wanogoe te pei kokoi sikai ni Utanilagi goo Farealapa doko
Leimaara

waina e doko paapaa paki masoso.

"Lawomidimiidi"
by
John Tarip Mariwota

[This is] the story of the chiefship of Farealapa.
The chief's title was Masenap̃au.
Masenap̃au had two m̃aau.
One was called
Lawomidimiidi.
The other was Lawopoaga.
These two m̃aau of Masenap̃au, used to go to other villages, and kill
    people,
and steal
yams, food and meat, then take it and present it to their chief–Masenap̃au.
On one particular occasion
they went to Utanilagi
and saw the chief of Utanilagi, Mariwota.
He had a great garden, of yams.
The people of Utanilagi had dug it and hung them all up for him [on poles]
when the two m̃aau came along at night–Lawomidimiidi and Lawopoaga.
They went and stole yams,
yams that belonged to Utanilagi's chief, Mariwota.
Then they took them and presented them to *mariki* Masenap̃au, their
    chief.
And Masenap̃au recognized the Utanilagi soil.
It wasn't the **same** as Farealapa's soil.
So he knew that it was Utanilagi soil and the yams Utanilagi yams.
And
then the m̃aau of chief Mariwota of Utanilagi, went back to his chief's

garden.

When he got there he saw

the rope with which they had tied up the yams, but the yams themselves
were gone.

Then Mariwota's ṁaau tied the rope back up again. He tied it up as a
notice.

He [did this] because in the olden days you could tie a rope to make a
message.

So what he was saying was, "Whoever you are who stole my chief's yams,
I am tying this rope as a warning to you."

So when the two ṁaau of Farealapa went back, to steal more yams, they
saw the tied rope.

They said, "So! Now they know a thief has stolen Mariwota's yams."

Then they took two more yams off the pole on which the yams had been
hung,

and undid the rope with which [Mariwota's ṁaau] had made the
message,

then re-tied it such that it was again a message, proclaiming, "We,
Lawomidimiidi and Lawopoaga, did the stealing."

So when

the Utanilagi people [next] went, they saw it and said, "So!

It's the ṁaau of Farealapa who came to steal."

So they did up the rope a second time to say:

"Come back again tomorrow;

come back and take some more yams tomorrow."

Then, [one of] the Farealapa ṁaau let them know, "Alright.

I'll come tomorrow,

I'll come at sunrise."

Yet before the sun was even up the next day, he had gone,

he'd gone, and was already waiting in the garden belonging to Mariwota
of Utanilagi.

He waited and waited, and eveeentually

the sun rose and the Utanilagi people climbed up to Mariwota's garden,
their chief's [garden].

Then they said, "Let's surround the garden!

Let's surround [it] before the ṁaau gets here."

But when they encircled the garden, the ṁaau was already there, and
said,

"It's me! Here I am already!"

Then they shouted, and went for the ṁaau, to kill him.

There were not two, but only one ṁaau who had come!

It was the one called Lawomidimiidi.

He went,

waited, then called out, "Here I am."

At that point they went for him to kill him, [but] he ran to one side, to the lower side of the garden!

Then they all **ran** to the **lower** side and he ran to the **upper** [side]!

So everybody ran back up again to the upper side and then he **ran** with all his **strength**!

He ran and vaulted over the fence, and **off** he raced!

They **tried to strike** him but **missed**, only managing to hit each other as the *m̃aau* sped in amongst them.

So he raced on and on until,

without even being touched, he **got past** them all and [raced] on towards [their] village.

Mariwota of Utanilagi had two wives who were always with him.

One stayed by his one side and the **other** by the other side.

The old chief was [always] in the middle between them.

And the Farealapa *m̃aau* ran [up to them] and **dragged off** one of these women,

then **ran** to the shore, and over the black rocks of Utanilagi,

running around [his pursuers]!

The old chief couldn't do a thing to stop the *m̃aau* from racing away with his wife and **disappearing**.

Then the word came from the bush–they said,

"The *m̃aau* who just came by! **Where** did he go?"

[The Utanilagi people] went to their chief, [and] he told [them], "He grabbed my wife and ran off with her!"

And [Lawomidimiidi] went oooon,

climbing over the rocks up and up until he reached Farealapa.

The Farealapa people spotted him and said, "**Look!**

Somebody's coming! It looks like he's carrying a **log** or [maybe it's] a **person.**"

They kept watching [and as he came closer], they said, "No!

It's the chief's *m̃aau!*

He's carrying a **woman!**"

And he bore her along until he got close to the village, then put her down and called for the old chief

to inform him that he, *m̃aau* of the chief of Farealapa, had captured the chief of Utanilagi's wife for him.

So Masenap̃au said to him, "Bring her here!"

They brought her forward and Masenap̃au accepted her.

The **chief** of **Farealapa** accepted her as one of his own women.

Eventually

word [of this] reached *mariki* Mariwota in Utanilagi,

and

Mariwota said, "Alright, then.

I would like my wife to be returned to Utanilagi, to my dominion."

So Masenap̃au told his people, "We'll take Mariwota of Utanilagi's wife
    back now and restore her to her **home**, to his dominion."
So they took the woman, going ooon until finally they let her,
Leimaara, go at the foot of an oak on the hill.
They left the chief's wife there.
Then
they said,
"This spot, shall mark the **boundary** between Farealapa and Utanilagi.
The chief's wife shall go back to her husband, Mariwota of Utanilagi."
Then Masenap̃au went back to the wives he already had.
So from that time on [that spot, called] Leimaara, has been the **boundary**
    between Farealapa and Utanilagi and it remains so up to this day.

(Reference: Mariwota-1. July 2, 1978, Tiki. Tape 9A, 52-70 & B, 0-1.)

Chapter Eight

Natukunoa Maaga

Tales

In contrast to the preceding chapter, the texts collected under the heading, *natukunoa*, are homogeneous in general form and content. Although all 6 inscribed here are taken from the vast repertoire of Kaltap̃au M̃asemata, and hence have a consistency of their own, as his, in all major respects they are very like those recorded by other narrators. Among others, Leisei Alick and Samuel Kalkoa perform narratives which fall into this category. Ultimately I hope to be able to bring their texts to the printed page, too, but for now perhaps they will forgive me, for the purposes of this volume and within its spatial constraints, for choosing to reproduce the entire body of texts recorded by Kaltap̃au M̃asemata. I do so in tribute to him as both a person and a wonderful raconteur and to make this record available to his family and kin, as the Ngunese say, as a "memory", a reminder or remembrance of a talented man much appreciated.

Text No.28:

"Oova"
pae
Kaltap̃au M̃asemata

Io, a ga woo noa
stori sikai nalo ni oova.
Ragi waina elau e maati,
goo oova e umai, poo doo dai naika kirikiri sikai waina eu soso e ki lawo.
E[u] doko luku maaga ni namaati.
Goo ragi wanogoe lawo eu dogo kite saa.
Goo eu noa naga, "O, ragi waia oova te ga marisaa ki puti gida, te ga
     kani puti gida!"
Goo ragi waina eu pano, goo eu pap̃ai nal[e]o mauri sikai waina e dakiusi
     rakum̃a. E kiiki.
Eu soso e ki m̃agougou.
Eu noa ki nia asa naga, "Ku mariatae silae gami kite?"
Goo e noa naga, "Io! A ga silae mu nasava?"
Goo eu noa ki nia asa, eu naga,
"Ragi waina oova e ga umai, p̃a maginami puasoki a.
Waina e umai e marisasaa ki gami."
Goo e noa kii da, e naga, "Io, e p̃ia."
Goo ragi waina ragi sikai oova e moro umai goo e doo dai lawo maaga pae
     natasi.
Goo ragi waina e umai paapaa e doko p̃ai m̃agougou sikai waina e sili
     doko.
Goo e **katisoki natuana!**
Ragi waina e katisoki natuana,
goo oova e doo **paruvaru,**
maa m̃agougou e kasua.

Goo ragi wanogoe,
oova e lega,
"M̃agougou rikii, m̃agougou lapaa,
P̃a torotoro au, toro au."
Goo ragi wanogoe m̃agougou e moro lega paki oova,
e noa naga,
"Lawooo sai ki ruukuu
pakinau, ta kati ko,
pakinau, ta kati ko."
Goo oova e doo mari pilosi naga e ga m̃elu.
Maa m̃agougou e kasua.
Maa e katisoki a doko paapaaa, elau e doo mua.
Goo oova e moro pasa ki m̃agougou pae nalegaana,
e noa naga,
"M̃agougou rikii, m̃agougou lapaa,
P̃a torotoro au, toro au."
M̃agougou e moro pasa pae nalegaana paki oova,
"Lawooo sai ki ruukuu
pakinau, ta kati ko,
pakinau, ta kati ko."
Goo e doo mari pilosi paapaaa, elau e mua.
Ragi waina elau e mua, goo natasi e umai
poo saramule oova.
Goo ragi wanogoe m̃agougou e doropusi a.
Goo ragi waina m̃agougou e doropusi a, oova e sale paki euta. Te mate.
Ragi waina e sale paki euta goo
katou maaga, eu rumai poo gani a waina e sale doko naworaone.
Tea waia e noopu.

"The Heron"
by
Kaltaḡau M̃asemata

Yes, I will tell
a story about the heron.
When the tide is out,
the heron comes, and catches small fish called *lawo*.
They live in holes in the reef.
This particular time the *lawo* were upset.
They said, "When the heron comes it will kill us all and eat us!"
Then they went, and found an animal like a crab, small.
They call it a chiton.
They said to him, "Can you help us?"
And he said, "Certainly! How can I help you?"
They replied,
"When the heron comes to kill us, you catch hold of him for us."
And he said, "Fine."
So, later, the heron came once more to the sea to catch the *lawo*.
He came alooong, until finally he was [standing] right beside the chiton
    who was hiding.
And [the chiton] **caught hold of his leg!**
When it grabbed his leg,
the heron **struggled,**
but the chiton was [too] strong.
Then
the heron sang,
"Little chiton, big chiton,
Let me go, let me go!"

Then, in turn, the chiton sang to the heron,
he said,
"The *lawo* spoke secretly
to me, I [should] trap you.
to me, I [should] trap you."
And the heron struggled **desperately** to free himself!
But the chiton held tight.
And he held onto him until... eventually the tide began to **come** in.
Then the heron addressed this song to the chiton,
he said,
"Little chiton, big chiton,
Let me go! Let me go!"
Once again the chiton sang his reply to the heron,
"The *lawo* spoke secretly
to me, I [should] trap you.
to me, I [should] trap you."
He kept struggling and struggling but, finally, the tide **came in.**
When the tide came in, the sea rose
and flooded over the heron.
Only then did the chiton release its hold.
When [he] let go of it, the heron floated to shore. It was **dead.**
It floated ashore and
the crabs came, and when it came to rest on the sand, they ate it.
That is the end.

(Reference: Kalo-10. April 19, 1978, Unakapu. Tape 4A, 0-10.)

Text No.29:

"Rakum̃a goo Kusue"
pae
Kaltap̃au M̃asemata

Io, a ga woo atuusi
natukunoa sikai
rakum̃a goo kusue.
Ero mari roara.
Goo ero marigoro sara naleo maaga waina ero lawo ra. Ero mari nakoro.
Goo ragi waina
navinaga adeada maaga te matua, goo waago mila sikai e doko gani
  navinaga adeada waina ero lawo e doko roara adeada.
Goo ragi sikai ero pano kite waago wanogoe e doko roara adeada. E doo
  ganikani.
E doo gani nawii goo sara naleo maaga waina ero lawo ra doko roara
  adeada.
Goo kusue e noa ki rakum̃a, e naga,
"Niigo p̃a dokogoro namata,
maa kinau a ga kopasi a.
A ga kopasi a daliepu roara anigida."
E naga, "Io, kinau a ga woo dokogoro namata tokora waina e pae asa paki
  roara anigida."
Goo e dokogoro namata.
Goo kusue e kopasi a dalitaliepu
roara adeada, paapaa e naga e ga vaki katama,
tokora waina rakum̃a e dokogoro e.
Ragi waina e pano, goo rakum̃a e katisoki natuana.
E katisoki natua ni waago wanogoe.
Goo e pei waago warua!

Ragi waina e katisoki a, goo kusue e pano,

goo ero puasoki a.

Ero puasoki a paa[paa], kusue e kati a paapaa doko katipunue a.

E kati lake namanuna.

Goo ero puati a paki katama maa, ero daa dape masimasi.

Goo ero punusi nakapu sikai e doo asua elagi ni tokora waina ero doko asa.

Goo ero naga, "E! Nakap[u] sikai wanae e doo asua. Toro ga vano.

Toro ga tatagovi a masimasi e ga tua gida asa naga toro ga tovai waago waia asa."

Goo ragi waina ero pano,

kite e daa pei naatamooli,

maa, loriki wanogoe e pei

naatamate tuai sikai, waina e doko tokora wanogoe e doko valea ni vaatu.

Goo ero noa ki nia asa, goo e naga, "Io, a peani masimasi, maa a ga woo palooti manimu dovai a."

Goo naatamate wanogoe e puati naala warua aneana goo e siwo.

E siwo umai punusi ra goo e madeada dovai a.

    Ragi waina e dovai a,

paapaa e noopu,

e pai napokasina maaga paa[paa] e noopu paki naala warua aneana.

Maa e dua ra namaritana mooli.

Goo tea rua ero dape namarita wanogoe

poo paki elau.

Maa ero midoaki saa ki nia,

"Aai!

Napokasina wia maaga waina mariki waina te dape a pano.

Maa e pei tea mooli. Toro ga woo moro umai gani a."

Goo ero sasari a namarita wanogoe paapaa e noopu, ero mari a e maaso, ero gani sua e.

Maa tero leosoki sua tokora waina mariki wanogoe e doo pauri a asa.

Goo ero madoko elau,

goo tero atae noa naga, "O! Ragi waina napokasi waina mariki waina e dao nia te maaso."

Goo ero pesivesi pae epua.

Ero pesivesi pae epua paapaa ero pa duasai tokora waina mariki wanogoe e dao ni napokasi wanogoe asa.

Goo ero duasai pai uupu waina e dao ni napokasi asa.

Goo ero gani napokasi maaga wanogoe!

Ero doo gani a gani a paapaaa, e noopu!

E pei navatuna mooli e doko.

Goo ero gani a paa[paa] e noopu poo titau uupu.

Paapaa naga nia e noopu ero moro liliu, poo moro totoni liliu tokora waina ero pae asa e pei napuada.

Goo mariki nae e doko paapaa ragimelu, e naga, "Oo! A ga ko pukesi nap̃okasi aginau.

A ga ko pukesi nap̃okasi aginau poo purasa gani a."

Goo ragi waina e puke—

nae e midoaki nia naga nap̃okasi e doko—

ragi waina e puke,

e daa punusi nap̃okasi ni waago wanogoe sikai maau. E pei navatuna m̃ooli e doko.

Goo e pei natai ni kusue goo natai ni rakum̃a mamau waina e doko uupu.

Naara tero gani sua e goo e naga, "Ooo! Tea rua waina!

Ero pae esava umai gani nap̃okasi waia?"

Goo ragi waina e leo, goo e punusi napuada waina ero pae asa.

Goo natukunoa waia e noopu.

"The Crab and the *Strongbak*"[1]
by
Kaltap̃au M̃asemata

Alright, I'll tell
a tale
of the crab and the *strongbak*.
The two of them made a garden
and fenced in everything that they had planted. They built an enclosure.
And when
everything ripened, a wild pig went and ate the food they had planted in
    their garden.
On one particular occasion they went and the pig was in their garden,
    eating.
It was eating yams and everything else they had planted there.
So the *strongbak* said to the crab [*whispering*],
"You go and block the entrance,
and I'll chase it.
I'll chase it around our garden."
He replied, "Fine, I'll block the gateway, where it got in."
So he blocked off the gateway.
And the *strongbak* chased it around and around
the garden, until it tried to escape,
right where the crab was blocking it off.
As it went [by him], the crab grabbed its leg,
caught hold of the pig's leg.
And it was a big pig!
Once he had caught hold of it, the *strongbak* came up
and they both held onto it.

They kept holding ooon, and finally the crab bit it, bit it to death.
He bit the base of its throat.
Then they carried it out of the garden but, they had no knife.
Then they saw the smoke from a fire up above where they were.
So they said, "Hey! There's smoke from a fire. Let's go.
We'll borrow a knife to butcher the pig."
So off they went,
but it wasn't a person;
rather, that thing was
an ancient spirit who lived there in a hole in a rock.
They told him [what they wanted] and he replied, "Yes, I have a knife,
    but I'll come and cut it up for you."
So the spirit went and got his big basket and then went down.
He went down to them and cut it up for them.
When he had finished butchering it,
and it was all cut up into pieces,
he filled his big basket with all the meat.
And all he gave them was the entrails—nothing more.
So the two of them took them
and went down to the shore.
But they were angry.
"Aai!
That old man took all the good meat.
But, no matter. We'll get to eat it yet."
So they split open and cleaned the entrails until that was all done, then
    they cooked it, and ate it.
But they remembered seeing the spot where the old man had his oven.
They stayed on the beach
and, knowing this, said, "Alright! By now the meat the old fellow baked
    will be done."
So they tunnelled underground.
They tunnelled along until eventually they reached the place where the
    old man had the meat in baking.
They came out right at the oven where he was baking the meat.
Then they ate the meat!
They ate and ate until it was all gone!
All that was left was the bones.
And, having finished eating it, they shat on the oven.
Having done that, they went back and filled in the place they had come
    from, their route.
And that old man waited there until evening, and he thought, "Oh! I
    must take out my meat.
I must take out my meat and leisurely eat it."
And when he opened it—

thinking that the meat was there—
when he opened it,
he didn't see a single piece of pork. There was nothing but bones.
All there was, all over the oven, was the shit of the *strongbak* and the
crab.
The two had eaten everything, and he said, "Oooh! Those two!
How did they manage to get in to eat my meat?"
Then he looked, and he saw the route they had taken.
And that is the end of the tale.

Footnotes

1. When discussing this tale, informants distinguish *kusue* (in Bislama,
   the *strongbak*) as a variant of *kukusue* or "chiton" from *kusue*
   meaning "rat".

(Reference: Kalo-14. May 20, 1978, Unakapu. Tape 5A, 31-40.)

Text No.30:

"Navakalo ni Naika"
pae
Kaltaρau Ñasemata

Io, a ga woo atuusi, a ga woo atuusi natukunoa, nalo ni naika, doko ragi
ni **tuai, tuai, tuai.**
Goo ragi waina naara eu doko goo,
eu doo midoaki nia naga eu ga mari navakalo. Goo sikai e noa naga e
pakilagi goo sikai e noa naga e pakilagi.
Goo ragi wanogoe eu doo saisai.
Eu duasai raki naga seei e ga woo pei nawota adeada.
Naga e ga woo pasaρotae naga "E! Tu ga taa mari navakalo" kite "Tu ga
woo mari navakalo".
Goo eu doo saisai paka **laapa.**
Eu doo saisai goo eu dape sara naleo ni navakalo adeada maaga.
E pei naio,
naasu,
naaρe, sara naleo maaga
paki tokora waina eu saisai asa.
Goo ragi sikai eu moro pano,
goo naika sikai nae e daa doko sikoti ra ragi waina eu doo saisai.
E pei **taura.**
Goo ragi waina e dogo naga naara eu doo saisai goo e umai punusi ra.
Goo e noa kii da asa, e naga, "Ku doo saisai nasava?"
Goo eu noa ki nia asa, eu naga, "Au doo saisai raki navakalo,
naga au ga tuñagami mari navakalo paki gami."
Goo taura, e noa kii da, e naga, "Ee, kinau a daa suasua.
Kinau a pei naika waina a ρarua **doliu** mu waina a doko natasi,
doko maramana mamau.

260

E pei kinau a pei naika waina a p̃arua doliu.

Goo a daa suasua naga ku ga mari navakalo.

Tu ga tum̃agida p̃ia ki gida!"

Goo naika maaga mamauputi eu pasa paki taura, eu naga, "Maa sara
naleo maaga waia,

sara naleo makalikali maaga waina au dape a, au ga kasaa ki nia?

Au ga tua seei asa?"

Goo naika sikai waina e doko, e naga, "Sara naleo mamauputi

sara naleo ni navakalo animu maaga, ku ga tua au asa, a ga masikigu
dape a."

Goo eu dua naika wanogoe asa.

Goo sara naleo maaga wanogoe waina naika wanogoe e dape a,

e doko paapaa paki masoso.

Naika wanogoe nagisana e pei p̃akai,

waina nadiuna e laapa e pei

sara naleo ni navakalo ki naika maaga waina eu midoaki nia naga eu
masau naga eu ga tum̃ada mari ra ara maa e noa naga, "Ku ga tua au
asa. A ga masikigu dape a."

Goo nae e dape sara naleo makalikali maaga wanogoe doko paapaa paki
masoso waia.

Natukunoa vuru waia e noopu nea.

"The War of the Fishes"
by
Kaltap̃au M̃asemata

Alright, I will tell, tell a tale, about fish, that is from long, long, long ago.
There they were and
they decided that they would make war. And one said that he was higher
and another said that he was higher.
So then they gathered to discuss it.
They came together to discuss **who** would become their chief.
So that he would make the decision and say, "No! we won't go to war" or
"We shall go to war."
So they discussed [it] **many** times.
And they took all their weapons:
spears,
bows,
clubs, and everything else
they took to the place where they were discussing it.
And this one time they had gone there,
but there was one fish who had not been with them when they were
meeting.
It was the **whale**.
When he heard that they were meeting, he came to see them.
And he asked them, "What are you discussing?"
And they replied, "We are discussing war-
whether we should make war on each other."
So, the whale said to them, "No. I do not agree to it.
I am the **biggest** fish of all of you in the sea-
even in the whole world.

It is I who am the biggest of all.
And I will **not** allow you to make war.
We must be good to each other!"
So all the fish said to the whale, "But **what** are we to do with all these
    dangerous things we've brought?
To whom can we give them?"
Then one of the fish said, "Give me
all of your weapons for war. I alone will bear them."
So they gave them to that fish.
And everything they gave that fish
remains to this **very** day.
The name of the fish is *ɓakai*[1],
whose many spines
originated when they decided to make war on each other but he said,
    "Give them to me, I'll bear them", so that all those weapons of war
    became his spines.
He took all those dangerous weapons and they are still there to this day.
That is the end of this short tale.

Footnotes

1. With apologies to ethnographic ichthyologists, I can only say that
    ɓakai is likely the Ngunese equivalent of "blowfish".

(Reference: Kalo-15. May 7, 1978, Unakapu. Tape 5A, 40-48.)

Text No.31:

"Tamadawota goo M̃aata"
pae
Kaltap̃au M̃asemata

Vitariki **sikai**, naara maa naanoai aneana
ero mari **roara** doko lake ni noai sikai.
Goo sara ragi waina ero pano ero punusi naga naadi adeada e doo mami.
Goo
lomauri sikai e doo gani a!
Goo naara ero doo midoaki nia naga e pei **marae**.
Goo ero doo pano, maa ero daa pap̃ai navatuuna waina e doo gani naadi
   adeada.
Goo ragi sikai ero moro pano, poo pap̃ai naga
marae sikai e pagi doko naadi, waina e mami, e doo gani a.
Maa e **daa** pei **marae**, e pei m̃aata.
Goo m̃aata wanogoe p̃ilana nae e pagi doko napaga, elagi.
Goo e doo punusi natuna waina e pagi doko naadi wanogoe poo doo gani
   a.
Goo ragi waina tamadawota ero pano,
goo mariki e punusi a, e naga, "Oo, toro poo pap̃ai loriki waina e doo gani
   naadi anigida!
Masoso toro ga woo p̃okati a poo paki sum̃a poo pa dao nia."
Goo ragi wanogoe vitariki, e puati naala aneana—
e pei **vigira**—
waina e puati a paki m̃aladigi goo mariki e p̃okati m̃aata wanogoe, e
   midoaki nia naga e pei marae.
Maa e pei m̃aata.
Goo ragi waina e dae naadi, goo e soki goo e p̃okati m̃aata wanogoe goo
   vitariki e pai a paki naala aneana goo e **pura**.

Goo mariki e dape naadi wanogoe goo ero paki esum̃a.

Goo ero pano poo **pauri** a, pilake natuna maaga, e peani natuna maaga eu **laapa**.

Maa p̃ilana e doko napaga e doo punusi a waina ero paki sum̃a pano.

Paapaa eu pauri a paa[paa] e noopu, eu dae kotokotovi a paa[paa]..., eu mari nakoau asa goo eu **koovu** asa.

Paapaa eu ganikani pa p̃oogi, teu gani sua nap̃okasi adeada.

P̃oogi, eu dogo e kite tokora e **saruru!**

E pei p̃ilana te ga m̃elu.

Te ga varaki naatam̃ooli maaga waina eu gani **natuna**.

Goo ragi waina p̃oogi eu doo maturu, eu dogo e kite natano te **saruru** umai paki m̃aladigi ki nasum̃a adeada.

Maa nasum̃a adeada e pei sum̃a m̃ooli.

Goo ragi waina e umai,

nap̃auna e pae taleeva goo napuena e pae taleeva goo ero pa pitip̃a namata!

Goo piakirikiri maaga wanogoe **tamada** e noa kii da asa, e naga, "A ga ko paki katama!"

Goo ragi waina e naga e ga vaki katama,

e marisaa pakalau paki katama nalakena m̃aata wanogoe e p̃arua!

Goo e marisaa pakalau asa, goo teu paka sikai maau doko ekopu.

Maa m̃aata wanogoe e **doo soli nasum̃a wanogoe.**

E doo soli a paapaa e **solikotokotovi nakau kakana maaga**, paa[paa] e noopu.

Naara eu duleana duu paka sikai maau goo e soli naatam̃ooli maaga waina eu doko ekopu ni nasum̃a wanogoe!

E soli ra paapaa e noopu!

Ragi waina eu mate, goo e moro dum̃ana peresi a, paapaa e gani sua tea mamauputi maaga waina eu doko ekopu wanogoe, poo moro liliu paki **naliana** waina e pae asa umai, napaga warua waina e doo maturu asa.

Natukunoa waia e noopu.

"The Husband and Wife and the Snake"
by
Kaltap̃au M̃asemata

There was a **woman**, and her husband
who made a **garden** at the foot of a certain pool.
And every time they went there they noticed that their bananas were
   ripening.
But
some creature kept eating them!
The two thought that it was an eel.
And they kept going, but they could never find the thing that was eating
   their bananas.
On one particular occasion they went back again, and found
an eel climbing a ripe banana tree, eating [the fruit].
But it was **not an eel**, it was a snake.
And the snake's mother had climbed up high, in a banyan tree.
She was watching her child as it climbed the banana and ate.
When the couple got there,
the husband saw it and he said, "Oh, now we see the creature that's been
   eating our bananas!
Today we shall kill it and then go home and bake it."
So the wife took her bag—
her **shoulder-basket**—
and brought it up close while her husband killed the snake, thinking that
   it was an eel.
But it was a snake.
So he cut down the tree, it fell and he killed the snake, then his wife put
   it into her basket which filled it **right up**.

Then the husband picked up the bananas and they went home.

They went and baked it, along with all of its young. It had a lot of babies.

But its mother was still up in the banyan and saw them going home.

Eventually it was done baking, they cut it all up into pieces, then made a coconut pudding with it and made it into *koovu*[1].

Eventually they ate, and it was night by the time they had finished eating their meat.

During the night, they heard a sound as if the whole place were shaking!

It was its mother coming out [of her place].

She was going after the people who had eaten her child.

So in the night as they slept, it seemed as though the shaking of the ground was coming closer to their house.

And theirs was only a *kastom*[2] house.

When she got there,

she put her head went round one side and her tail round the other and they met in the middle across the doorway!

The children's father said to them [*whispering*], "I'd better go outside!"

But when he tried to get out,

he was unable to get over the snake because it was so enormous!

He couldn't climb out over it, so they all remained inside, every one of them.

Then the snake started squeezing the house.

She squeezed and squeezed... until finally she snapped off all the house-posts,

and then it was over.

So they all stood up together inside the house and then she squeeeeezed the people inside [it]!

She squeeeeezed them... until it was all over!

Once they were dead, she released herself again, and ate everyone who was inside, then went back to her place, the big banyan where she slept.

That is the end of this tale.

Footnotes

1. *Koovu* is a special sub-set of *nakoau* or coconut pudding, being pudding into which bite-sized pieces of meat or fish—or, as in this case, snake—are placed before baking.
2. A "*kastom haus*", or *(na)suma mooli*, refers to the traditional-style, wood and thatch dwelling as opposed to the more solid, modern con-crete-block and corrugated sheet iron variety.

(Reference: Kalo-20. June 26, 1978, Unakapu. Tape 8A, 31-33.)

Text No.32:

"Tokopea,Vonu goo Kusue"
pae
Kaltap̃au M̃asemata

A ga woo noa natukunoa sikai, ni manu sikai, nagisana e pei tokopea.
Ragi sikai e madoo surata pae namalasi, paapaa goo uusa e p̃owo p̃arua.
Goo e pagi doko nakau sikai waina e doo sale pae noaisara warua sikai.
Goo ragi waina e pagi nakau wanogoe, e dogo m̃ata ki nia waina noai e
  doo sara ki nia paki elau.
Goo e lawo doko nakau wanogoe doko, paapaa e sara paapaa doko paki
  natasi, doko paki uvea!
E paki uvea goo e midoaki naga e ga moro diri liliu paki navanua,
maa, e pei uvea saaa.
Goo e naga, "Io, a ga tiri pano maa nadivarugu e ga mamale a ga woo
  mate."
Maa te madoo sale pano, paapaa goo e punusi naika warua sikai e umai.
E pei pakoa.
E noa ki nia asa naga, "Pakoa! Ku mariatae silae au paki euta, kite?"
E naga, "Io, a mariatae, maa, kinau e pei waina a daa sava pae lina.
A sava pae epua ni natasi.
Goo ragi waina a ga sava pae epua ni natasi, p̃a woo marisaa likosokisoki
  au."
Goo te madoo sale pano.
Te midoaki naga te ga mate.
Goo te madoo sale pano paapaa e pap̃ai naika sikai waina eu soso e ki
  masoni.
Tea warua kakana e pei takeo.
Goo e moro noa ki nia asa naga, "Takeo! Ku mariatae silae au paki euta,
  kite?"

E naga, "Io, a mariatae silae ko, maa kinau e daa pei waina a sava pae lina,

maa a sava pae epua.

Goo waina a ga sava pae epua, ku marisaa likosokisoki au."

Goo te doo sale.

Goo te leopuoli ki navanua!

Goo ragi waina e sale, goo te punusi vonu sikai waina e doo sava paraki nia umai.

Goo e noa ki nia asa naga, "Vonu!

Ku mariatae silae au, kite?"

E naga, "Io!

Kinau maa a doo paki navanua, goo ragi waina a midoaki naga a ga tao nadi ki atolugu goo a doo paki malo garagara.

A mariatae silae ko.

Goo a mariatae sava pae epua kite a mariatae sava pae elagi ni natasi."

Goo ragi wanogoe, manu wanogoe e doropusi nakau, poo lawo paki nap̃au ni vonu wanogoe, nam̃aduna.

Goo e doo sava, e sava paraki euta.

Manu wanogoe e peani nalaelaeana waina e doko nam̃adu ni vonu.

Ero sava paapaa ragi waina ero paki euta, maa vonu te noa ki nia asa naga,

"Ragi waina toro ga vaki euta

naatam̃ooli eu marisaa p̃okati au?"

Goo e naga, "Eee, eu marisaa."

Nalakena vonu e dum̃ana atae naga nae maa e pei nap̃okasi wia sikai.

Naatam̃ooli eu masau gani a.

Goo manu e noa ki nia asa naga "Eee", eu marisaa maripunue a.

Maa tero pano, tero pano paapaa ragi waina tero paki euta goo te naga te ga toropusi manu.

Goo naatam̃ooli laapa ni natokoana eu paki elau, eu puati naio, naga eu ga araika, eu ga tokogoro naika maaga.

Goo eu punusi vonu wanogoe e doko euta, goo eu puati a.

Eu puati vonu wanogoe.

Goo eu dape a paki esum̃a.

Maa natokoana adeada e daa pei uvea ki elau, e doko m̃aladigi.

Goo manu e diri pano doko doo punusi vonu wanogoe, e dodomi a, nalakena nae e peea silae a.

Pano paa[paa] goo ragi waina eu doropusi a, goo manu wanogoe e paki nam̃asua ni nakau sikai waina e doko leana ki tokora waina eu doropusi vonu asa.

Goo e doo kai, e doo kai poo doo sale.

Maa ragi waina e pano doko punusi kusue sikai.

Goo e noa ki nia asa naga, "Kusue!

Ku mariatae silae au? goo a ga woo pakotovi ko ki naadi mami waia.

Naadi mami waia a ga woo dua ako asa."
Goo e naga, "Maa a ga maniigo mari nasava?"
Goo e naga, "Ku punusi vonu waia, eu solisoki a madoko.
Kinau, a ga too sale nam̃asua ni nakau goo naatam̃ ooli maaga wanae eu
    ga too punusi au.
Maa niigo, p̃a too katikotovi natali waina eu solisoki vonu asa."
Goo ragi wanogoe, manu nae e doo kai poo doo sale, nam̃asua ni nakau,
    goo naatam̃ooli maaga eu doo leosoki manu wanogoe waina nae e doo
    sale.
Maa kusue nae e doo p̃osiwosi.
E doo katikotovi natali maaga wanogoe.
Paapaa ragi waina manu e doo punusi vonu
paapaa ragi waina vonu e doo sole pano paapaa te paki natasi,
goo manu te diri.
E diri umai doko moro umai punusi kusue, doko naga,
"Naadi mami waia a dua ko asa."
Maa vonu te pano!
Maa ragi waina naatam̃ooli maaga eu moro pa punusi vonu adeada kite
    te pueli.
Eu naga, "O, manu waina e soro gida.
E soro gida naga tu ga too punusi a maa navatuuna sikai waina e
    marikotovi natali ni vonu waina tu soli a asa.
Maa e pei kusue."
Goo ragi waia ku pe toropusi naadi mami, e pe toko ekopu,
e pe toko *sef,* kite e pe toko esava, maa kusue e ga woo gani a.
Nalakena manu te dua kusue naadi mami naga e ga vei navinaga
    aneana.
Natukunoa waia e noopu.

"The Dove, the Turtle and the Rat"
by
Kaltaᵽau M̃asemata

I shall tell a tale, about a bird, named the **dove**.
This particular time he had been journeying through the bush, when it
    started raining **hard**.
So he climbed onto a tree that was floating along in a big river.
It felt good being up on the tree, as it began floating down toward the
    seashore.
So he stayed there, standing on the tree ... and eventually it was swept
    out to sea, far out to sea!
It went a long way out and he began thinking that he ought to fly back
    to dry land.
But, it was already toooo far.
He thought, "Oh, it's really much too far. If I try to fly back my wings will
    surely give out and I'll be killed."
So he kept on drifting... and after a while he saw a large fish coming
    along. It was the **shark**.
He said to him, "Shark! Can you help me get back to shore?"
He replied, "Yes, I can, but I don't travel in the open air.
I travel in the depths of the sea.
If I were to travel underwater, you wouldn't be able to hang onto me."
So he kept on drifting.
He thought he was going to die.
And so he drifted on until he found a fish called **masoni**–
actually, the larger type, [called] **takeo**.
So once again he said to him, "Takeo! Can you help me get to shore?"
He replied, "Yes, I can help you, but I don't travel in the open air,

I travel in the depths of the sea.

If I were to travel underwater, you wouldn't be able to hang onto me."

So he kept on drifting.

He lost sight of land!

And as he drifted, he saw a turtle travelling toward him.

So he said to him, "Turtle!

Can you help me?"

He replied,

"Yes!

I often go to dry land. When I want to lay my eggs and bury them, I
always go to a dry place.

I can help you.

And I can travel either under the sea or on top of the sea as well."

So then the bird abandoned the tree, and sat on the turtle's head, [and
then] on his back.

And he started off, he headed for land.

The bird was so happy to be up on the turtle's back.

The two of them travelled along... until finally they were about to go
ashore, and the turtle said to him, "When we go ashore

people won't kill me, will they?"

He replied, "No, of course not, they won't."

(For the turtle knew he was good meat.

People liked eating it.)

But the bird assured him that "No" people wouldn't kill him.

So they went on; they went on until they finally came ashore and he was
about to let the bird off.

There were a lot of people going to the shore, carrying spears for fishing,
for driving the fish [into their nets].

And they saw the turtle on the shore, and caught it.

They captured the turtle.

Then they took it home.

But their village was not far from the shore, it was quite close by.

So the bird flew off and kept watching the turtle, feeling so sorry for him,
because he had helped him earlier.

Finally, they put [the turtle] down, then the bird flew up into the crown
of a tree that stood right at the place where they had left the turtle.

And he cried out, he cried and danced.

As he did, he spotted a rat.

So he said to him, "Rat!

Could you help me, and I'll repay you with ripe bananas?

I'll give the ripe bananas to you."

He said, "But, what am I supposed to do for you?"

He replied, "You see the turtle they've left tied up here.

I am going to dance in the top of this tree and the people will watch me.

But you chew through the rope with which they've tied the turtle up."
So then, the bird sang out and danced in the crown of the tree, and [all]
    the people stared at this dancing bird.
But as for the rat—he was working.
He was chewing away at the ropes...
Until finally the bird, watching the turtle,
saw him begin to crawl away, and at last he crawled right down to the
    sea.
So then the bird flew off.
Then he flew back again to see the rat, and said,
"I give you these ripe bananas."
And the turtle was gone!
So when the people went to look at their turtle again, it had disappeared.
They said, "Oh, that bird tricked us.
It tricked us into watching it while something cut the rope with which we
    tied the turtle.
It was the rat."
So now, if you leave a ripe banana inside [the house],
or in the *sef*[1], or wherever it might be, a rat will eat it.
Because the bird gave ripe bananas to the rat to be his food.
That is the end of this tale.

Footnotes

1. *Sef* is the Bislama term for a food storage cabinet. These shelving
    units generally stand a few feet off the floor and are covered with wire
    mesh to keep out flies and other insects. They might be expected to,
    but do not, keep out rats and this tale suggests the reason why that
    may be so.

(Reference: Kalo-22. June 26, 1978, Unakapu. Tape 8A, 45-52.)

Text No.33:

"Tooa, M̃aata goo Makala"
pae
Kaltap̃au M̃asemata

Io!
A ga woo moro noa natukunoa sikai,
e pei natukunoa ni **tooa**.
Tooa sikai e pei tooa goroi.
E doko paa[paa] te pa mari veete, paa[paa] doko nadi ki **atolu**.
E nadi ki atoluna.
Maa e peani napaga sikai e doko tokora waina tooa wanogoe e doko asa,
    goo e peani m̃aata warua sikai nae maa e doko elagi.
Goo e doo punusi tooa wanogoe e doo dakovi atoluna.
E naga, "O, kinau maa a masau dakovi atolugu."
Goo tooa wanogoe ragi waina e pano e naga e nadi ki sua atoluna goo
te diri paki uvea goo te doo p̃akap̃akaata, maa m̃aata e doo punusi a.
Paapaa ragi sikai tooa e moro pano e dakovi atoluna paapaa e pano goo
    m̃aata wanogoe e m̃elu.
E pei m̃aata **warua**.
E m̃elu poo pa dakovi atolu ni tooa wanogoe, nalakena **nae** e masau
    dakovi atolu.
Goo ragi waina tooa e doko paapaa e moro paraki atoluna, naga e ga
    takovi a goo ragi waina e pano, e punusi a kite
m̃aata wanogoe te dakovi atoluna.
Goo e doo p̃akap̃akaata poo doo daliepu!
Maa seei e ga silae a poo maneana kopasi lua m̃aata wanogoe?
Goo e pano poo pap̃ai **waago**.
E pap̃ai waago sikai goo e noa ki nia asa naga,
"E! Waago!

Ku mariatae silae au?" E naga, "Nasava?"

E naga, "Ragi waina a pano ma m̃aata sikai e dakovi atolugu."

Maa tooa e midodoa liliu, "E! Ragi waina e ga vano goo ragi waina ero
 ga vile, goo, atolugu e ga woo mawora."

Goo e pano poo moro pap̃ai buluk.

Goo e noa ki nia asa, e naga, "Buluki!

Ku mariatae silae au kite?" Goo e naga, "A ga silae ko nasava?"

E naga, "Oo, a pano kite m̃aata sikai te dakovi atolugu."

Goo e midoaki nia naga, "Oo, buluki nam̃elena nae e poo p̃arua.

Ragi waina naara ero ga vile goo nam̃elena e poo p̃arua goo e ga woo
 paasisasaa ki atolugu."

Goo te doo daliepu paapaa e punusi makala sikai.

Makala kiiki sikai e umai goo e noa ki nia asa naga,

"E, makala!

Ku mariatae silae au kite?"

E naga, "Nasava?"

Goo e naga,

"Ragi waina a pano, naga a ga dakovi atolugu maa m̃aata warua sikai te
 dakovi sua e."

E naga, "Io,

a ga woo silae ko."

Goo makala e pano poo puati bel varea, varea adeada.

Goo ragi waina makala mamauputi eu saisai,

makala kirikiri, makala warua, eu saisai!

Eu paki manu paka manu!

Goo, eu paraki m̃aata wanogoe.

Ragi waina eu pano, kite e dakovi atolu ni tooa doko.

Sikai e pano doko kati napuena, sikai e pano [doko] kati nap̃auna.

Maa m̃aata e dogo e kite eu doo kati a, goo e doo parivaari.

Maa nae te midoaki nia naga te ga noopu, maa tea laapa eu poo doo umai.

Goo eu kati m̃aata wanogoe paapaa, e m̃elu dua ki atolu ni tooa wanogoe.

Goo eu kati a pano paa[paa] poo maripunue a, makala kirikiri maaga
 wanogoe eu maripunue m̃aata warua wanogoe.

Goo ragi waina m̃aata e mate,

e madoko paa[paa] e p̃oa, goo makala maaga wanogoe eu poo ova malo
 kirikiri maaga poo paki nasum̃a ni kiada maaga,

poo dape a e pei nap̃okasi adeada.

Natukunoa e noopu.

"The Chicken, the Snake and the Ant"
by
Kaltap̃au M̃asemata

Alright!
I shall tell another tale,
a tale about a chicken.
[It] was a hen.
[One daaay] she went to build a nest, and eventually she laid an egg.
She laid her egg.
And there was a banyan in the spot where the hen lived, and there was
    a big snake living up high in it.
He used to watch the hen sitting on her egg.
He thought, "Oh, I'd like to be sitting on my egg, too."
So when the hen had laid her egg
she would fly away and be clucka-cluck-clucking, and the snake would
    watch her.
Finally one time the hen again went to sit on the egg, then she went away,
    and the snake came out.
It was a big snake.
He wanted to sit on an egg, so he came out and sat on the hen's egg.
So when the hen came back for her egg, she saw
the snake sitting on her egg.
And she clucked and clucked and ran in circles around it!
Who could help her and chase the snake away for her?
So she went off and found a pig.
She found this pig and said to him,
"Hey, pig!
Can you help me?" He said, "What is it?"

276

She said, "I went [to my nest] and there was a snake was sitting on my
    egg."
But then the hen had second thoughts, "Oh, no! If he goes and they fight,
    my egg will get broken."
So she went on and next she found a bull.
And she said to him, "Bull!
Can you help me?" He said, "How can I help you?"
She said, "Well, I went [to my nest] and there was a snake was sitting on
    my egg."
But then she thought, "Oh, but the bull's foot is so big!
If they fight his foot is so big he'll crush my egg to pieces."
So she kept going around in circles until she found an ant.
The little ant came along and she said to him,
"Hey, ant!
Can you help me?"
He said, "What is it?"
And she said,
"When I went to sit on my egg there was a great big snake sitting on it."
He said, "Alright,
I'll help you."
So the ant went and rang the bell at their meeting-house.
And then all of the ants gathered,
little ants, big ants, they [all] came!
There were a thousand times a thousand!
Then, they went off after the snake.
When they arrived, he was still sitting on the hen's egg.
[So] one went and bit his tail; [and] another went and bit his head.
The snake felt them biting, and he began to move about.
And he thought that was all there was to it, but there were so many they
    just kept on coming.
They kept biting the snake until finally he got off the egg.
And they kept biting and biting him until they killed him—all those little
    ants killed that great big snake.
So when the snake was dead,
it lay there until it stank, then the ants shouldered it in tiny pieces and
    carried it back to their homes,
taking it for their meat.
That is the end of the tale.

(Reference: Kalo-24. June 26, 1978, Unakapu. Tape 8A, 52-70.)

Chapter Nine

The Voices:
Profiles of the Narrators

The following are brief sketches and photographs of those of the included narrators with whose personal histories I am well acquainted. I cannot speak of Thomas Tanearu's background, as I had little contact with him apart from a few occasions in which he participated in recording sessions. With the others I shared many hours, both in formal interviews and in more casual discussion in various kinds of contexts.

Ronneth Manutukituki

Referred to usually as Manutukituki, a title he bears as one of a small number of high chiefs (the *maanu*) who are closest to Nguna's paramount chief, Taripoaliu, Ronneth is a very busy person. In his mid 50s, he takes a very active and influential role in M̃atoa's village life, and in wider island affairs, being not only a high chief, but also a church elder and one of Nguna's three Government Assessors. This last is an intermediary, paralegal position created in 1953 to assist local District Agents. Although the "D.A." is now a thing of the past, Government Assessors remain, vested with discretionary powers to contact and consult with the central authorities in Port Vila regarding any serious crimes, e.g., rape, violent assault or murder, which might occur within their jurisdictions.

John Tarip Mariwota

After his father, André, John Mariwota was high chief of Tikilasoa village from 1968 until his death in 1980. Like many others of his generation, he spent a number of years in his youth working on steamers, cargo ships, out of Port Vila and in the Solomons. Thereafter, he spent three years in the British Police force in Vila. He then married, returned to Tikilasoa to start a family, and remained there for the rest of his life. One of his achievements was his village's communal re-building of its impressive *varea* (meeting-house) following its near destruction by a hurricane in the early 1960s.

Kaltaβau M̃asemata

Blind since his early youth, "Kalo" was a brilliant raconteur. Due perhaps to the handicap which prevented him from participating fully in productive activities in the gardens or in wage labour, he invested a great deal of energy in developing his talent for telling captivating stories covering the full range of types. Throughout my stay on the island I was inevitably joined by his wife and many of his family and co-villagers when I went to Unakapu to enjoy and record his accounts. When he died in 1979, his companions lost not only a beloved husband, father and dear friend, but also a masterful narrator whose stories, whether short, snappy and humorous or long, complex and dramatic, were invariably vital and utterly engaging.

Lui Taatalele

A frail and very softly spoken man in his 60s, Lui lives in his native inland village, Fareafau. A respected church elder, he uses as his surname his father's first or "small name". As he recounts in his text "The Origin of Mariamearaliu", his father was a chief of Fareafau. According to *kastom*, as his son Lui is the rightful possessor and narrator of that text.

Jack Tavim̃asoe

A former teacher and retired church elder for Nekaaβa village, where he has lived for most of his life, Jack has an unusual amount of experience dealing and working with outsiders. He worked on ships, dove for trochus, and did odd jobs for a number of local plantation owners in his youth. Married in 1930, he taught school on Nguna for 14 years. Later on, he laboured long for the church, first translating hymns with Kaloris, a boyhood friend, then intermittently for many years with more than one missionary to Nguna, translating the Bible. Later, he teamed up with a linguist, Albert Schütz (who wrote a preliminary grammar of Ngunese as well as <u>Nguna Texts</u>), a historian from Dunedin, Gordon Parsonson, and finally with myself to accomplish both language-related

and ethnographic goals. Though well into his 70s, Jack's work and
likewise his texts always show his mark: careful attention to detail and
recognition of the necessity of being clear and precise. He has a
remarkable memory and, most particularly, consistently approaches
whatever he is asked to do, be it tutoring in the Ngunese language,
transcribing texts (an exhausting task), or recounting texts, in a professional, entirely conscientious fashion. It has been my great pleasure to
know and to collaborate with him.

Thomas Tavirana

A former elder and teacher—one of the early graduates of the Tongoa
Training Institute—Thomas took pleasure remembering how strong and
active he was in his youth and manhood, playing football, cricket, diving,
shooting the bow and arrow skilfully, and so on. Toward the end he was
increasingly debilitated by Parkinson's Disease; yet his mind and spirit
remained lively. He continued to pursue actively familial concerns,
concerns regarding the community's spiritual life, village affairs, most
particularly the education of the young in Ngunese traditions or *kastom*
and, when he felt able, he continued his hobby of carving clubs and
canoes. He was extremely interested in my research on Ngunese history
and *kastom*, and we spent many hours conferring on these subjects in his
home in Tikilasoa. In the hopes that his family will see and read his text
included herein, I would like to convey to them the gratitude I feel toward
Thomas for his enthusiastic interest: even when he was unwell or when
I felt daunted by the research goals I had set for myself, his strength of
spirit buoyed us both up.

Plate Three: (l.-r.) Lui Taatalele, Ronneth Manutukituki, Jack Taviṁasoe

Plate Four: Thomas Tavirana (in foreground, with hat)

Plate Five: Kaltap̃au M̃asemata, with his wife, Leitagis

Plate Six: John Tarip Mariwota

Chapter Ten

Nguna Text And Culture

Variation

Now that one has read the texts, there is a final issue to consider: the question of inter-textual consistency. It has already been stated that in some texts the narrator employs one or more of a variety of rhetorical means whereby he/she establishes an air of veracity and historical authenticity about that text. Where several versions of what is apparently the same text were collected, generally only one has been represented in this volume, i.e., that which either seemed to be the most authentic based on local criteria, or had a reasonable claim in those terms and was also the more elaborate or more artfully crafted piece (in the editor's literary judgement). This is in no way intended to place greater emphasis on, nor to lend greater credence to one individual's version over another's, although this is an obvious and almost inescapable local consequence of an outsider making choices between different versions of a text. The fact that some individuals' renditions are engraved in printed form, while others' are not, may alone lead to a devaluation of those and any other contrasting versions.

In order to take into account this potential problem, while avoiding reproducing verbatim texts which vary little from one another, the instances of discrepancy or disagreement of which I am aware are cited below along with whatever contrasting information is involved. In this way, Ngunese narrators whose versions do not appear in the volume will be credited with "the facts" as they see them; and Ngunese readers, if they so choose, can judge for themselves which version they feel is most authoritative, a function which I feel is not the scribe/anthropologist's to perform.

In the concluding portion of Kaltaᵽau M̃asemata's text "The Origin of Tariᵽoamata and Tariᵽoaliu" (text #1), it is stated that the captured child of the *sagalegaale*, once civilized and grown to maturity as a woman, gives birth to a son and a daughter, the boy being Tariᵽoamata. The girl, sent to Nguna upon being betrothed, marries and gives birth to a boy who is the first Tariᵽoaliu. This differs from Jack Tavim̃asoe's version of the same story, which is found in Albert Schütz's collection, *Nguna Texts* (text #13). There the captured daughter of the *sagalegaale* gives birth to two boys. The first, named Tariᵽoaliu, moves to Nguna and becomes paramount chief there; the second is named Tariᵽoamata and remains as paramount chief on Efate. The present paramount chief of Nguna, Leith Tariᵽoaliu, himself recounted these events informally, his version agreeing with that of Tavim̃asoe.

Some interesting, non-conflictual variations exist between three accounts of the doings of the "new diviner": Kaltaᵽau M̃asemata's text (#12 herein); the version recounted by the late Marivurai of Farealapa village and that by Jack Tavim̃asoe, both of which are available in *Nguna Texts* (#20 and 21 respectively). It should be noted that Marivurai was himself a direct lineal descendant of the "diviner" in question, the latter being Marivurai's paternal grandfather (*tiia*). To the Ngunese mind, of course, this gives Marivurai's version a particularly direct, therefore compelling connection to the narrative "facts".

Neither Marivurai nor Tavim̃asoe supplies details regarding the way in which the new diviner initially acquires his powers, a discussion which constitutes a substantial portion of M̃asemata's text. All three versions do agree on the kinds of miraculous feats worked by the diviner; in Marivurai's, however, the new diviner attributes his miracle of the magically appearing coconut puddings to God:

> He said to them, "It was Jehovah who gave it to you. Uncover it and eat."... When they returned, they spread the news to those who stayed in the village—"Today we planted for the new diviner. He asked for some food, and there it was before us. He sent it to us that we might eat. He said it was Jehovah who gave it." And it was done at that place.(Schütz 1969a:210)

Tavim̃asoe's version, in which the new diviner is not named, corresponds closely to that of M̃asemata, with two exceptions. The former's conclusion has the diviner predicting the arrival on Nguna of the first book, a very special book—the Bible—introduced by the first missionary. Then, upon Rev. Milne's arrival (with said book), the following rather startling events are said to have transpired:

And when Peter Milne came to Nguna, he wanted to shake
hands with the diviner, but the diviner refused. But Milne
insisted that he shake hands with the new diviner. He still
refused, but Milne's words were forceful, and finally he shook
hands. But blood came from the new diviner's hands, and he
stayed [lived] but a short time, then died. They buried him,
and after the third day, they went to his grave and saw that
it was sunken in and the body of the new diviner was not in it.
He was the last diviner on Nguna. There have not been any
more. (Schütz 1969a:223)

A recurrent ethnographic and textual difference of opinion is that of
the traditional practice regarding the taking of chiefly titles. While the
adherents to each view tend to be adamant, their positions are neither
logically nor ethnographically irreconcilable.

In Kaltap̃au M̃asemata's "Making Chiefs" (text #7) he refers to the
acquisition of chiefly titles as a stepping–stone process in which a
successor may take a high title once his predecessor has "retired" from
active performance of his duties. Having given way to the younger man,
he is thereafter referred to by a third or "retired" name.

In the opinion of other Ngunese local historians, however, a new chief
would *not* take his successor's chiefly name while the latter was still
alive; they say that this is not the Ngunese way, but that of islands to the
north–Tongoa and others of the Shepherd Islands. Ngunese tradition
dictates, rather, that a chief remain chief, retaining his chiefly title,
until his death, at which point, and only at which point, his successor
may assume the chiefly title.

If one reads on in M̃asemata's narrative, however, it is clear that the
ritual ordination of a chief's successor presumes that his predecessor is
dead, in that the "spirit" with which the title is imbued must be "pulled
up" from the previous title-holder's grave. The discrepancy involved
here, then, is a minor one. M̃asemata is referring to a two stage process:
the younger man, as chief-designate, takes over the chiefly functions as
the aging incumbent grows unable to perform them; consequently, the
younger man may be treated *as if* he already bore that title. But it is only
when the chief is actually dead and buried that his successor can be
formally installed in the position and given the title.

A particularly fascinating case of variation concerns Kaltap̃au's "How
the Slit-Drum was Discovered" (#14). This brings up a significant
phenomenon in Ngunese narrative behaviour: some narrators recount
texts based on reference to their own, handwritten corpus of texts. It is

not unusual for one to be told accounts informally in a truncated outline or précis form, with the promise that, once the raconteur has reviewed the details thoroughly by reference to his own written documents, he will sit down for a formal recording session. All too often, unfortunately, for one reason or another, the future date is not set and the "full" text is never told. Kaltap̃au often operated this way, too; but he always had the next set of texts ready for performance by the time the ethnographer next came to call.

"How the Slit-Drum was Discovered", as a product of this process, is a historic and multi-layered phenomenon, a performance of a text of a performance of a text. What becomes interesting, then, is in what ways does the performance differ from the text that precedes it, and on which it is modelled, as an oral re-presentation? This is the inverse of the usual issue in textual re-production, with which much of this volume deals, i.e., in what ways does the text, as re-produced by the analyst/editor, differ from the original text as performed event?

It was long after I had recorded many of his accounts, including this one, that Kaltap̃au allowed me to examine his own compendium of texts. One of his relatives had the story transcribed back in 1919 and it came into Kalo's hands, by inheritance, in 1938. He then had this decaying document re-inscribed as part of his personal collection of texts in 1970; and I was permitted to peruse it in 1978.

The written text differs from Kaltap̃au's oral performance of it in two major respects: first, the main character's name, Matap̃esu, is included in the written version. It is fair to assume that, as often happens, the narrator momentarily forgot the individual's proper name in the heat of the narrative moment in front of an audience and a tape recorder. Second, the written version's ending goes slightly further than did the oral performance of it, providing the proper name of the first known dancing-ground, and generalizing about the spread of the inventions of making slit-drums and dancing-grounds, and dancing. It runs, in translation, as follows:

> [Having finished the slit-drums,] they constructed a dancing-ground. They called it M̃alamalonap̃arae [Place of the Sugar-cane Dancing-Ground]. Then they began to dance and to construct dancing-grounds all around Nguna, and they would dance on them to the slit-drums. They used to carve a certain number of them. There were a total of four [types]. (Author's Fieldnotes Vol.6: 57-8)

The two texts recounting the origins and ancestry of the M̃atoa high chief, Mariameara or Mariamearaliu are clearly the same text in terms of focus, but there numerous obvious discrepancies between them. In brief point form, the essential elements of each version are as follow:
Version One:
- the coming of Leiameara from Efate, from Tapumara, the Takara landing-place
- her landing at Vatup̃aunu, then assumption of the chiefly position in M̃atoa, as their first chief
- succession by Mantai (same matriclan: yam)
- succession by Manaatamate (yam clan)
- succession by Marikoroi of Rewoka village, Sapuraki meeting-house (also yam clan)
- succession by Taatalele, Marikoroi's sister's son, of Rewoka-napua
- succession by his son, Kenneth (a shift away from the yam clan)
- succession by his son, Abel.

Version Two:
- Manaatamate is the first chief of M̃atoa
- succession by Mantai
- succession by Marikoroi
- Leiameara comes from Takara, landing at Vaatup̃auna
- succession by her daughter's son, Taatalele
- succession by his son, Nap̃ileitia.

While it is important to point these differences out, one walks a delicate line in doing so. Narrators on Nguna take pride in recounting texts to which they consider themselves the legitimate heirs. They do not lightly engage in telling accounts which they feel "belong" to others. In this case, by virtue of ancestry, place of birth and title, both of these individuals felt properly placed and even therefore, in some sense, obliged to tell the "facts" as they know them. Consequently, having no other, external sources for comparison, I will make only a few observations about what is common to both accounts. They agree on these fundamental elements: the name, gender, place of origin, clan membership and route taken to reach Nguna by the new chief, Leiameara; the names of the four members of the yam clan who were chiefs of M̃atoa (although the order of the first two is reversed from one version to the other); and, the point at which succession moved out of the yam line, i.e., the shift from uncle-to-nephew to father-to-son succession.

It is sufficient to say that the fundamental difference is where, in the sequence of succession, the first Mari-ameara appeared. As with other examples of variation discussed above, there are no "objective" historical sources or documents available which might be brought to bear for comparison. So any assessment of the relative authority of these two texts must necessarily be left to those who tell and those who hear them; and, indeed, in my view this is how it should be even were such documents available.

Textual Re-presentation as Ethnography

As Gregory Reck (1984:4) put it, "Humans are story–telling animals. We domesticate our past, our present, and our future with narrative." I might also add that all too often the ways in which outsiders manipulate, control and re-present the oral literary performance of other cultures has nothing to do with how they might themselves choose to present or have it presented. Insiders might well like a chance to domesticate/control the folklore and other kinds of materials written on or about them and read by others of the world community. The "natives" would like to be able to domesticate their own narrative or literature, too.

With this in mind, I have refrained from performing some of the routine anthropological operations on the foreign corpus, such as what is little more than a rating of accounts on an extrinsic true/false scale: for example, "this is a tale because it clearly could not be true" [i.e., it offends or deviates too greatly from the researcher's belief system]; or, "this story is a legend, because it is possible that it might have really happened; and this one is history, but this one can only be a myth", etc. Instead, I have analyzed and presented the indigenous criteria employed in assessment of historical authenticity, while making every effort not to impose my own, external (and cultural) judgements regarding the historicity of any given text.

Similarly, foreign texts virtually always appear in anthropological works in English only (or French, or whatever happens to be the writer's mother tongue), but certainly not verbatim in the indigenous language. It is as if the texts' very existence, and certainly their comprehensibility, were only made possible via the foreign (civilized/civilizing?) language. My argument is that it is imperative to convey the contrary impression, that is, a vivid sense of the fact that these texts, a body of cultural thought in textual form, are part of a lively contemporary culture, and have their purest realization via that culture's own language, a fully functional, living and working language. For these reasons, this volume supplies full transcriptions of the texts as they were recorded in "live" perform-

ance, in the Ngunese language. It also includes a complete glossary/
dictionary of the more than 1100 items of grammar and vocabulary that
are used in the texts.

It would seem logical that, as writing and performing, in any culture,
are about cultural self-definition, so too is textual re-presentation. But,
of course, it isn't. It is actually about cultural other-definition, as is all
ethno-graphic writing. It is the domestication or definition—still euphem-
istically referred to as "description"—of one group's past, present and
even future by one or more members of another group.

According to Gatewood, four variables figure into the enterprise of
"ethnographic description":

> In sum, for ethnographic description, there are four separable
> constraints on the form and content of the final product. First
> is what natives do and what they think... A second constraint
> is the ethnographer's own values, motives, life ambitions,
> theoretical prejudices, and so on... Third is the author's
> estimation of the intended audience, that is, what the author
> thinks the readership will accept and respond to. The last
> constraint is the currently preferred literary form. (Gatewood
> 1984:5)

True. But, to these four constraints, I suggest a fifth be added: the
"*natives'* " understanding and estimation of the intended audience, in
combination with the "*natives'* " own values, motives and life ambitions,
as well as their cultural self-perception. This must also be accompanied
by a rider—that, if last, this is most certainly not the least of these
constraints or factors. Its reality and massive significance are recognized in the form and content of the present volume.

Just as no ethnographic fieldwork in the participant–observation
style could be accomplished without the participation of those who are
"observed", neither could this ethnographic piece have been created
without such mutual participation and observation. In short, while as
author/editor I have chosen to produce a volume of a particular type
because, for my reasons and purposes it pleases, interests and effectively
"does the job", its final shape and texture is in large part dependent upon
the reasons, purposes and interests of those who participated in its
creation. And this is, in my view, wholly appropriate.

Appendix:

Two Inter-linear Translations

Text #7, "*Namariana ni Naveinawotaana Maaga*/Making Chiefs".

A poo masau stori nalo ni stori ni na-vei-na-wota-ana goo
I Comp want recount subject of story of chief and

na-vei-na-wota-ana maaga doko Nguna, goo P̃ele goo Efate na-gisa
chief PL on Nguna, and P̃ele and Efate name

e dolu-toolu. Ragi waina na-vei-na-wota-ana sikai e pei naga e
it three. Time that chief one it is that it

ga woo duu oli tama-na. Goo ragi waina e ga veani
Int will stand instead father-his. And time that he Int have

na-gisa veea wanogoe. Goo e ga umai dape na-gisa ni m̃aleoputo
name first that. And he Int come take name of middle

na-gisa veea e ga woo nadi ki nia madoko. Maa ragi waina
name first he Int will throw Obj Mkr it away. But time that

e pe toko paapaa e pe matua. Goo natu-na e pe vaataka wia.
he if live until he if old. And child-his he if enough quite.

293

E ga woo moro dape na-gisa ni m̃aleoputo maa tama-na e ga
He Int will in-turn take name of middle but father-his he Int

tape na-gisa ke-toolu e pei "retired" na-gisa. Waina te noopu.
take name Ord Mkr-three it is "retired" name. That he finished.

Goo ragi waina eu doko paa[paa] eu masau dovi na-vei-na-wota-ana
And time that they stay until they want ordain chief

wanogoe. Eu piragi a pa-ki weede. Maa peea na-vei-na-wota
that. They lead him go-to throne. But first chief

lake-sikai-ana. Dakiusi e ga umai poo puasike a. Dapala waina
related. Such he Int come and pull-up him. Like that

e peani na-vatuuna sikai waina na-wota veea e mate e pei
there is thing a that chief first he dead it be

naleo mauri sikai waina e doko matigo waina eu pa doni a
thing living a that it live grave that they go bury it

pilake na-p̃atoko. Na-vuasike-ana e pei na-wota lake-sikai-ana
with corpse. Ordination it is chief related

waina e ga tape te na-vatuuna seara sikai umai dapala waina
that he Int take any thing some a come like that

e puasike naleo mauri wanogoe e pei sup̃e ni na-vei-na-wota-ana.
he pulls-up thing living that it is god of chief.

Poo sili na-ata-m̃ooli wanogoe waina eu poo moro dovi
And enter person that who they Comp again annoint

na-p̃au-na goo na-wosi-ana aneana e ga woo moro kasua p̃ia.
head-his and work his it Int will in-turn strong good.

Goo ragi waina e ga vuasike a. Peea goo tea aneana maaga
So time that he Int pull-up him. First and person his PL

e pe vei tukurau waina e doko kite tai-na maaga kite
it if is widow who she remain or brother-his PL or

gore-na maaga maa e-daku eu ga woo pusi a. Eu ga woo
sister-his PL but after they Int will escort him. They Int will

pusi na-gisa wanogoe. Poo dua na-ata-m̃ooli waina e ga woo
escort name that. And give person that he Int will

ova na-gisa wanogoe. Goo ragi waina eu pusi a pano e-daku
carry name that. And time that they escort him go after

eu ga woo piragi a pa-ki weede. Waina e pei vaatu sikai e
they Int will lead him go-to throne. That it is stone a he

ga woo pei tea tovi-ana asa. Goo ragi waina na-wota wanogoe
Int will be one annointed on-it. And time that chief that

e pe toko paapaa e pe mate doko ragi ni tuai e pe naga e
he if remain until he if dead in time of old he if think he

pe mate. Eu ga woo pitua ki na-vasa-ana pa-ki sara
might die. They Int will send Obj Mkr word go-to every

na-ata-m̃ooli, Nguna dali-viri kite naure kite Efate. Goo eu poo
person, Nguna around or island or Efate. And they Comp

umai dagi-si na-wota wanogoe. Maa ragi waina eu ga umai
come mourn chief that. But time that they Int come

na-wota wanogoe e daa pei tea lesiana dakiusi ragi waia.
chief that he not is one lain-down like time this.

Maa eu ga woo mari a e ga ovi doko naara ni na-sum̃a
But they Int will make him he Int lean on wall of house

aneana e ga woo dapala tea mauri sikai. Goo eu ga woo
his he Int will like person living a. And they Int will

puati waago warua sikai waina na-pati-na e puri paka-ruua. Poo
bring pig big a which tusk-its it pierce time-two. And

liko soka-sokaari viria maaga wanogoe poo umai liko-ti naru ni
tie one-to the-other vine PL that and come tie arm of

na-vei-na-wota-ana wanogoe asa. Eu ga liko-ti a paki
chief that with-it. They Int tie it to

naru-na ni matua. Goo ragi waina eu pe tagi paapaa e
arm-his of right. And time that they might wail until it

pe maligo. Goo eu ga woo pa ova ki nia. Eu ga
might be-dark. They they Int will and bury Obj Mkr him. They Int

woo pa ova ki nia maa tea aneana maaga eu ga woo
will and bury Obj Mkr him but relative his PL they Int will

doko eu ga woo pali na-aleati-a rua-lima-liima. Goo na-p̄oogi-ana
stay they Int will fast day two X five X five. And night

wanogoe eu ga woo dape na-vinaga seara poo doropusi a matigo.
that they Int will take food some and leave-at it grave.

E pei waina eu ga vaga-ni a asa. Goo ragi waina mali-p̄oogi
It is that they Int feed it with-it. And time that morning

eu pano eu daa punusi te na-vinaga seara e doko matigo. Maa
they go they not see any food some it on grave. But

e lagoro pei koria kite puusi kite na-sava e gani a. Goo naara
it perhaps is dog or cat or what it eat it. And they

eu midoa ki nia naga na-ata-mate e gani a. Eu ga toko
they think Obj Mkr it that spirit it eat it. They Int stay

paapaa kup̄a lima kite na-kup̄a rua-lima-liima. Goo nae te
until day five or day two X five X five. And that-one she

ga woo paki na-tasi poo loloso. Ragi waina eu midoa ki
Int will go-to sea and wash. Time when they think Obj Mkr

nia naga eu ga va-ki matigo dapala nigida ragi waia tu doo
it that they Int go-to grave like us time this we Prog

p̄osiwosi ki nia doko kup̄a lima maa naara e pei na-kup̄a
work Obj Mkr it for day five but they it is day

rua-lima-liima kite na-kup̄a p̄onotia-sikai. Goo ragi waina eu
two X five X five or day hundred X one. And time that they

ga va-ki matigo tea mamau-puti eu ga vano. Goo ragi
Int go-to grave person all they Int go. And time

waina eu pa-ki matigo eu midoa ki nia naga eu ga
that they go-to grave they think Obj Mkr it that they Int

vavano na-tasi. Goo ragi wanogoe eu ga naga, "Itoo!
wash sea. And time that they Int say, "Good-bye!

Itoo! Taroa itoo!" Ragi wanogoe eu sava naga eu ga
Good-bye! Everyone good-bye!" Time that they run that they Int

kisi-p̄ai na-tasi; seei e ga veea kisi-p̄ai na-tasi. Maa eu midoa
touch sea; who he Int first touch sea. But they think

ki nia naga tea waina e e-daku saatana ki
Obj Mkr it that person who is last devil of

na-vei-na-wota-ana wanogoe e ga kisi-p̄ai a goo nae e ga
chief that it Int touch him and that-one he Int

woo mate. Goo ragi waina eu ga woo mamau-puti sava kisi
will die. And time that they Int will all run touch

na-tasi. E pe vei euta maaga maa eu masau naga eu ga sava
sea. It if is inland PL but they want that they Int run

poo kisi na-tasi. Eu sava poo gaegae maa tea waina e
and touch sea. They run and puffing but person who he

kasua e kisi-p̄ai na-tasi peea. Goo ragi waina eu pa-ki sum̃a.
strong he touch sea first. And time that they go-to home.

Eu mari na-vinaga warua goo eu moro dovi na-p̄au ni
They make food big and they again annoint head of

na-vei-na-wota-ana sikai waina e ga tuu oli tama-na waina
chief a who he Int stand instead father-his who

te mate sua waina eu ova ki nia. Goo stori kiiki waia te
he dead Comp who they bury Obj Mkr him. And story little this it

noopu tokora waia.
finished place this.

Text #8, "*Wota ni Manu*/Chief of the Birds".

Vaatu sikai na-gisa-na e pei wota-ni-manu. Goo tuai, tuai,
Stone one name-its it is chief-of-bird. And long ago, long ago,

tuai, ragi waina e doko Eromago e pei na-ata-m̃ooli. E pei
long ago time that it stay Eromago it is person. It is

na-ata-m̃ooli waina e pei na-ata-m̃ooli araika e doo dali-viri
person who he is person fisher he Prog around

na-vanua ni Eromago. Goo ragi waina e umai paki taleeva ni
land of Eromago. And time that he came to coast of

Efate, e punusi na-gisu varau sikai waina na-gisa-na e pei
Efate, he saw point long a which name-its it is

Maniura goo e naga, "O! A leo-m̃ata ki na-gisu wa-nae.
Manuira and he said, "Oh, I look-well of point over-there.

A masau pa lawo na-ika asa maa a ga vae e-sava pano?
I want go spear fish on-it but I Int by where go?

E pei uvea saa." Goo e pano poo sara ki naio varau sikai
It is far very." So he go and cut Obj Mkr spear long a

waina na-tua-na e parau. Goo ragi waina e doko Eromago e nadi
which shaft-its it long. And time that he stay Eromago he threw

ki na-vinaga ni naio wanogoe e doko na-wora-one ni
Obj Mkr head of spear that it stay beach of

Eromago. Na-tura ni naio aneana e umai p̃oka na-gisu ni
Eromago. Shaft of spear his it came strike point of

Maniura goo ragi wanogoe e sai lua naio aneana. Goo e atulake
Maniura and time that he pull out spear his. And he start

poo lawo na-ika pae Maniura poo umai paki taleeva ni P̃au.
and spear fish from Manuira and come to coast of P̃au.

Goo ragi waina e umai paki P̃au e punusi tama-da-wota
And time that he come to P̃au he see husband-and-wife

sikai ero doko. E pei na-vei-na-wota-ana ni P̃au. E pei
a they-two stay. It is chief of P̃au. It is

mariki Valea-wia goo na-goroi aneana e pei Lei-wia. Goo ragi
old-man Valeawia and wife his it is Leiwia. And time

wanogoe e doo lawo na-ika goo e dape a pa-ki sum̃a ni ki-ada.
that he Prog spear fish and he took it go-to house of theirs.

Goo na-goroi ki na-vei-na-wota-ana wanogoe e mari na-ika
And wife of chief that she cook fish

wanogoe e ma-aso goo ero doo gani a. Goo ragi sikai e
that it cooked and they-two Prog eat it. And time one he

doo disu umai pae taleeva ni One-sua paki E-pule. Goo e doo
Prog move come from coast of Onesua to Epule. And he Prog

liliu pano punusi tama-da-wota paapaa ragi sikai e umai doko
return go see husband-and-wife until time one he come and

do-liu paki taleeva ni E-mua e punusi na-goroi sikai natu ni
pass to coast of Emua he see woman a child of

Ma-na-lae-sinu, na-gisa-na Lei-na-sei, e naga e ga vautu.
Manalaesinu, name-her Leinasei, she think she Int bake.

E noa ki nia, "Aleati-wia!" goo e puati na-ika seara goo e dua
He say to her, "Good morning!" and he catch fish some and he give

na-goroi wanogoe asa. Maa tama-na goo p̃ila-na ero
woman that of-it. But father-her and mother-her they-two

surata pu-oli goo ragi waina ero pa-ki sum̃a ero
gardening gone and time that they-two go-to house they-two

dogo na-p̃o ni na-ika. Goo ero naga, "Seei e dua ko
perceive smell of fish. And they-two say, "Who he give you

na-ika?" Goo Lei-na-sei e naga, "Na-ata-m̃ooli sikai. E lawo
fish?" And Leinasei she say, "Person a. He spear

na-ika umai paapaa e dua au asa maa te moro liliu." Goo
fish come until he give me of-it but he again return." And

matamai ki nia e moro pano na-lake-na e punusi koroi
tomorrow of it he again go because he see girl

wanogoe goo te masau na naga e ga vei na-goroi aneana
that and he want her that she Int be wife his

natu ni Ma-na-lae-sinu. Goo matamai ki nia te moro pano.
child of Manalaesinu. And tomorrow of it he again go.

Goo p̃ila-na goo tama-na ero moro surata. Goo ragi
And mother-her and father-her they-two again gardening. And time

wanogoe e moro dua e na-ika, e naga, "P̃a umai toro ga
that he again give her fish, she say, "Imp come we-two Int

rua paki e-kopu." Goo ragi waina p̃ila-na ma tama-na
two go-to inside." And time that mother-her and father-her

ero moro liliu, ero naga, "Na-p̃o ni na-ika wanogoe."
they-two again return, they-two say, "Smell of fish that."

E naga, "Na-ata-m̃ooli waina e moro umai." Maa ero naga,
She say, "Person that he again come. And they-two say,

"Te paki e-sava pano?" E naga, "E doko e-kopu." Goo naara
"He to where go?" She say, "He stay inside." And they

ero pano poo taloova ki nia. Goo eu mamau doko maa
they-two go and greet Obj Mkr him. And they all stay but

na-ata-m̃ooli wanogoe e pei na-ata-m̃ooli ni na-ika na-ata-m̃ooli
person that he is person of fish person

araika. Goo sara ragi e mari-saa pa-ki na-malasi maa e doo
fish. And every time he unable go-to bush but he Prog

araika dali-viri Efate. Goo e doo dape na-ika umai paapaa
fish around Efate. And he Prog catch fish come until

goo tama-da-wota wanogoe. Eu doko eu datuuta ki
and husband-and-wife that. They stay they promise Obj Mkr

nia naga na-tau vaau eu ga woo sike na-vei-na-wota-ana
it that year new they Int will raise chief

vaau, Ma-na-lae-sinu ni E-mua. Goo tea laapa eu doo
new, Manalaesinu of Emua. And person many they Prog

mari-soki-soki eu doo uɱa. Goo vitariki e umai goo
prepare they Prog clear-bush. And old-woman she come and

e noa ki natu-da asa e naga, "Te-koro pa mamale saa
she say to child-their of-it she say, "You-two so lazy very

maa kinami au doo p̃osi-wosi kasua saa pae na-malasi
but we we Prog work hard very in bush

na-lake-na tu ga mari na-vei-na-wota-ana sikai, na-tau vaau."
because we Int make chief a, year new."

Goo koroi kiiki wanogoe e noa ki mariki aneana asa, e noa
And girl little that she say to husband her of-it, she say

ki Wotanimanu asa goo e noa ki nia asa, e naga, "P̃a noa
to Wotanimanu of-it and he say to her of-it, he say, "Imp say

kii da asa naga matamai ero ga tua gida masimasi
to them of-it that tomorrow they-two Int give us knife

sikai, toro ga va uɱa." Goo ragi waina tama-da-wota
a, we-two Int go clear-bush. And time that husband-and-wife

ero dua ra masimasi kau-ɱelu sikai na-kau-na e ɱelu.
they-two give them knife handleless a handle-its it off.

Goo ero puati a poo pa-ki taava naga ero ga
And they-two took it and go-to hill that they-two Int

uɱa. Goo koroi wanogoe e peea ki nia goo ero
clear-bush. And girl that she in-front of him and they-two

pano goo e naga, "Niigo pa punusi tokora waina e matemate
go and he say, "You go see place that is level

paki uvea." Goo ero pano poo dae-lua na-kau sikai maau
to far." And they-two go and pull-out tree one just

poo puti-lua na-ɱenau sikai maau poo nadi ki nia, goo
and pull-out grass one just and throw Obj Mkr it, and

ero moro liliu umai paki e-suma. Goo ragi waina ero
they-two again return come to house. And time that they-two

umai paki e-suma goo tama-da-wota ero moro liliu
come to house and husband-and-wife they-two again return

p̃ila-na ma tama-na, "O! Nimu koro surata dapale sava?
mother-her and father-her, "Oh! You you-two garden like what?

Te-koro moro umai paki e-suma." Maa koroi kiiki e daa pasa.
You-two again come to house." But girl little she not speak.

E moro lawo na-ika paapaa tero pauria paa[paa] tero
He again spear fish until they-two build-fire until they-two

dao sua. Eu ganikani sua ragi-melu, mali-p̃oogi tero
cook Comp. They eat Comp evening, morning they-two

moro pano. Ero moro pa-ki tokora wanogoe waina ero
again go. They-two again go-to place that which they-two

uma e. Ragi waina ero pano na-enuma warua waina eu
clear it. Time that they-two go clearing-party large that they

madeada uma e. Ragi wanogoe te pei tea mari-m̃ata-ki-ana raki
for-them clear it. Time that it is one readied for

eu ga tokoni a na-lake-na e peani na-rei eu laapa.
they Int burn it because there are people they many.

Wota-ni-manu e peani na-rei laapa. Goo matamai ki nia ero
Wotanimanu he has people many. And tomorrow of it they-two

moro pano. Ero moro pano poo punusi te kokolo p̃ia.
again go. They-two again go and see it dry good.

Goo ero dape na-lisere sikai poo nadi ki nia asa.
And they-two take leaf one and throw Obj Mkr it on-it.

Goo ero dokoni-dogo e te madoko maa tero liliu paki
And they-two burn it it remain but they-two return to

e-suma. Goo ragi waina ero liliu umai paki e-suma
house. And time that they-two return come to house

goo na-vasa-ana sikai maau tama-da-wota ero moro
and message one just husband-and-wife they-two again

noa ki nia asa. "Nimu koro pa mamale saa." Maa koroi
say to her of-it. "You you-two so lazy very." But girl

kiiki e daa pasa na-lake-na e maaga na-wosi-ana waina
little she not speak because she astonished work that

e doo pei tea mari-ana roara adeada. Goo matamai ki nia
it Prog is one done garden their. And tomorrow of it

ero moro pano maa e pei tea tokoni-sua-ana. E pei tea
they-two again go but it is one burnt-off. It is one

mari-m̃ata-ki-ana raki waina teu ga lalawo. Wota-ni-manu
prepared for when they Int plant. Wotanimanu

noa ki Lei-na-sei e naga, "P̃a noa ki tama-m̃a goo p̃ila-m̃a
say to Leinasei he say, "Imp say to father-your and mother-your

asa naga ero ga tua gida na-wii e ga sikai maau,
of-it that they-two Int give us yam it Int one just,

goo sara naleo mamau-puti waina eu pei tea lawo-ana doko
and every thing all that they are one planted in

lolua maaga naga eu ga tua gida e ga sika-sikai." Goo eu
garden PL that they Int give us it Int one-one." And they

dua ra asa. Goo ero pano poo lawo taki na-wii sikai
give them of-it. And they-two go and plant stalk yam one

maau goo tea maaga wanogoe ero nadi ki nia ma-doko.
just and one PL those they-two throw Obj Mkr it remain.

Goo ero moro pano matamai ki nia ero punusi naga
And they-two again go tomorrow of it they-two see that

na-wii maaga eu lawo e tokora wanogoe. Eu pura ki sara
yam PL they plant it place that. They full of every

na-leo, maniok goo na-adi, noopa, na-p̃arae, na-maloku, sara
thing, manioc and banana, cabbage, sugarcane, kava, every

na-leo mamau-puti eu pura. Goo e doko paapaa ragi waina
thing all they full. And it stay until time when

na-wii te matua goo teu datuuta, naga, "E pei atelagi vaau
yam it ripe and they promise, that, "It is month new

tu ga mari na-vei-na-wota-ana goo eu doo magi sara
we Int make chief and they Prog for every

na-ata-m̃ooli maaga ni E-mua tea laapa." Woli e doo kai
person PL of Emua person many." Conch it Prog cry

eu doo madeada dape na-vinaga maaga pa-ki e-sum̃a, eu mari
they Prog for-them take food PL to house, they make

vaala pae na-sum̃a maaga; maa te na-ata sikai ni E-mua e daa
rack by house PL; but some person one of Emua he not

punusi roara adeada wanogoe paapaa adeada maaga eu noopu.
see garden their that until theirs PL they finished.

Maa koroi kiiki noa ki p̃ila-na goo tama-na asa e naga,
But girl little say to mother-her and father-her of-it she say,

"E! Waasa! Tu ga woo magi-nami surata roara
"No! The-day-after-tomorrow! We Int will for-us gather garden

agi-nami pa-ki e-sum̃a." Goo naara ero noa ki nia asa
our go-to house." And they they-two say to her of-it,

ero naga, "E! Aro mataku! Tu ga vano poo dape na-sava?
they-two say, "Oh! We-two afraid! We Int go and get what?

na-lake-na nimu koro pei tea mamale." Goo koroi kiiki e
because you you-two are person lazy." And girl little she

noa ki tama-na asa e naga, "E pei tea m̃ooli. Tu ga vano.
say to father-her of-it she say, "It is one nothing. We Int go.

Waasa! Woli e ga woo kai goo tea laapa
The-day-after-tomorrow! Conch it Int will cry and person many

tu ga woo pano. E pei na-masau-ana agi-nami." "Io." Maa naara
we Int will go. It is wish our." "Yes." But they

ero peea pano masoso goo matamai ero moro pano.
they-two first go today and tomorrow they-two again go.

Ero mari-soki-soki uupu maaga naga ragi waina eu pano
They-two prepare oven PL that time when they go

eu ga veea gani na-vinaga ma-aso veea maaga. Poo e-daku
they Int first eat food cooked before PL. And after

dape tea mata eu ga woo umai paki e-suma. Goo ragi waina
take one raw they Int will come to house. And time when

ero pano ero mari-soki-soki tea maaga wanogoe. Goo
they-two go they-two prepare one PL that. And

waasa woli e poo kai goo tea laapa eu
the-day-after-tomorrow conch it Comp cry and person many they

poo pano. Goo ragi waina eu pano taoa maaga eu doo sui
Comp go. And time when they go oven PL they Prog smoke

na-lake-na na-rei aneana maaga teu mari sua tea maaga wanogoe.
because people his PL they make Comp one PL that.

Na-rei ki Wotanimanu. Goo e naga, "Tu ga too ganikani pae
People of Wotanimanu. And he say, "We Int Prog eat by

na-suma maaga." Eu puke. Eu tuturi pae na-suma maaga. Paapaa
house PL." They open. They divide by house PL. Until

e noopu. Na-vinaga maaga waina eu ga woo dape a eu kili
it finished. Food PL that they Int will take it they dig

sua e. Go ragi waina eu ganikani sua, na-goroi maaga eu
Comp it. And time that they eat Comp, woman PL they

pai na-vinaga ma-aso na-ala adeada maaga eu pura. Goo ragi
fill food cooked basket their PL they full. And time

waina e noa kii da asa tea mata wanae e duu. Eu dape
that he say to them of-it one raw there it stand. They take

sika-sikai mooli maa sara na-leo mamau-puti eu ma-duu
one-one only but every thing all they remain

na-lake-na teu pai tea ma-aso te toliu. Goo ragi wanogoe
because they fill one cooked it surpass. And time that

e noa, "Tea m̃ooli tu ga va-ki sum̃a." Maa tea mata maaga
he say, "One nothing we Int go-to house." But one raw PL

waia e ga tuu na-rei aneana eu ga woo maneana dape a
this it Int stand people his they Int will for-him carry it

umai pa-ki e-sum̃a. Maa ragi waina p̃oogi na-rei aneana eu ga
come go-to house. But time when night people his they Int

woo maneana dape a umai paki e-sum̃a. Goo eu sawa ki
will for-him carry it come to house. And they load Obj Mkr

nia paki vaala e pura pilake waago rua-lima-sikai maau waina eu
it to rack it full with pig two X five X one just that they

dape a umai pilake na-vinaga maaga wanogoe pa-ki e-sum̃a goo teu
take it come with food PL that go-to house and they

datuuta naga na-aleati-a waia e ga vei na-aleati-a ni naleoana
promise that day this it Int be day of feast

warua. Goo teu dovi na-vei-na-wota-ana wanogoe. Goo ragi
great. And they annoint chief that. And time

waina na-vei-na-wota-ana e noopu. Eu doko kiiki goo tea
that chief it finished. They stay little and person

ni E-mua eu maeto ki nia na-lake-na na-vinaga aneana e doliu
of Emua they angry at him because food his it more

na-ata-toko maaga kite waago maaga e doliu na-ata-toko maaga.
native PL or pig PL it more native PL.

Goo eu atulake poo pasa ki nia eu naga, "O! Niigo ku pei
And they begin and speak to him they say, "Oh! You you are

na-musasake eu pei na-m̃enaki goo ku umai poo mari doliu gami.
driftwood they are stranger and you come and do more us.

Ragi waia au karae kita ko. P̃a vano." Goo na-goroi p̃ota
Time this we reject Obj Mkr you. Imp go." And woman different

sikai e moro liko wotanimanu e pei na-goroi ke-rua ni
a she also cling-to Wotanimanu it is woman second of

Lei-na-sei. E piragi na-rup̃a. Goo ragi wanogoe mali-p̃oogi e noa
Leinasei. He took lover. And time that morning he say

kii da asa e naga, "Ta ga m̃elu, ta ga m̃elu tokora waia."
to them of-it he say, "I Int leave, I Int leave place this."

Goo naara eu dodomi p̃arua ki nia. Goo ero m̃elu poo
And they they love much Obj Mkr him. And they-two leave and

umai paki taleeva ni matigo ni E-mua, paki taleeva ni Saam̃a.
come to side of graveyard of Emua, to side of Saam̃a.

Goo e naga, "Tokora waia ta ga loloso asa." Goo na-goroi dua
And he say, "Place this I Int swim at-it." And woman two

ero madoo kai tokora wanogoe, ero dagisi a, maa nae
they-two remain cry place that, they-two mourn him, but he

te m̃elu. E loloso duagoto umai paki Nguna. Maa tea dua
he leave. He swim cross come to Nguna. But person two

ero ma-doko na-maati ni tokora wanogoe eu soso e ki
they-two remain reef of place that they call it Obj Mkr

Na-wewele-ki-na-rup̃a. Na-goroi dua wanogoe ero doko
Bed-of-lover. Woman two that they-two remain

paapaa masoso e pei vaatu dua waina ero doko tokora
until today it is stone two which they-two remain place

wanogoe doko. Eu soso e ki Na-wewele-ki-narup̃a maa nae
that remain. They call it Obj Mkr Nawewelekinarup̃a but he

e umai poo sake Tikilasoa poo pa-ki taava [ni] lake
he come and come-ashore Tikilasoa and go-to hill [of] stump

na-kimau. E poo doko tokora wanogoe e naga, "O! Ragi
nakimau tree. He Comp stay place that he say, "Oh! Time

waia a doko p̃ia." Ragi wanogoe te pei vaatu. Te daa pei
this I stay well." Time that he become stone. He not is

na-ata-m̃ooli maa te pei vaatu. Goo ragi waina e doko e dogo
person rather he is stone. And time that he stay he hear

e kite na-ka ni Tikilasoa maaga eu p̃oka-ti na-kp̃ea p̃oogi
it that people of Tikilasoa PL they beat slit-drum at-night

e mari-saa maturu. Goo na-ka ni M̃ala-lolo maaga goo na-ka ni
he cannot sleep. And people of M̃alalolo PL and people of

M̃ala-liu goo e naga, "O! A doko tokora waia a daa maturu p̃ia
M̃alaliu and he say, "Oh! I stay place this I not sleep well

p̃oogi. Eu p̃oka-woka a-leati goo p̃oogi. A dogo saa ki
at-night. They beat daytime and at-night. A feel badly from

nia na-p̃au-gu e pitinu asa goo na-p̃ele-gu e pitinu. A
it head-my it hurt from-it and stomache-my it hurt. I

mari-saa maturu p̃ia. A ga woo lagoro m̃elu." E doko kiiki
cannot sleep well. I Int will perhaps leave." He stay little

goo e m̃elu, e m̃elu poo pa-ki taleeva ni Unakapu, doko
and he leave, he leave and go-to side of Unakapu, stay

na-toko-ana e doko e-tano maa nae e doko e-lagi kaka-na. Goo
village it stay below but he he stay above of-it. And

tokora waina e m̃elu asa doko Tikilasoa eu soso e ki
place which he leave from-it at Tikilasoa they call it Obj Mkr

M̃oru-ni-wota e doko paapaa paki masoso. Goo e moro m̃elu
Pit-of-chief it remain until to today. And he again leave

pa-ki taleeva ni Unakapu goo tea ni Unakapu maa eu p̃oka
go-to side of Unakapu and person of Unakapu but they beat

na-kp̃ea. Goo e mari-saa maturu, "Eee! A dogo-kite saa.
slit-drum. And he cannot sleep, "No! I feel badly.

Na-p̃au-gu pitinu. A daa doo maturu p̃oogi elagoro a ga woo
Head-my hurt. I not Prog sleep at-night perhaps I Int will

m̃elu." Goo e moro m̃elu tokora wanogoe goo e moro m̃elu poo
leave." And he again leave place that and he again leave and

pa-ki taleeva ni Mere. "O! A doko taleeva waia a leo p̃ia paki
go-to side of Mere. "Oh! I stay side this I look well to

na-tasi paki na-talova-na-maladi. Goo elo e sake a punusi m̃ata
sea to horizon. And sun it rise I see well

ki nia ragi waina e sake mali-p̃oogi. A poo doko p̃ia." Goo
Obj Mkr it time that it rise mornings. I Comp stay well." And

tokora wanogoe e m̃elu asa doko Unakapu nae maa na-gisa-na
place that he leave from-it in Unakapu he but name-its

e pei M̃oru-ni-wota e doko masoso. Goo e dasake tokora
it is M̃oruniwota it remain today. And he settle place

wanogoe. Ragi waina e doko kiiki na-ka ni Mere, na-ka ni
that. Time that he stay little people of Mere, people of

M̃ala-liu, na-ka ni M̃atoa, na-ka ni Rewoka, na-ka ni Sau-wia
M̃alaliu, people of M̃atoa, people of Rewoka, people of Sauwia

maaga eu p̃oka-ti na-kp̃ea p̃oogi goo e daa maturu. E naga,
PL they beat slit-drum at-night and he not sleep. He say,

"A doko tokora waia maa e paataka-sikai, e-lagoro a ga woo
"I stay place this but it exactly-the-same, perhaps I Int will

m̃elu, a ga woo m̃elu pa-ki na-tasi." Goo ragi waina e m̃elu e
leave, I Int will leave go-to sea." And time that he leave he

pa-ki na-taku ni Mataso poo doko tokora wanogoe. Goo e peani
go-to behind of Mataso and stay place that. And there were

na-rei laapa waina e peani ra doko asa doko masoso. Na-rei
people many which it has them on it there today. People

maaga wanogoe waina eu doo maneana p̃osiwosi ki roara
PL those who they Prog for-him work Obj Mkr garden

aneana doko E-mua. Goo masoso tu punusi manu maaga wanogoe
his on Emua. And today we see bird PL those

eu doo diri pano maa sala veea eu pei na-ata-m̃ooli. Goo
they Prog fly go but time first they are person. And

manu wanogoe waina na-ka ni Mataso eu doo gani ra. Goo
bird that which people of Mataso they Prog eat them. And

stori waia e noopu tokora waia.
story this it finished place this.

MUSICAL TRANSCRIPTIONS

#7, Namariana ni Naveinawotaana Maaga/Making Chiefs and **#13,**
Nadu Dua/The Twins

1- too 1- too taaaa - roo -- aa

------------ i - too !

#14, Takana Waina Eu Pap̃ai Nakp̃ea/How the Slit-Drum was Discovered

Ta - pe - su ma - ra ta -

pe - su ma - ra. lo wee-- ta - pe

e - su ma - ra. le - ro pa - ki ro - a raa, ie - ro pa - ki

ro - a - ra. lo wee ta- pe - su ma - raa.

le - ru sa - ri sa - ri, ie - ru saa - ri sa - ri lo -wee

---- ta - pe-- su ma - ra. le - ru sa - ri na - pa - rae, ie - ru

sa - ri na - pa - rae, lo wee ta - pe - su ma - ra.

I - o ! Swa-- le - le ! We !

#24, **Tamataida Rualimasikai goo Rovemao/The Ten Brothers and Rovemao**

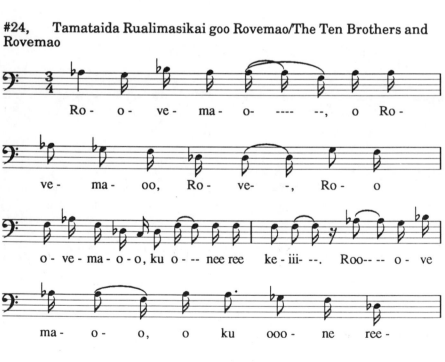

Ro- o - ve - ma - o- ---- --, o Ro -

ve - ma - oo, Ro - ve- -, Ro - o

o - ve - ma - o - o, ku o - --- nee ree ke - iii- --. Roo-- -- o - ve

ma - o - o, o ku ooo - ne ree -

ke - ii. Re - ke -- i si - i- - li die - le

ka - a- a- -- ta ma - ii-- --. Re - kee - i - i-- -- si - li di - e -

le - goo - ro - e.

#26, Vaatu ni M̃aatoa/The M̃aatoa Rock

Na - u, na - a - u, na - u, daa - gi - si aa.

Na - u, na - u-- -- u, na - u, daa - gi - si aa.

Na - pa - gaa ma - ri - ee- - ri - e, na - pa - ga

ma - ri - ee-- - ri - e.

#28, Oova/The Heron

Plea:

Ma - gou - goo- -- u-- -- rii -

kii, ma - gou - goo - - - u

la - paa, Pa to - ro - to - ro a - u. to - ro a - u.

Reply:

La - a- -- woo-- -- -- sa - i-- --- ki

ruu - kuu pa - ki - nau, ta ka - ti -

i - ko, pa - ki - nau, ta -kaa - ---- ti - ko.

Glossary

a — I

adeada — their

agi — of, belonging to

aginami — our

aginau — my

ai — [an exclamation, akin to] "Oh, no!"

ako — (to) you (sing.)

aleati — morning; daybreak

aloa — uncle (MB, for example)

anagoroi — his wife

anawota — her husband

aneana — his

anigida — our

anigo/aniigo — your (sing.)

animu — your (pl.)

ara — (to) them

araa — branch

araika — (to) fish

aro — we (two, exclusive)

asa — (to) him/her/it

asilua — (to) scrape/cut out

asua — (to) smoke [as of a fire]; (to) steam

atae — (to) know

ataeana — known

ataesuaana — already known

atavi — chiefly assistant

atelagi — moon; month

atolu — egg

atu/atugi — to hit, strike (intransitive/transitive)

atulake — (to) start, begin

atuusi — (to) tell, recount

au — (to) me; we (more than two, exclusive)

beelo — bell [Bislama]

buluk/buluki — bull [Bislama]

da — them

daa — not

daap̄otae/dap̄otae — (to) divide, break apart, separate

315

daare   (to) crow; white
daareare   all/very white
dae   (to) cut
daelua   (to) cut out
daep̃orae   (to) cut up, in pieces
dagi/dagisi   (to) mourn, wail (intransitive/
                               transitive)

daki   (to) turn, shift
dakidarogo   (to) stay still, quiet
dakidorogo   (to) listen
dakimata   (to) glance, peek
dakiusi   like, similar
dakovi   (to) sit on [as in a chicken
                               sitting on her eggs]

daliali   slowly
daliepu   (to) go around, circle
dalitaliepu   (to) circle around and around
daliviri   all around, throughout
dalivirigoro   (to) surround
dam̃alua   (to) jump
dao/daoni   (to) bake (intransitive/
                               transitive)

dapala   like, as if
dape   (to) take
dapepele   (to) drop, lose
dapesoki   (to) hang onto
dapetape   (to) carry
dapilagona   (to) get stuck, caught up (on)
dapiri   (to) break, violate [a rule or
                               prohibition]

dapu   sacred, holy
dapugoro   (to) consecrate
dap̃a   empty
dap̃ara/dap̃araki   (to) burn (intransitive/
                               transitive)

dap̃olaga   (to) open
dap̃otae   [see: daap̃otae]
dara   (to) shine [as in, the sun
                               shines]

daragi   (to) heat
darasa   (to) call, shout
daratara   (to) stagger, stumble, reel;
                               fully/sound (asleep)
dasake   (to) sit down

dasuru	(to) hide
datagau	(to) fish (with hook and line)
datago/datagovi	(to) ask (for) (intransitive/ transitive)
datuuta	(to) promise; set a date
dau	(to) hang down
daulua	(to) buy, pay for
dausi	(to) follow
dautau	sparkling clean or white
dave	(to) go out; (to) excrete
dekei	(to) decorate
diele	to call out
diena	pregnant
digi	(to) point
digo	(to) herd, drive, push (ahead of one)
dika/diika	nothing
dipe	(to) shoot (with bow and arrow)
dip̃a	against; (to) send, command; (to) fight
diri	(to) fly
diro	(to) sink (intransitive)
diroa	(to) sink (transitive)
disu	(to) move, shift
ditipe	(to) shoot (with bow and arrow) repeatedly
doa	(to) turn; (to) change, transform
dodomi	(to) love
dogo/rogo	(to) hear; feel
dogoatae	(to) recognize
dogorogo	(to) listen; (to) hear (talk) of
doitoi	(to) envy, be jealous (of)
doko	(to) live; stay, remain
dokodorogo	(to) do nothing, be inactive, stay still
dokogoro	(to) block
dokoni	(to) burn (transitive)
doliu	(to) pass; surpass
dolu/doolu	three
dolutoolu	three (each)
doni	(to) bury
doo	[progressive tense verbal marker]

doropusi	(to) put, place
dorotoro	(to) sweat
dosadusugi	(to) submerge (transitive)
dosagi	(to) drag/pull (along the ground), beach (a canoe)
dovai	(to) cut up, butcher
dovi	(to) annoint; ordain
dowo	(to) fall
dua	(to) give
dua/duua/rua/ruua	two
duagoto	(to) cross
dualele	straight through, without pausing or stopping
duasai	(to) emerge, appear
duki	(to) pound, thump
duleana	(to) stand up
dumu	pool
dum̃ada	themselves
dum̃agami	ourselves (more than two, exclusive)
dum̃agida	ourselves (more than two, inclusive)
dum̃amu	yourselves (pl.)
dum̃am̃a	yourself (sing.)
dum̃ana	himself/herself/itself
duoli	(to) replace, take the place of
dusugi	(to) chase
duti	(to) tie (a knot in); (to) tie together
duturi	(to) sew; (to) divide, distribute
duu	(to) stand
duua	[see: dua]
e	he/she/it
edaku	after; behind; later
ee	no
eelo	[see: elo]
ekopu	inside
elagi	above; inland
elagoro	perhaps
elau	shore, seaside
elo/eelo	sun
epua	deep
erasa	cliff
ero	they (two)

esava	where [interrogative]
esuũa	at home; in the house
etano	down; seaward
eu	they (more than two)
euta	shore
famli	family [Bislama]
ga	[verbal intention marker]
gaegae	(to) puff, be out of breath
gami	us (more than two, exclusive)
gani/kani	(to) eat (transitive)
ganikani/kanikani	(to) eat (intransitive)
garagara	thirsty
gida	us (more than two, inclusive)
go/goo	and, then
goa	spear
gona	stuck
gonasokisoki	stuck tight
goo	[see: go]
gora	(to) snore
gore	brother [female speaking]; sister [male speaking]
goro	against
goroi	female
guũa	package; heap, bunch
iero/ieru/ioro	yes [emphatic]
iita	[an exclamation, akin to] "Aha!"
io	yes
ito/itoo	good-bye
kai	(to) cry; [generic term for] clams/limpets
kaikai	food [Bislama]
kakada	of/about them
kakagida	of/about us
kakana	of/about he/she/it
kalau	(to) climb, clamber over
kali	digging-stick
kalukalu	package, parcel
kanao	boy
karae	(to) refuse
karau	large sp. of clam
karopuludoa	(to) mix
kastom	custom, tradition; traditional [Bislama]

kasua	strong; tough; hard
katama	outside
katea	the side of a canoe opposite the outrigger
kati	(to) bite, chew
katikotovi	(to) bite through, off
katipunue	(to) bite to death
katisoki	(to) bite onto
katou	hermit crab
kau	handle
kaum̃elu	handle-less
kavuti	(to) wrap, cover up, pack
keekee	[an exclamation of extreme fear and/or pain]
kelarua	seventh
kelatesa	sixth
kelima	fifth
kelugoro	(to) wrap up
kerua	second
ketolu/ketoolu	third
kevaati	fourth
ki/kii	of, belonging to
kiada	their home/place
kiagida	our home/place
kiagu	my home/place
kiana	his/her/its home/place
kiedaku	aft
kii	[see: ki]
kiiki	small, little
kili	(to) dig (with an implement)
kilikili	(to) dig, continously or repeatedly
kinami	we (more than two, exclusive)
kinau	I
kirikiri	little [of a plural subject]
kisi	(to) touch
kisiƥai	(to) hit squarely, precisely
kita	perhaps?/isn't it so?
kite	[question marker]
kivea/kiveea	fore
ko	you (sing., obj.)
kokoi	boundary
kokolo	dry, withered
kokoti	(to) cut up in pieces

kolopu	(a) length/section (of bamboo); forearm
kooro	enclosure
koovu	coconut pudding with chunks of meat or fish in it
kopasi	(to) chase
koriia	dog
koro	you (two)
koroi	girl
kotokotovi	(to) cut up, continuously or repeatedly
kove	(to) fan (a fire, with one's hand); (to) blow/play (a bamboo flute)
ku	you (sing., subj.)
kukusue	chiton
kup̃a	day [as "in three days hence" or "on the fifth day after"]
kup̃e	(to) kick; (to) hit, strike
kurati	(to) kick (at)
kusue	rat
laaga	(to) search, look for
laago	fly
laago vuvuaa	"bluefly"
laapa	many, lots
laasa	half coconut shell; cup
laelae/laelaea	(to) be happy
laen	[see: line]
lagalaga	(to) search, look for (continuously or repeatedly)
lake	base; foot, stump (of a tree)
lakesikaiana	of common origin or source
laki	(to) marry [only said of a woman]
lalawo	(to) plant, continuously or repeatedly
larua	seven
latesa	six
latolu	eight
lau	leaf
lawo	(to) plant
lawoana	planted
lawoduu	(to) stand fast
lawopele	(to) miss with a spear throw

leana	right, straight; proper
lega	(to) sing
legaana	sung
lei	(to) pick (fruit or coconuts)
leimule	large type of banana
leleo	(to) look at
leo	(to) look
leoatae	(to) recognize (visually)
leogoro	(to) watch for, expect (someone)
leoṁata	(to) like (the looks of)
leoparaati	(to) look after, care for
leopuoli	(to) lose sight of
leosoki	(to) stare at
leousiusi	(to) look over, examine
lesi	papaya/pawpaw
lesiana	laid down
liina	(in the) open; apparent
liko	(to) cling to
likosokisoki	(to) cling tightly to
likoti	(to) accompany
liliu	(to) return; go/come back; (to) end
lima	five
line/laen	matriline, matriclan [Bislama]
liṗa	(to) put (someone) ashore
liu	past, beyond
loa/looa	dark; black
lofeti	nine
lolo	sweet
loloa	completely/very black
lolomana	(to) come to fruition, be fulfilled
loloso	(to) bathe; (to) swim
lolua	garden
lomau	true, real
lomauri	animal; living thing
looa	[see: loa]
looga	pen, sty
loopu	bamboo
loṗai	(to) spot, catch sight of
loriki	thing
lowia	good thing [as in something edible]

lua	(to) vomit
luku	hole
lulu	(to) wrap
lulugoro	(to) wrap up
lulusi	(to) follow (along a path)
ma/maa	but; and
maaga	[plural noun marker]; (to) gape (open); (to) be amazed, astonished
maanu	(high-ranking) chiefly position (serving Tarip̃oaliu)
maaso	cooked
maau	[see: mau]
madeada	for them
mado/madoko/madoo	remain/continue (in a given place or state)
maduu	remain standing
maeto	angry
magi	for
maginami	for us (more than two, exclusive)
maginau	for me
magona	stuck, caught up (on/against)
makala	ant
makali/makalikali	sharp [of a sing./pl. subject]
makoto	broken
malaadi	cold; deserted, devoid
malakesa	blue/green
malasiviri	species of fish
maleepu	widowed
maligo	dark
malip̃ogi/malip̃oogi	morning
malo	place, spot
mama	father
mamale	lazy
mamau	all, whole
mamauputi	all, every
mami	ripe
manaunau	(to) be appalled, shocked
maneana	for him/her/it
mani	(to) grate
manigida	for us (more than two, inclusive)
maniigo	for you (sing.)
manimu	for you (pl.)

maniok	manioc [Bislama]
manu	bird
manukavina	sp. of small songbird
manumatua	clever, intelligent
mapula	hawk
marae	eel
maraka	all
maraki	(to) lead
marama	(to) shine
maramana	world
maramara	(to) rule
maraverave	quickly
mari	(to) do, make
mariana	done, made
mariatae	(to) be able to
maridip̃a	(to) fight, attack
maridogo	(to) try, attempt
marierie	"is falling down" [archaic or poetic form]
marigoro	(to) enclose, fence in
mariki	fellow; [title of respect, akin to Mr.]
marikini	axe
marikotovi	(to) cut
marimatua	(to) succeed; (to) conquer, beat
marim̃ata	(to) complete, finish
marim̃atakiana	all/well done/finished
maripueli	(to) get rid (of), wipe out
maripunue	(to) kill
maripunueana	killed
marisaa	(to) be unable to
marisara	(to) struggle, try desperately
marisasaa	(to) destroy, ruin
marisokisoki	(to) prepare, get ready, assemble
maromaaro	(to) rest
masale	without; except
masau	(to) want, need
masikigu	I alone, by myself
masikina	he/she/it alone, by him/herself
masimasi	knife
masoni	sp. of fish
masoso	today
masua	top, tip

mata	raw
matadoko	giant clam
mataku	afraid
mataloa	large type of pig
matamai	tomorrow
matau	(to) be afraid (of)
mate	unconscious; dead
matemate	gentle; quiet
matigo	grave
matua	mature; old
maturu	(to) sleep
mau/maau	at all; scarcely; only
mauri	(to) live; alive, living
mauti	(to) keep, hang onto, hoard
mavatu	sp. of fish
mawora	broken/torn; having a hole in it
melu	shade
menae	(to) lick
meso	(to) decay, rot
miala	red
midoaki	(to) think
midodoa	(to) worry
misi/miisi	missionary; Reverend
mila	wild
mimi	aunt (FZ, for example)
momoaa	smooth, highly polished
moro	again; next
mu	you (pl., obj.)
mua	(to) come in, rise [said of the tide]
munu/munugi	(to) drink (intransitive/ transitive)
munuai	diviner
muru	(to) laugh
musagi	(to) ferry, transport
musamusa	(to) flee in haste by canoe
musu	(to) dive; sink; set [said of the sun]
musuvi	(to) dive for
ñaata	snake
ñaau	champion warrior
ñagougou	chiton
ñaladigi	near, close
ñalala	dancing-ground

m̃aleoputo	middle
m̃ata	well, proper(ly)
m̃elu	(to) leave, move out
m̃oli/m̃ooli	just, only; nothing
m̃olim̃oli	round
m̃oogi	day [as in "three days hence"]
m̃ooso	channel
m̃oru/m̃ooru	hole, pit, grave
m̃orua	punctured, broken open
naadi	banana
naala	basket, bag; purse; coffer
naaleatia	day
naanoai	man
naap̃e	club
naara	they (more than two, emphatic)
naasi	jaw; chin
naasu	bow
naata	spirit; unknown person [as in *te naata*, "someone"]
naatamate	spirit of the dead
naatam̃ooli	person; human
naatatoko	native, local inhabitant
naatuusiana	story, account
naau	reed
nadaa	blood
nadagidagiana	wailing; mourning
nadaleo	voice
nadaliga	ear
nadamami	sp. of banana
nadi	(to) throw; (to) lay [of a chicken laying eggs]
nadigi	side
nadiu	spine; spike; internal, small fish-bones
nadom̃o	end [of an object having length]
nadoomariana/natoomariana	custom, tradition; manner, behaviour
nadue	twin
nae	he/she/it (emphatic)
naenum̃a	communal clearing and planting [for one's chief, or for one village or dominion by

	another village or dominion]
naga	(to) say; as, so that, in order to
nagai	almond tree (*canarium indicum*)
nagisa	name; title
nagisu	nose; point, peninsula
nagole	mouth; opening
nagole ni natasi	the sea's edge; high-water mark
nagoroi	woman
naika	fish
naio	spear
naita	sp. of ficus tree
naka	people [of a particular chief or place]
nakainaga	matriline, matriclan
nakaniana	meal
nakanikaniana	eating, [unusually large or lengthy] meal
nakapu	fire; firewood; "a light" (i.e., a match or lighter)
nakara	sp. of seaweed [used to treat sores when dried to a powder]; sp. of nettle-tree
nakaroa	itching sores
nakasuaana	strength
nakau	wood; tree
nakaulootu	gun
nakim̃au	"Pacific teak" tree (*intsia bijuga*)
nakoa	root
nakoau	coconut pudding; [in Bislama] *laplap*
nakonoti	nut
nakopesi	sp. of tree
nakoro	fence; windbreak
nakp̃ea	slit-drum/gong
nakup̃a	day [as in "on the fifth day from today"]
nalae	sail
nalaelaeana	pleasure, happiness, joy
nalagi	wind
nalagiatu	hurricane
nalake	foundation; root, reason

nalakena	because
nalakiana	wedding, marriage [only with reference to women]
nalalawoana	planting
nalegaana	song
naleo	thing
naleoana	celebration; [in Bislama] *singsing*
naleoparaatikiana	care, protection
nalia	(habitual/usual) place, position
nalikolikoana	sticking
nalisere	coconut frond
nalo	about, concerning
nalolu	hair
nalootuana	worship; religion; Christianity
nalua	arrow
namaati	reef
namadau	tunnel, shaft; the empty space left when the roots of a tree have rotted away
namagovai	half; part
namalasi	bush, jungle
namaleepu	widow
namalo	the inside(s); trunk (of a tree)
namaloku	kava
namalopaa	sky; gap, empty space
namanu	throat
namarakiana	dominion; rule
namariana	behaviour
namarisaakiana	destruction; wrongdoing, sin
namarita	guts, intestines
namariu	sp. of tree *(acacia spirorbis)*
namasauana	desire, need
namasu	harvest-time, peak fruit season, time of plenty
namata	door; face, eye; source; replacement, look-alike or another (of something)
namatai	bread; breadfruit
namatap̃ago	end [of an object having length or duration, e.g., a stick, a story)
namatarau	matrilineal descent group; family (in a very extended sense)

namataruana	end; cessation
namateana	death
namauriana	life
namavesi	person's second name [derived from the father's clan name]; paternal inheritance
namelesi	sp. of tree
namena	tongue
nameura	dew
namidoakiana	thinking, thought; opinion
namidodoaana	worry, concern
namidoakiparaatikiana	memory; remembrance
namnam	(to) eat [slang or archaic]
namusasake	driftwood
nam̃adu	back
nam̃asua	top, peak (of a rock, hill); crown (of a tree, of a person's head)
nam̃audu	field [i.e., large communal garden]
nam̃aβe	"Tahitian chestnut" tree (*inocarpus edulis*); chestnut
nam̃ele	sp. of palm tree
nam̃elevara	coal
nam̃eluana	origin, source; departure
nam̃enaki	stranger
nam̃enau	grass
nam̃o	green coconut (with no meat, only water); heart
nanatu	offspring; (succession) from father to son
naniu	coconut
nanoaana	meaning; speech; saying
nanoaβotaeana	meaning; explanation
naone	ocean-floor, sea-bed
naosi	green coconut (with some "meat" in it)
napaga	banyan tree
napalala	ration/portion of food [especially that which is a condiment or side dish to the main dish]
napanipani	armband
napapitaata	in between

napati	tooth, tusk; seed (of a plant); pearl; core (of a pimple)
napatiira	cliff
napetau	breadfruit
napilelu	sp. of tree
napu	heap, bunch
napua	road, path; route; way, means
napue	tail; cigarette butt
napuka	"canoe tree" (*gyrocarpus americanus*)
napuku	price, cost
napura	halves of a clam shell; afterbirth
napuraru	sp. of plant
napuri	tubers baked in slices
nap̃alau	belly; (a person's) insides
nap̃aloa	creek
nap̃anu	mat
nap̃arae	sugarcane
nap̃atoko	body
nap̃au	head; boss; devil-spirit
nap̃aunako	upper side (of a garden); front end (of a canoe)
nap̃eka	sp. of hard yam
nap̃ele	stomache, belly
nap̃o	(to) smell; smell, scent
nap̃oaana	smelled
nap̃ogiana/nap̃oogiana	night
nap̃okasi	meat, flesh
nap̃olo/nap̃oolo	large type of basket; thatch wall (of a house)
nap̃oro	edge, verge
narae	face; in front of/before (someone)
naraperape	similar, closely related [as of two words]
narei	(a chief's) people
naririmata	tear
nariwota	ancestry
naru	arm
narup̃a	"concubine"; second wife/woman
nasaga	fork (of a stick or tree, in the road)

nasaiana	promise
nasakesakeana	distribution
nasaleana	dance, dancing
nasama	outrigger
nasava	what; what [interrogative]
naseana	request
naseati	firebrand
nasei	(magical) spell
nasorosoroana	deceit, deception, trickery
nasum̃a	house; (immediate/nuclear) family
nasum̃ili	meat of a clam
nasurataana	journey, voyage
natagoto	lower side of a garden
natai	faeces, shit; vegetal powder [once used as a dye for bodily decoration]
nataku	the far/other side
natale	taro
natali	rope
natalie	sp. of hardwood tree (*terminalia catappa*)
natalovaana	greeting, handshake
natalovanamalaadi	sunset
natam̃ate	peace; perfectly calm sea
natam̃ateana	peace ceremony
natano	ground, earth
natapetapeana	carrying
natapua	prohibition, restriction
natapuana	sacredness, holiness
nataputea	leaves
natasi	sea, ocean
natau	year; sp. of fruit
natavara	breaker; wave
natip̃a	arrow; spine (of a fish); horn (of a bull)
natoara	grass
natoga	foreign lands
natokoana	village; inhabitant
natoomariana	[see: nadoomariana]
natoto	sp. of softwood tree
natu	child
natua	arm; leg
natukunoa	story, tale

natukutukumena	sp. of nut-tree
natura	shaft (of a spear)
natusuña	old village, former dwelling-place
natuturiana/natutuuriana	division (of food at a feast, by village)
natuuta	promise, agreement
nau	wild cane; bamboo flute
naulu	leaf; price
naure	island
naureure	group of islands, archipelago
navago	mixture of faeces and food (e.g., breadfruit)
navaivaiaana	indication, sign
navakalo	war; battle
navanua	land; country
navarakale	family of (many) brothers
navare	sprouting coconut (suitable for planting)
navasaana	word; language; message
navasap̃otaeana	decision
navasua	pile; portion, allotment
navatu	bone
navatuuna	thing
navavakaworaana	descendants
naveaniana	first fruits; possession(s), belongings
naveele	sp. of vine [thick, often found on banana trees]
naveinawota	chief
naveinawotaana	chief; chiefship; control, authority
navidi	rib
naviila	sp. of nut tree (*barringtonia edulis*)
navilalu	rubbish [e.g., leaves that have been used in baking]
navinaga	food; point/head (of a spear)
navinoso	cork, stopper
navitawiriana	wedding, marriage
navitoloana	hunger; famine
navuasikeana	installation; installation
navusuñakiana	discussion, conversation
nawaa	fruit

nawaanoai	whole coconut shells tied together in groups of four to six, for holding and transporting water
nawaritau	the edge of the shallows [i.e., spot where the dark blue, deep sea meets the lighter, shallower water]
nawii	yam
nawili	skin, peel
nawoka	mouth (of a cave)
nawokawokaana	killing, slaughter (continuous or repeated)
nawora	landing-place; reef-passage; harbour
naworaone	sand
naworearu	family of (many) sisters
nawosaia	path, trail
nawose	paddle
nawosiana	work, job; act, deed
nawota	chief; leader
nea	here
nearu	ironwood tree or casuarina
nelikau	weapons
ni	of
nia	him/her/it (obj.)
nigida	we (more than two, inclusive, emphatic)
niigo	you (sing., subj., emphatic)
nimu/niimu	you (more than two, emphatic)
noa	to say, tell
noai	water
noasai	(to) announce, inform, tell
noasi	"native cabbage"
nogo/nogoe	that, forementioned
noopa	"native cabbage"
noopu	done, finished
nunu	picture; reflection; shadow
oli	instead/in place of
one	(to) lie, stretch out on; to have to, must
oova	sp. of heron
ova	(to) carry (on the back); (to) bury

ovakiana	carried (on the back); buried
ovi	(to) lean
pa	[see: pano]
paapaa	until
paasi	(to) step on; (to) walk (the reef)
paasisasaa	(to) crush
paataka	enough; sufficient; appropriate
paati	four
pae	from; with, by, via
pagani	(to) feed
pagarae	(to) dry (oneself)
pagavaga	(to) feed, continuously or repeatedly
pagi	(to) climb
pai	(to) fill, load
paivai	(to) indicate, be a sign (that/of)
paka	times [as in "three times": paka doolu]
pakalaapa	many times, often
pakalau	(to) climb over
pakaruua	twice
paki	to, toward
pakilagi	up, upwards
pakilina/pakiliina	(to) emerge, appear
pakinau	to me
pakitaku	(to) defecate
pakoa	shark
pakotovi	(to) buy, pay for
pali	(to) fast [and observe other restrictions for a set period of mourning]
palo	up high, in the air
paloni	(to) remove, eradicate
paloti/palooti	(to) go/come along; move
paluse	(to) paddle, row
panako	(to) steal
pano	(to) go
panoꝑota	different; another; odd
paꝑai	(to) find, discover
paraki/parakii	for (with movement toward)
parau	long; tall
parivari	(to) move (around)
paruvaru	(to) struggle
pasa	(to) speak, talk

pasadara	(to) answer, reply
pasalea	(to) get/step out (of)
pasap̃otae	(to) judge; decide
pativaati	four (different kinds)
pau	(to) weave
pauri/pauria	(to) build a fire/oven for baking (transitive/intransitive)
pautu/pautui	(to) draw (water) (transitive/intransitive)
pavaga	(to) be inflamed, raw (said of a wound); (to) catch fire, light
pavagoda	(to) fish for/gather shellfish or octopus
pavano	(to) wash off (oneself)
pe	if; might
pea/peea	first
peani	(to) get, have, possess
pei	(to) be, become; (to) come [in the inland dialect]
peni/peeni	(to) roast (on top of a fire)
peresi	(to) release, free; untie
peresiana	released, freed; untied
pesi	(to) dig (with the hands)
pesivesi	(to) dig (with the hands), continuously or repeatedly; (to) beget
pevera	(to) spread out, scatter; (to) drop off or break into bits
piakiiki	infant, child
piakirikiri	infants, children
piisa	(a) few; how much/many [interrogative]
piiti	joint (e.g., of a finger); knot (of bamboo, cane or wood);blade/sliver (of bamboo)
pilake	with, accompanying; (to) put on (a loincloth)
pilasaisai	(to) gather/call together, assemble
pile	(to) fight, argue
pilokisai	(to) poke out, cut out (with the point of a knife), drill
pilosi	(to) be angry; (to) hate; (to) hit (with the hand)

pinisomi	(to) cork, stop/block (a hole)
pioso	(to) call
pipia	baby
piragi	(to) bring; (to) marry (some-one)
piragisoki	(to) welcome
pisari	beside
pisei	(to) show, indicate
pisou	(to) sprout, grow
pitautau	(to) invite
pitinu	(to) hurt
pitip̃a	(to) meet each other, meet together
pito	lame; halt
pitolo	hungry
pitua	(to) give, return, share; (to) give forth, spread out
pivilake	(to) get/be pregnant
pivitinu	hot
ple	(to) play [Bislama]
poo	and; [completive tense verbal marker]
pua	maternal grandfather; deep; (to) split (a coconut) in half
puasike	(to) pull up, erect; (to) invest, install
puasoki	(to) grasp, take hold of
puati	(to) pull; hold
pue	(to) pour on/over
pueli	(to) be gone/out; (to) be missing/lost
puka	(to) swell up; (to) be full
pukai	(to) pry (up)
puke/pukesi	(to) open (an oven and remove the baking) (intransitive/transitive)
pule	giant; person who knows nothing, is ignorant
punue	(to) kill
punusi	(to) see
puoli	gone, missing
pura	full
purasa	gently
puri	(to) pierce, come through

puripuri	pile
pusake	(to) ordain, install
pusi	(to) bring, lead; (to) deliver, hand over
pusum̃aki	(to discuss, chat, converse
pusuusu	(to) ask, question
puti	(to) pull
puusi	cat [variation of the Bislama term *puskat*]
puuti	(to) weed
p̃a	[imperative tense verbal marker]
p̃ai	precisely, exactly
p̃akai	sp. of fish [probably "blowfish"]
p̃akap̃akaata	(to) cluck
p̃aku/p̃akuti	(to) pick, pluck (intransitive/transitive)
p̃alo	empty; ignorant
p̃alua	hole
p̃arap̃aaro	doing nothing [i.e., to be without plans, having no particular intention]
p̃arowaro/p̃arowaaro	(to) play
p̃arua	big
p̃asi	(to) wash; (to) adopt; (to) break
p̃asilua	(to) break/snap off, pluck
p̃elemata	nephew/niece
p̃ia/wia	good; very
p̃ila	mother
p̃ili	(to) close one's eyes; (to) be blind
p̃ilikaroa	sp. of lizard
p̃oa	(to) stink
p̃oka/p̃okati	(to) work; (to) hit, beat (with an object) (intransitive/transitive)
p̃okalua	(to) knock out
p̃okapunue/p̃okatipunue	(to) kill, beat to death
p̃okapupugi	(to) submerge
p̃okawoka	(to) beat, kill, continuously or repeatedly
p̃olo	(a type of) basket; testicles, scrotum
p̃onoti	(to) square up, pay off (a debt)

p̃onotia	a hundred
p̃oogi	night
p̃ora	(to) grow
p̃ori	(to) break/snap off; (to) break (e.g., a wave on the beach)
p̃oruru	(to) coo
p̃osiwosi	(to) work
p̃ota	other; different
p̃owo	(to) rain
p̃owolau	(to) steer, direct
ra	them
raewia	pretty, attractive
ragi	time; weather
ragimelu	afternoon
raki/rakii	for, in order to
rakum̃a	sp. of sand crab
rarua	canoe, boat, ship
ravitavuru	short side of the meeting-house (where the roof/wall comes to within approx. 2 feet of the ground)
rekei	[see: dekei]
ri	good, nice
roaleo	dialect
roara	garden
rogo	[see: dogo]
rogom̃atakiana	sounding just like
rua	[see: dua]
rualima	ten
rualimadoolu	thirty
rualimaduua	twenty
rualimaliima	fifty
rualimasikai	ten
ruatu	East wind
rumai	(to) come (in large numbers), gather, assemble
ruua	[see: dua]
ruukuu	secretly
saa	bad, evil; very
saatana	devil-spirit
sagalegaale	humanoid spirit-being
sai	(to) promise
saiki	(to) push off (a canoe, boat); (to) catch

saiki ruuku	(to) speak to secretly [in the sense of plotting]
saisai	(to) meet
sake	up; (to) go up, ascend
sakesake	(to) divide, distribute
sala	time [in an ordinal sense, as in "the fifth time"]; (to) rub, brush off
salagisa	(to) name
sale	(to) float, drift
salea	(to) set adrift, afloat
saovi	(to) visit
sapura	(to) spread out, spread all over
sap̃o	wrong, by mistake
sara	(to) flow; every
saralomau	(to) believe
saramule	(to) flow over, cover
sarapaa	aimless, without interest or purpose
sarasara	each
sari	(to) cut, carve (with a chisel); (to) strain (a liquid)
sarisari	(to) peck, continuously or repeatedly
saruru	(to) shake, rumble
sasama	cheek
sasam̃oliwia	the/that very same
sasari	(to) gut and clean
sau	(to) blow [as of the wind]
sava	(to) run, flee
save	(to) pick (e.g., bananas)
savelua	(to) break/snap off, pluck
savi	(to) sharpen; (to) cut (with an axe)
sawa	(to) hang up
sea	(to) ask
seara	some
seasea	(to) spread out, covering over
seei	who
sef	food-safe/cupboard [Bislama]
seve	which, what [interrogative]
sikai	a, one
sikasikai	one by one, each
sike	(to) choose; (to) set (something)

sikoti	with, alongside; (to) accompany, be with
silae	(to) help
sili	(to) enter, go in; hidden
siwo	down; (to) go down, descend
soka	(to) stick/poke out
sokari	(to) join, add (to), extend; (to) continue, keep on (doing something)
sokasokari	one-after-the-other
soki	(to) fall [said of a tree]
soko	(to) reach, come up to (a set figure or total)
sole	(to) creep, crawl (on all fours)
soli	(to) carry; (to) tie
solikotokotovi	(to) snap off [i.e., break off by wrapping something about an object and pulling]
solipunue	(to) hang (oneself)
solisoki	(to) tie up tight
solisoli	(to) bind together
soogi	violence; vengeance
sooro/soro	(to) burn, be burning
sorosoro	(to) lie, deceive, trick
sorovi	(to) growl
soso	(to) call, name
sosoana	called/named
stori	story [Bislama]
sua	(to) meet, encounter; already; [perfective or completive tense verbal marker]
suasua	(to) agree
sugoro	clothes; umbrella
sui	(to) blow [as of the wind]; (to) fan a fire by blowing
suisui	gun; (to) shoot
sulagai	(to) break out (of)
sum̃a	house
sup̃e	spirit; God
surata	(to) walk; (to) go to the gardens; (to) travel;
susu	breast
suui	(to) be warm/hot [of the weather]

ta	I (emphatic)
taa	[see: daa]
taapu	[see: dapu]
taare	[see: daare]
taareare	[see: daareare]
taaro	we (two, exclusive, emphatic)
taaroa	[meaning unknown- archaic and/or poetic]
taata	maternal grandmother
taatapera	scattered, spread out
taava	hill, mountain
tae	[see: dae]
tagali	hook; arthritic spider conch
tagi	[see: dagi]
tagida	our friend
tagona	generation
tai	brother/sister [i.e., same-sex sibling]
taikesa	graveyard, cemetery
takalapa	firstborn/eldest child (in a family)
takana	how, in what way
takarausia	secondborn/ second eldest child (in a family)
takariki	lastborn/youngest child (in a family)
takeo	sp. of fish
taki	[see: daki]
takovi	[see: dakovi]
talakea	owner, proprietor
taleeva	side
taliepu	[see: daliepu]
taliviri	[see: daliviri]
talova	(to) greet, shake hands (with)
tama	father
tamadawota	husband and wife
tamataida	brothers/sisters
tamate	and/plus
tanari	his friend
tao	[see: dao]
taoa	oven
tapala	[see: dapala]
tape	[see: dape]
(tea) tapenelikau	warrior

tapetape	[see: dapetape]
tapu	[see: dapu]
tap̃esu	sp. of bird (possibly "Purple Swamp Hen")
taro	we (two, exclusive, emphatic)
tasake	[see: dasake]
tatagau	[see: datagau]
tatagovi	[see: datagovi]
tau	[see: dau]
taua	heap, pile; group
taulua	[see: daulua]
taumako	wild taro
taura/tavura	whale
tautau	[see: dautau]
tautaua	(individual, separate) groups
te	a, some
tea	(a/one) person
teele	perpetual, eternal
teete	mother
tekei	[see: dekei]
tero	they (two, emphatic)
tetu	we (more than two, inclusive, emphatic)
teu	they (more than two, emphatic)
tipe	[see: dipe]
tip̃akiana	sent
tiri	[see: diri]
tiroa	(to) sink
titau	to defecate, shit
tivinivinikopai	(a particular kind of) bush spirit
toko	[see: doko]
tokogoro	[see: dokogoro]
tokoni	[see: dokoni]
tokonisuaana	burnt
tokopea	dove
tokora	place, spot
tokotano	West wind
toliu	[see: doliu]
too	[see: doo]
tooa	fowl
toolu	[see: dolu]
toro	we (two, inclusive)

toropusi	[see: doropusi]
torotoro	[see: dorotoro]
totoni	(to) fill in
totowo	(set) amount, total
tovai	[see: dovai]
toviana	annointed; ordained
towo	[see: dowo]
tu	we (more than two, inclusive)
tua	[see: dua]
tuagoto	[see: duagoto]
tuai	old, former, past
tukurau	(chief's) widow
tuṁada	[see: duṁada]
tuṁagami	[see: duṁagami]
tuṁagida	[see: duṁagida]
tuṁaṁa	[see: duṁaṁa]
tuti	[see: duti]
tuturi	[see: duturi]
tuu	[see: duu]
umai	(to) come
uṁa	(to) clear bush (for gardens)
usi	(to) take, follow (a path)
usuraki	around, throughout
uupu	oven
uusa	rain
uvea	far, distant
va	[see: pa]
vaala	rack, platform
vaasi	[see: paasi]
vaataka	[see: paataka]
vaatu	stone, rock
vaau	new; next [as in "next month"]
vae	[see: pae]
vagani	[see: pagani]
vagavaga	[see: pagavaga]
vagi	[see: pagi]
vai	[see: pai]
vaivai	[see: paivai]
vakavuroana	fulfilled
vaki	[see: paki]
vakilina/vakiliina	[see: pakilina]
valea	cave
valoti/valooti	[see: paloti]
vanako	[see: panako]

vano	[see: pano]
vap̃ai	[see: pap̃ai]
vap̃aiana	found, discovered
varaki	[see: paraki]
varau	[see: parau]
varea	meeting-house
vativaati	[see: pativaati]
vauria	[see: pauria]
vautu/vautui	[see: pautu]
vavano	[see: pavano]
vea/veea	[see: peea]
vei	[see: pei]
veni/veeni	[see: peni]
venive	crest (of a wave)
vete/veete	nest
vigira	type of basket (carried by women, on the back, by a line hooked around the temples)
vile	[see: pile]
viragi	[see: piragi]
viria	vine, rope
vitariki	(mature, married) woman; wife
vitautau	[see: pitautau]
vitawiri	[see: pitawiri]
vitolo	[see: pitolo]
vivilake	[see: pivilake]
vonu	turtle
vuasike	[see: puasike]
vuasoki	[see: puasoki]
vuati	[see: puati]
vuka	[see: puka]
vukesi	[see: puke/pukesi]
vunusi	[see: punusi]
vuru	[see: puru]
vuuti	clump (e.g., of taro)
waago	pig
waasa	the day after tomorrow
waia	this
waina	that [said of something far off]; which, when
wanae	that [said of something nearby]
wanana	that, those

wanogoe	that (previously mentioned)
warua	[see: p̃arua]
weede	bed; platform, seat
wenaga	that, those
wia	[see: p̃ia]
wiita	octopus
woli/wooli	shell-trumpet, triton conch
woo	will [future tense verbal marker]
woosa	coconut pudding
wootu	wound, scar; spotted
wora	place; vagina
wosiwosikiana	worked; prepared, done

Index of Narrators

The following texts, by number, were narrated by:

Ronneth Manutukituki: #5, 19, 20, 21, 22
John Tarip Mariwota: #27
Kaltaᵽau Māsemata: #1, 2, 3, 7, 8, 9, 10, 11, 12, 13, 14, 15, 16, 28, 29, 30, 31, 32, 33
Lui Taatalele: #4, 17, 18
Thomas Tanearu: #25, 26
Jack Taviñasoe: #6, 24
Thomas Tavirana: #23

Scholarly Works Cited

Buse, J. E.
1960   Rarotongan personal pronouns: form and distribution.
            Bulletin of the School of Oriental and African Studies
            23:123-137.

Camden, William
1977   *A Descriptive Dictionary. Bislama to English.* V i l a :
            Maropa.

Counts, Dorothy A.
1982   *The Tales of Laupu/Ol Stori Bilong Laupu.* Boroko,
            PNG: Institute of Papua New Guinea Studies.

Don, (Rev.) Alexander
1927   *Peter Milne of Nguna.* Reprinted 1977, Dunedin:
            Foreign Missions Committee, Presbyterian Church of
            New Zealand.

Facey, Ellen E.
n.d.   The Customs of Nguna/*Natoomariana ni Navanua
            ni Nguna.* Ms. deposited in the Vanuatu Cultural
            Centre, Port Vila, Vanuatu.

1983   Ideology and Identity: Social Construction of Reality on
            Nguna, Vanuatu. Ph.D. Diss. Sydney, Australia:
            University of Sydney.

Gatewood, John B.
1984   A Short Typology of Ethnographic Genres: Or Ways to
            Write About Other Peoples. *Anthropology and Human-
            ism Quarterly Special Issue* 9(4): 5-10.

Howard, Alan
1970   *Learning to be Rotuman: Enculturation in the
            South Pacific.* New York: Teachers College Press.

Hymes, Dell
1981   *"In vain I tried to tell you": Essays in Native
            American Ethnopoetics.* Philadelphia: University of
            Pennsylvania Press.

Jolly, Margaret A.
1982   Birds and Banyans of South Pentecost: *Kastom* in
            Anti-Colonial Struggle. In Roger M. Keesing and
            Robert Tonkinson, eds. *Reinventing Traditional
            Culture: The Politics Of Kastom In Island
            Melanesia. Mankind* Special Issue 13(4): 338-356.

Keesing, Roger M.

1982a   *Kastom* in Melanesia: An Overview. In Roger M.
               Keesing and Robert Tonkinson, eds. *Reinventing
               Traditional Culture: The Politics Of Kastom In
               Island Melanesia. Mankind* Special Issue 13(4):
               297-301.

1982b   *Kastom* and Anticolonialism on Malaita: 'Culture' as
               Political Symbol. In Roger M. Keesing and   Robert
               Tonkinson, eds. *Reinventing Traditional Culture: The
               Politics Of Kastom In Island Melanesia. Mankind*Special
               Issue 13(4): 357-373.

Keesing, Roger M. and Robert Tonkinson, eds.

1982   *Reinventing Traditional Culture: The Politics Of
               Kastom In Island Melanesia. Mankind* Special Issue
               13(4).

Larcom, Joan

1982   The Invention of Convention. In Roger M. Keesing and
               Robert Tonkinson, eds. *Reinventing Traditional Cul-
               ture: The Politics Of Kastom In Island Melanesia.
               Mankind* Special Issue 13(4): 330-337.

Layard, John W.

1942   *Stone Men of Malekula.* London: Chatto and Windus.

Lindstrom, Lamont C.

1982   *Leftamap Kastom:* The Political History of Tradition on
               Tanna (Vanuatu). In Roger M. Keesing and Robert
               Tonkinson, eds. *Reinventing Traditional Culture: The
               Politics Of Kastom In Island Melanesia. Mankind* Spe-
               cial Issue 13(4): 316-329.

Lini, Father Walter H., ed.

1980   *Vanuatu.* Institute of Pacific Studies, University of the
               South Pacific and South Pacific Social Sciences Associa-
               tion.

Maud, Ralph

1982   *A Guide to B.C. Indian Myth and Legend: A Short
               History of Myth-Collecting and a Survey of Published
               Texts.* Vancouver: Talonbooks.

Patterson, Mary C.

1976   Kinship, Marriage and Ritual in North Ambrym. Ph.D.
               Diss. Sydney, Australia: University of
               Sydney.

Reck, Gregory G.

1984   Introduction to the special issue. *Anthropology and
               Humanism Quarterly Special Issue on Ethnographic
               Writing* 9(4): 3-4.

Schütz, Albert J.
1969a   *Nguna Texts.* Honolulu: University of Hawaii Press.
             Oceanic Linguistics Special Publication No.4.
1969   *Nguna Grammar.* Honolulu: University of Hawaii Press.
             Oceanic Linguistics Special Publication No.5.

Seitel, Peter
1980   *See So That We May See: Performances and Interpre-
             tations of Traditional Tales from Tanzania.*
             Bloomington and London: Indiana University Press.

Tedlock, Dennis
1972   *Finding the Center: Narrative Poetry of the Zuni Indians.*
             Translated from performances in the   Zuni by Andrew
             Peynetsa and Walter Sanchez. New York: Dial, 1972;
             Lincoln: University of Nebraska Press, 1978.
1982   Anthropological Hermeneutics and the Problem of
             Alphabetic Literacy. In Jay Ruby, ed. *A Crack in the
             Mirror.* 149-161. Philadelphia: University of Pennsyl-
             vania Press.
1983   *The Spoken Word and the Work of Interpretation.*
             Philadelphia: University of Pennsylvania Press.

Tonkinson, Robert
1981   Church and *Kastom* in Southeast Ambrym. In Michael
             Allen, ed. *Vanuatu: Politics, Economics and Ritual in
             Island Melanesia.* 237-267. Sydney: Academic Press.
1982a   *Kastom* in Melanesia: Introduction. In Roger M.
             Keesing and Robert Tonkinson, eds. *Reinventing Tradi-
             tional Culture: The Politics Of Kastom In Island
             Melanesia, Mankind* Special Issue 13(4): 302-305.
1982b   National Identity and the Problem of *Kastom* in
             Vanuatu. In Roger M. Keesing and Robert Tonkinson,
             eds. *Reinventing Traditional Culture: The Politics Of
             Kastom In Island Melanesia, Mankind* Special Issue
             13(4): 306-315.